PRAISE FOR *EYES OF THE GORGON*

Depth psychologist C. G. Jung famously wrote that "the gods have become our diseases," but how may we truly understand the mythic meaning of this insight? Grounded in her own life story and leading-edge multidisciplinary scholarship, Dr. Jaffa Frank brilliantly elucidates how we may understand the archetypal significance of endometriosis. By personifying this malady in relation to the Gorgon Medusa and the goddess Athena, she provides women who suffer the disease with an embodied, healing process that offers not cure, but the means by which they may experience healing, resilience, and an empowered relationship to the sacred that inheres in their bodies.

> ~Dr. Patrick Mahaffey, Professor and Associate Chair of the Mythological Studies Program at Pacifica Graduate Institute and author of *Integrative Spirituality: Religious Pluralism, Individuation, and Awakening.*

Not only do mythic stories matter but, more deeply, they can and do appear in matter as matter. Dr. Jaffa Frank's personal, yet well-researched rendering of the Gorgon Medusa's myth within her own challenging and life-threatening experience of suffering through the pains of endometriosis, reveals an entirely new form of describing and defining illness through the mythic imagination. *Eyes of the Gorgon* is a revelatory, original and elegantly rendered story of a heroic journey through the landscape of somato-mythic illness. It should be read by all students of myth as well as physicians to broaden the truth of mythic presences in our lives.

> ~Dennis Patrick Slattery, PhD, Emeritus Professor of Mythological Studies at Pacifica Graduate Institute and author of *The Wounded Body: Remembering the Markings of Flesh* and *Riting Myth, Mythic Writing: Plotting Your Personal Story.*

Vaclav Havel wrote: "Hope is not the conviction that something will turn out well but the certainty that something makes sense, regardless of how it turns out." It is a rare thing today for someone to painstakingly re-search the mythological face of her own illness. Dr. Jaffa Frank has given us an extraordinary journey as she plumbs the depths of the goddess, Gorgon Medusa, as hidden in her suffering with endometriosis, a disease affecting some 176 million women worldwide. Thank you Dr. Frank for gifting us with your soul-searching wisdom and hard-won truths. Your journey will help many to make sense of their own lives and sufferings.

~Alexander John Shaia, PhD, speaker, Jungian Sandplay Therapist, and author of *Heart and Mind: The Four-Gospel Journey for Radical Transformation* and *Returning From Camino*.

EYES OF THE GORGON

ENDOMETRIOSIS,
MYTHIC EMBODIMENT,
AND FREEDOM

JAFFA VERNON FRANK, PhD

ISBN: 978-1950186068

Front cover art by Keziah Grace Baltz
Back cover photo by Dale R. Baltz

Cover and interior design by Jennifer Leigh Selig
(www.jenniferleighselig.com)

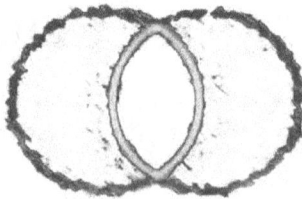

MANDORLA BOOKS
WWW.MANDORLABOOKS.COM

DEDICATION

For Dale, Keziah, Rachel, Frederick, and Ely

TABLE OF CONTENTS

FOREWORD

Why would any modern woman claim the ancient Gorgon Medusa as her Goddess of Endometriosis? What's the point of such a bizarre approach to coping with disease? It's a long, complicated story, which ultimately landed me in a PhD program in mythological studies and depth psychology. But, the simplest answer comes from my experience of the disease as being so existentially challenging as to *feel* like a sacred visitation. Endometriosis, like some sort of old-time deity, has demanded nearly everything of me. As to my choice of the Gorgon, she is a hybrid, a paradox, a transgression, shattering ideas of feminine wholesomeness with her serpentine hair, mesmerizing eyes, gaping mouth, and lolling tongue and fangs. Endometriosis is the same sort of paradox, its blood wreaking havoc rather than supporting life.

In fact, the mythology of the Gorgon is filled with stories of hybrid, transgressive creatures which juxtapose qualities in ways that disconcert or even terrify; they are often monstrous to our norms and expectations. Medusa's lineage includes the horrific half-woman, half-viper Echidna; Cerberus, the three-headed Hell-hound with a mane of serpents; and the gigantic, regenerating, snake-headed Hydra. Medusa herself combines aspects of woman and serpent, and traditionally has wings and owl eyes. Like the Gorgon Medusa for whom it is named, this book is a multidisciplinary hybrid. And to some, it may seem slightly monstrous—that is deconstructive of our standard rules of argument and narratives of reality. The work is personal and collective, concrete and metaphoric, scholarly and experiential, rational and imaginal; in a word, Medusan. The purpose is to make meaning of an experience that feels meaningless—the suffering of endometriosis, a destructive, misunderstood, chronic, painful, frustrating disease. Making meaning is not a linear process controlled by the ego and the rational mind. It is a mythopoetic activity that asks the intellect to collaborate with imagination and bodily experience, including emotion, to reveal and narrate significance, which facilitates psycho-spiritual healing; a reconciliation and integration of lived experience that rejects nothing and still manages to empower.

For me, mythopoesis requires that I lay out the components, one by one, so that the disparate parts can link together into a cohesive, coherent form. First, I describe endometriosis in detail so that it is known as intimately as a lifelong partner, which it often is for women with the disorder. Next, I reconstruct Medusa from her ancient representations and myths. Her paradoxical masks of beautiful victim, apotropaic protector, and emblem of the Evil Eye and menstrual taboos emerge. In the process, Athene announces her own trickstery presence as the overt and covert protagonist in Medusa's story. Through Athene, I meet her childhood nursemaid Aidos, Goddess of Shame, and untangle a web of shame, power, and embodied misogyny. It is through the eyes of this hybrid Gorgon—part Medusa, part Athena, part myself—that I reexamine my previously hopeless experiences of suffering endometriosis and find a deeper story of transformation through love, redemption through acceptance, and creative freedom.

As I finished work on this book, my daughter was diagnosed with endometriosis; unfortunately taking her place in a lineage of pain carried genetically through me, my mother, and most likely, our grandmothers and great grandmothers unknown. Medical research shows that endometriosis runs in families.

I share this extension of "my" endometriosis story because it throws into relief the truth that there are as many narratives as there are women who suffer with the disease. What I offer in this book is concurrently mine and also part of a chorus of millions. Collectively our lament embodies both pathos and release. The paradox of our simultaneously individual and collective reality has served as ballast against the doubt that my story, and the ways I weave it, might be too specific and esoteric to be of service to anyone else. But, it seems to me that the capacity to create meaning and beauty from suffering is a gift of soul and a triumph of the creative imagination—as heritable as our diseases—which potentiates healing, our mythopoetic legacy.

I don't know how the disease will play out for my daughter, what her endometriosis story will be, but I do understand that it is already a force in her life—both destructive and creative. While receiving medical treatment, she has begun to mythopoetically give voice to her experience of endometriosis, adding her lyric to our collective song and manifesting her human ability to narrate its anguish and wisdom:

July 31st, Laparoscopy

Renegade tissue weaves
its web inside of me with such
determination I am paralyzed
by leaden, lacerating pain—
scarring filaments shackling my ovaries
to pelvic walls.

I cut away the web, free
my strangulated ova,
but leave my organs scrambled,
swollen, and confused. I fool
the endometriosis to be still—
or at least to slow its greed—
halting the cyclic bleeding of my body
losing its rhythmic sense of time.

I am left to feel prepubescent,
post-menopausal,
to be perpetually pregnant
with absence—a nothingness
that fills my womb, postponing pain
of the leaking tissue's eager, biting threads.

But by deferring suffering, my body falls
dumb. Post-surgery, I ache
with unfamiliar discomfort—muscles'

muffled speech inarticulate
compared to the once unmistaken scream
of my diseased pelvic cavity, demanding
I oblige the body's need
for luxuriating rest.

It is the sacrifice I choose—the necessary action
to prevent endometrium
from garroting my guts—this ultimately female
disembodiment.

My scars fade, retreating
deep within my navel—
surgery of womanhood sliced
through trauma of my birth.

Now, the button of my belly represents
not just severance from the mother but
diagnosis of my complex maturity,
my diseased womb upholding the maternal tradition—
daughter's bane—of endometriosis.

by Rachel Baltz

CHAPTER 1

A MYTHIC ENGAGEMENT OF DISEASE

The way we understand and narrate experience is shaped by and shapes our sense of self and reality. While the material facts of "what happened" have objective concreteness, it is the contextualizing reflective, creative, and integrative articulation of events through the mind that transforms facts into coherent, meaningful stories—life stories. Through stories we co-create our well-being and dis-ease. Collectively, the arts and myths of humankind demonstrate the power of creative narrative formation to construct and deconstruct what we experience as real. When facing life's most challenging aspects—illness, loss, alienation, physical or psychological pain, death—the stories we embrace are instrumental in our restoration. The capacity to engage the experiencing body, creative imagination, and narrating mind in a healing collaboration in response to pain and loss is a form of grace; a mystery that transforms the experience of hardship without denying the truth of suffering.

For me and over 176 million other women, our story is dominated by endometriosis. Endometriosis is a disease of inflammation in which tissue similar to that lining the uterus occurs elsewhere in the body where it reacts to monthly hormone fluctuations by swelling and bleeding. The simple irony of endometriosis is that the female blood which nourishes new life in the womb becomes the misplaced blood of destruction. Often misunderstood and minimized, this disorder is a leading cause of pelvic pain, infertility, and female hospitalizations. During the 45 years that I have suffered from this chronic, incurable disease, it has wreaked pain, loss, and even death. Like most women with endometriosis, I experienced increasingly intense menstrual pain as a teenager. However, the disorder is far more complex and destructive than typical cramps. In my case, the disease caused a uterine arterial rupture and hemorrhage that resulted in the stillbirths of the twins I was carrying and my own near death. Years later, invasive endometriosis strangulated my ureters, threatening my kidney function, and penetrated my colon causing perilous blockages. Diseased tissue infiltrated my bladder and uterus and encased my reproductive organs in a calcified condition called "frozen pelvis." I have undergone multiple abdominal surgeries because of endometriosis and lived with debilitating chronic and acute pain, and myriad complications. In addition to the physical suffering, I, like so many women with endometriosis, have faced a perplexing medical and psycho-social landscape dominated by uncertainty, misconceptions, ignorance, contradiction, and shockingly dismissive misogynistic attitudes and taboos. Because of its ubiquity and the existential threat endometriosis has posed to my life, I am compelled to understand the disease; not simply its physiology, but its meaning, its story.

As a scholar of mythology and archetypal psychology, I approach endometriosis as a significant mythic visitation. I ask myself: "Who is visiting and what is the myth—the big story—that is playing out?" I want to metaphorically personify and elicit the symbolic meaning of the disease so that I can relate to my endometriosis experience in mythopoetic ways that transcend personal details and offer context and insight. As a mental health professional with training in grief and trauma therapy, I offer my narrative to provide women diagnosed with endometriosis hope for finding a psychologically healing story that transforms the meaningless suffering and loss engendered by the disease.

While my work is to narrate a mythopoesis of endometriosis, I do not argue that stories literally cause illness. The veracity of that claim is beyond my expertise and the stance too easily slips towards dismissiveness, scorn, and blame in the context of female disease experience; there exists a devastating tradition of averring endometriosis and other enigmatic disorders as "all in your head." However, by engaging mythic material and the body through a multidisciplinary approach that integrates psyche, soma, and relationship, I facilitate meaning-making, incubate new stories beyond victimhood, and create psycho-spiritual resilience and healing, even though medical cure of endometriosis is not currently possible.

Through the Eyes of the Gorgon

The snapshot of my endometriosis experience recounted above may give the impression that I have had an extreme case of the disease. But, it is the very extremity of my situation that excites my curiosity. The iconoclastic psychologist, James Hillman claims that the "insights of depth psychology derive from souls *in extremis,*" and I would argue from bodies as well.[1] In addition, the facts I have recounted are not unrepresentative of other women's stories shared in online forums, memoirs, and testimonials. So, how do we find restorative stories expansive enough to both validate the objective realities of living with disease and give the meaningless anguish illness engenders a significance that supports growth? It is by turning to the mythic imagination that we discover such stories—psycho-spiritual truths and symbolic guides for reconfiguring our most painful experiences into life affirming narratives. In the great, archetypal stories we find clues to who is visiting and why.

So, who is the Goddess of Endometriosis and what does it mean to encounter her? The answer crept into my awareness through my endometriotic symptoms, dreams, and intuitions where I met the Gorgon Medusa. Her serpent hair, silent scream, and glaring eyes fascinated my imagination such that, while the text of my endometriosis story is the afflicted female body, the metaphoric narrator is Medusa. Very briefly, the Gorgon represents the often vilified, sometimes rageful, multivalent face of unmitigated feminine potency, including the numinous *tremendum*: the aspect of sacred power experienced as so overwhelming it can be terrifying— petrifying. As my mythic guide, hers is the archetypal face expressing my experience of endometriosis. I sense the Gorgon Medusa's presence in many of the physical aspects of endometriosis, including the way it essentially turns the female reproductive organs—the biological center of feminine creativity—into stone and the nature of

Medusa's blood, which, like that of endometriosis, is simultaneously destructive and creative. I feel the Gorgon's proximity in the psycho-social typing, misogynistic assumptions, and female anger that I encounter as a patient and when reading about the disease.

Although these connections began as personal intuitions and associations, the links between Medusa and endometriosis find synchronistic grounding in myths of the Gorgon. An imaginal dialogue between the mythology of Medusa and the lived experience of endometriosis discloses an understanding of feminine creative and destructive power as it has been apprehended for thousands of years by Western consciousness and as it expresses itself symbolically through endometriosis. Hillman argues that symptoms of both psychological and physical disease are meaningful expressions of archetypal energies in the psyche[2] and that we must "restore the disease its God and give the God its due."[3] In other words, illness becomes a messenger and a means to recover archetypal realities alive, but hidden within us. What might this kind of recovery look like and how can one benefit from a mythic perspective of illness and hardship? By way of an answer, I offer a restorative story of the Gorgon Medusa, a Goddess of Endometriosis, who can be seen as incarnating in millions of women across the world.

Because it is the Gorgon Medusa that energizes my story, I must understand the possible meanings of her archetypal presence, which I perceive in endometriosis. Her identities and their denotations and connotations must be explored. I focus on the ancient Medusa as parallel to primal levels of human experience and development in body and psyche. Therefore, I do not address her modern representations in pop culture and elsewhere. The first step in healing is reaching back and down into the formative experiences of understanding and wounding. And so, I begin with the imagery and origins of the Gorgon from her Neolithic appearances through the Greco-Roman period. I uncover her ancestry, predecessors, and ties to so-called Great Goddess traditions around the Aegean, in North Africa, and Crete as well as her cultural connections to Old Europe and the Minoan-Mycenaean civilization, which heavily influenced ancient Greek culture. As I dig deeply into the mythic past, other great goddesses are evoked: Athene and her mother Metis, Innana and Ereshkigal, and the Bird/Serpent Goddesses of the Neolithic. Even prior to her union with Athene in Greek and Roman tales, the Gorgon is linked to complementary aspects of archetypal powers traditionally expressed through multifaceted Great Goddesses or goddess complexes like the Triple Goddess, who manifests as maiden-mother-crone such as Persephone-Demeter-Hecate. Medusa's emblematic head—its terrible and generative aspects—is associated with the Evil Eye, daemonic sacred, demonic feminine, sacred vulva, shame, menstrual taboos, and the experience of embodied misogyny. The Gorgon's evolving representations; dual, liminal nature; and links to other chthonic goddesses and traditions reveal psycho-spiritual and socio-cultural significance related to characterizations of femaleness and feminine archetypal power.

Moving beyond her visual representation, I investigate Medusa in the narrative tradition from archaic Greece with Homer and Hesiod into the Greco-Roman period. Literary depictions provide descriptions of events and details about Medusa's appearance, origins, family, offspring, and divine associates, expanding and contextualizing her image, power, and role in ancient Greece and beyond. Multiple mythic and historic versions of episodes demonstrate Medusa's multiplicity and complexity, and a tradition of ambivalence toward her, expressed in the Gorgon's paradoxical linking of destruction and creation, repulsion and attraction, which resonates with experiences of endometriosis within the context of sexual tyranny engendered in patriarchy. The changing interpretations and roles of Medusa are examined to expand understanding of the socio-cultural and archetypal evolution of the feminine and femaleness. Ancient Greek socio-cultural and mythic issues surrounding menstruation, female roles and agency, and feminine nature and power are analyzed as contributors to the foundations of modern misogyny and its deep roots in the body.

Imperative to comprehending Medusa is a familiarity with Athene, upon whose breastplate or *aegis* the Gorgon's snaky head is consistently represented. Medusa is inextricably interconnected with Athene in Greek mythology. Probing Athene's connection with Medusa entails tracing their bond back into their pre-Greek origins. My focus on Athene is delimited by her association with Medusa such that it is primarily through Medusa's story that I meet and understand Athene. I analyze Athene's mythology as it relates to Medusa's rather than for its own sake. For it is through Athene's repeated, sometimes puzzling interventions into Medusa's story that the Greek Gorgon is created. Athene, that iconic female defender of patriarchy emerges as a trickster with deep and enduring roots in the chthonic feminine sacred. Aspects of each goddess's true nature are revealed in the context of their relationship and this connection is essential to the sort of healing—as meaningful, reconciling integration—which I champion.

Working with Myth

Both my approach to working with mythology and the healing activity I articulate in this book are interdisciplinary. In terms of mythography, this stance follows the position expressed by preeminent myth scholars such as William Doty, who argues for "a multilayered, multifunctional mythography that folds in ritual studies as well as iconography."[4] Through this interdisciplinary diversity of perspectives I plumb symbolic meanings, metaphysical truths, and psychological wisdom expressed in mythic material. In particular, depth and archetypal psychology and archeomythology inform my reflections on and analysis of mythic material, as does the commentary of classical scholars who lean toward psychological and mythopoetic interpretations. The function and form of mythic material in and across cultures are also relevant. Underpinning my thinking is a feminist perspective: belief in and advocacy for equality of value of the so-called feminine and female experiences as forms of truth. This stance does not negate the masculine; rather it asserts the equal validity and veracity of the feminine. Because I conceive of endometriosis as more than its biological reality—as reflective of feminine identity and power issues—I engage feminist perspectives to contextualize mythic, cultural, historical, and biological implications of Medusa within gender-driven power constructs. As I sort through Medusa's mythic legacy, I pursue threads that counter those tending toward exclusively demonizing interpretations or primarily patriarchal perspectives that give ascendency to the male/masculine. My approach allows interplay between academic rigor, intellectual skepticism, and intuitive curiosity and possibility. I avoid literalism so that I can uncover the latent truths within my intuition of Medusa as a face of endometriosis.

In defining literalism, I follow the conceptual leads of C.G. Jung and Hillman. Literalism is a way of understanding that equates meaning with external form; literalism rigidly limits and calcifies understanding, renouncing the creative imagination. While material reality manifests concretely, the concrete also signifies an underlying meaning, that is, an archetype. Archetypes can be thought of as the energies of all life including those manifested from the organs of the body, their powers, and conflicting needs.[5] Beyond this embodied but somewhat materialist conceptualization of archetypes, is the understanding that archetypes are fundamental energy patterns of potential psychological response. These patterns of potential are understood as inherent to psyche as instincts are to biology. While the particular form in which an archetype emerges is personally, culturally, and historically specific and influenced, the essence of the archetypal energy is independent of that form. An archetype includes all of the qualities of its essence such that within an archetype is its opposite or shadow aspect *in potentia*. When an archetype manifests, it tends to appear in a specific form with strong positive or negative associations. For example, the Mother archetype may be expressed in images of the Virgin Mary, ideas of the natural world as benevolent, or experiences of being nurtured. The opposite or complementary aspect may constellate as the Wicked Witch, "dark" nature, or the *vagina dentata*. We perceive archetypes through emotionally-charged motifs, ideas, experiences, and behaviors. Anyone who has felt the inebriating elation of love knows Aphrodite's touch, just as Demeter surely dwells in the stupefying agony of grief. From the depth psychological perspective, reality includes not only the concrete and explicit, but also the archetypal and implicit. Literalism denies the archetypal such that a complex symbol forsakes its protean dynamism and numinosity and becomes simply a sign. By working with mythic images and stories archetypally, both the specificity of the explicit and the universality of the implicit are employed to discern multiple truths.

An Embodied, Psycho-mythic Approach

Psychologically, the healing process I present is primarily grounded in the depth and archetypal tradition of Jung and his successors. This lineage recognizes the multiplicity of the psyche, including the expression of that multiplicity in myth and art, and supports a varied and inclusive apprehension of psychic experience. A cornerstone of my work is the idea that it is valid and efficacious to engage the archetypal pattern of a disease, whether it be endometriosis or cancer or lupus; that such an effort can and ought to be employed via the mythopoetic action of the creative imagination. In practical terms, techniques of Jungian active imagination, dream work, and other forms of reflective, meditative inner work serve as ways to encounter, interact with, and integrate content and experience. While mythic material and mythopoetic processes are viewed as symbolic renderings of archetypal patterns, these phenomena also have a *psychoid* reality—partaking of both the psyche and matter. Therefore, to complement the psychological and engage the wisdom and role of the body, other therapeutic perspectives more overtly championing the psycho-physiological and somatic come into play.

Modern trauma theory is a multidisciplinary endeavor linking developmental, attachment, and psychodynamic theories with biological and relational frameworks. As such, the approach provides a theoretical link between mind and body. Typically, suffering from a disease like endometriosis may not be seen as traumatic in comparison to other harrowing events, such as being the victim of violence. However, this incurable, chronic, and painful disorder often causes extreme, debilitating stress. Its inextricable link with reproductive processes and femaleness is such that the illness is a lightning rod for misogynistic attitudes—including documented stereotyping and psychopathologizing of afflicted women as over-achieving man-haters, manipulative needy narcissists, or sexually frigid hypochondriacs—which can contribute to the overwhelming nature of endometriosis. Associated surgical interventions as well as infertility and other complications can evoke physiological and psychological trauma responses in those who suffer from the disease.[6]

Trauma is a physiological process of the mammalian nervous system in response to overwhelming stressors and has psychological and physical repercussions. Much of current theory situates traumatic activation in a biological understanding of resilience in the face of suffering and pain through observations of other mammals. This perspective reveals the innate wisdom of nature carried, and potentially available, in the human body as well. In addition, interpersonal neurobiological perspectives offer an integrative model wherein psychological healing is conceived of as the linking of differentiated parts into a functional whole, an idea that heavily influences my understanding of healing as reconciliation and integration. The interconnection and power of personal and collective, and inner and outer narratives in wounding and healing comes into focus through this unified psycho-physiological perspective that brings the body explicitly into the picture. The neurobiological focus of much of trauma theory balances the tendency of depth psychology to emphasize non-somatic aspects of psyche. It is not my intention to abandon mystery for biological reductionism. However, including voices from the natural sciences provides balance by ensuring that the body and embodiment are material parts of the discussion and by engaging the analytic rigor and elegance of rational cognition in a dance with the inspiration and transcendence of mythic consciousness.

In addition to the modern pursuits of understanding embodiment represented by trauma theory and neuroscience, I rely upon more ancient, indigenous models expressed in shamanic traditions and conceptualized in ritual theory. Such frameworks provide theoretical grounding and practical tools from thought systems that unify body and mind and validate imaginal realities. The inclusion of indigenous wisdom requires an attitude of deep respect and self-awareness. Archetypal patterns are culturally as well as individually influenced, so it is important to be conscious and respectful of the fact that others' traditions are first and foremost, their own, while constructs like archetypes and depth psychology are Western. Any insights arising from a psychological reading of indigenous material should be recognized as a "cross-cultural borrowing" colored by Western perceptions, values, and ideas.[7] However, such understandings and applications revitalize Medusa's shamanic roots claimed by scholars including the archeomythologist Marija Gimbutas and offer a wisdom bridge reuniting experience sundered by dualistic paradigms that undermine healing. Research by Michael Winkelman,[8] under the guidance of indigenous practitioners, supports shamanic ritual's efficacy within the neural circuits of the human brain and asserts the capacity of shamanic ritual, and other embodied ceremony, to integrate physiological experience and perception with the imaginative mind. Shamanic practice provides access to the *psychoid* realm. Embodied apprehension can be understood as "neurognostic," that is, based in biological structures and features of the brain, its processes and their physiological responses which interact through preverbal perception and enactment—enactment that can be activated through ritual behavior.[9] This approach is congruent with my lived experience of Medusa manifest in my body and imagination.

Another therapeutic idea vital to the healing process I portray is the proposition that narrative formation can be curative. I am arguing for the efficacy of re-story-ing as healing such that an understanding of the power and function of stories as healing, harming, and relational is necessary. Story happens when events are conceived of as meaningful experiences—cohesive, interrelated, and causal. Narrative formation is a neurologically integrative process utilizing both hemispheres of our brains and is the primary meaning-making mechanism for reconciling the difficult events of life; in profound ways, my reality is shaped by the way I see and narrate my experiences to myself and others. The archetypal nature and power of mythopoesis energizes and deepens experience through understanding and may engender health or harm.

In this book, I do not write about the literal curing of endometriosis. Rather, I offer a story to complement medical treatment—a narrative which engages therapeutic concepts and practices that connect relational, psycho-physiological, and mythopoetic realities. Relationship, as a concrete and imaginal phenomenon, is both creative and deconstructive and is the field in which we are wounded and healed. Through the principle of relatedness, I challenge the conceptualization of mind as split from and superior to body, and the myriad repercussions and extensions of this central conception of reality. Perhaps our most fundamental relationship is with our own bodies; we live in bodies and are therefore embodied. Human experience—even psychological experience—occurs within or in relationship to the body; even so-called out-of-body experiences infer embodiment by way of disembodiment. The body, as material and archetypal, is an essential source of information and wisdom, but one must learn to listen to its language of symptom, sensation, intuition, affect, and dream.

The dissociation of mind from body echoes a deeper split wherein human consciousness reacts to duality through aversion or attraction, rupturing relationality, denying interconnection and interdependence, and creating suffering. The split in consciousness divorces cognition from embodied ways of knowing, compromising the integrity of both. I work to re-harmonize the intellect with other ways of knowing; to embrace each form of perceiving as valuable, limited, and essential. Other ways of knowing include interpretations of experience that validate mythopoesis, subjective embodied experience, and the imaginal realm. These "other ways of knowing" conceptualize reality as consisting of multiple, interrelated, teleological complex systems that move into and out of harmony. Healing in this context is psycho-spiritual, fundamentally reconciliatory and integrative; the emergence of harmony and meaning from disharmony and meaninglessness. This healing is mediated through generated, creative, relational fields that are essentially mythopoetic; fields that can be concrete and imaginal, interpersonal and archetypal, human and nonhuman.

Endometriosis and Menstruation

Given that my story focuses on endometriosis, a concrete understanding of the disease is needed. Even among women who have endometriosis and health practitioners who treat it, large gaps in up-to-date knowledge are typical, as are lingering, incorrect opinions and beliefs. A recapitulation of the disease story is an essential thread in the tapestry of healing. While many comprehensive guides as well as websites and other sources are available, I provide an overview of symptoms, diagnosis, treatment options, and issues of infertility and other aspects of the disease. I also highlight and challenge some aspects of conventional wisdom and medical misinformation commonly encountered when dealing with endometriosis. I offer an historical review of medical conceptualizations of the disease, as well as relevant socio-cultural issues. Problematic attitudes surrounding female reproductive processes, identity, gender bias, cultural norms and taboos around menstruation, "female" pain and sexuality, guilt, grief, victimization, relational implications, and feminism influence nearly every aspect of the way endometriosis is understood, treated, and experienced. As a fuller image of the disease emerges, a Medusan presence begins to enliven the physical and her divine paradox is evident not only in endometriosis but in the cycles of menstruation experienced by most women.

Archetypes and Gender Considerations

Mythic images, including deities, constellate archetypal energy patterns or archetypes. While archetypal energy patterns are not gendered, archetypal motifs, including mythic imagery, typically are sexed. Further, a particular manifestation as female, male, androgynous, or hermaphroditic illuminates some sort of psycho-spiritual and/or socio-cultural truth. Therefore, gendered language and psycho-cultural constructions of gender and sex are part of the story. The words and even the very idea of feminine and female—and masculine and male—are currently undergoing cultural deconstruction. However, because I am working with gendered archetypal personifications and also given the fact that endometriosis is an estrogen-reactive disease, that is, biologically a female disease, my story both benefits from and is limited by language and conceptualizations that may sometimes feel incomplete or untrue to the experience of some readers. While an offering to the larger collective, my story bears the burden and the blessing of reflecting one woman's experiences, amplifications, interpretations, musings, thoughts, and analysis. As the author, I elucidate one framework of many for exploring the so-called feminine principle in relationship to the female body. I relate insights into feminine creative and destructive power and its connection to the so-called masculine principle from a psycho-mythic perspective reflected through and delimited by my individuality.

Mythologizing Healing

The embodied, psycho-mythic healing process moves from the relative objectivity of "my story" into mythic "mystory" and links embodied and psychic experience relationally, facilitating the examination of creative, procreative, and destructive power in the context of the female body and psyche. Reflections on the relationship between victim and victimizer; development of a female identity and body; the experience of embodied misogyny; trauma as a portal to the numinous; and lessons of the chthonic feminine, split and reconciled, are explicated against the backdrop of the experience of endometriosis. This effort allows myth and body to interpenetrate, providing coherence and wisdom. I also reflect on the implications of "restoring the disease its god" for one's attitude toward and experience of illness, death, and life. I mythopoetically weave together threads of endometriosis, Medusa, and Athene on the loom of my lived experience of the disease, imaginative and embodied reflection the weft and warp of a life tapestry. By personifying endometriosis as Medusan, pathology is rendered sacred. By contemplating what it means to be a human woman in embodied relationship with the divine, I provide a psychological and spiritual model of healing while living with chronic illness. I do not profess the Truth, but offer my truths; truths that will continue to deepen and morph with lived experience and greater understanding. By beginning with the examination and transformation of one body and soul, I offer one possible path toward well-being. While I focus on endometriosis, the process demonstrates how suffering can be integrated without denying or rejecting the lived experience of it, thereby finding ways to access healing, resilience, and even joy by relating to dis-ease through the mythic imagination.

CHAPTER 2

ENDOMETRIOSIS: MEDICAL MASK AND ARCHETYPAL FACE

A Brief Overview

Before a meaningful link is made between Medusa and endometriosis, the disease and its effects must be described. In fact, an in-depth explication of endometriosis not only illuminates the enigmatic nature of the disorder, but highlights cultural sex and menstrual taboos and misogyny, and underscores perplexing antagonism among medical professionals, as well as between doctors and patients regarding the disease. Even the name "endometriosis" is somewhat of a misnomer, since it reflects a bias toward a particular theory of pathogenesis that is not universally accepted as accurate.[10, 11]

I review the prevalence, morphology, presentations, symptoms, pathogenesis, diagnosis, and treatment of endometriosis according to the Western model and provide a brief summary of Traditional Chinese Medicine's understanding of the disease. At times, the medical description may feel complex or even tedious. However, the biology of endometriosis provides a critical ground and complement to my later mythic and imaginal exploration and is worth the effort. My explanation of the disorder is influenced by the fact that I am not trained in medicine, which circumscribes my understanding of medical texts. The research is heavy with citations for the sake of transparency; I do not claim to be a medical authority. Rather, I delve into the biology of endometriosis because I am deeply curious and value the perspective of the scientific paradigm as one form of truth. Many medical professionals are dedicated, caring, and competent—I would not be writing today if not for successful and sometimes heroic interventions built on scientific rigor and human compassion. However, as I unwittingly discovered, medicine has documented its all too frequent misogyny for all to see. As a woman and a patient, my subjective experiences of being dismissed, shamed, and medically under-treated prohibit me from feigning indifference to the more egregious claims and characterizations found throughout supposedly scientific materials. My primary goal is to provide some understanding of the physical, psychological, and socio-cultural faces of endometriosis so that the rational mask prescribed by the Western medical paradigm can be removed and an archetypal face revealed.

Briefly, endometriosis is an estrogen-dependent disease of inflammation typically defined by tissue similar to that within the uterus appearing ectopically, that is, elsewhere in the body.[12] Experientially, endometriosis is most often a disorder of menstruation with implications for fertility; that is, endometriosis is a disease inextricably linked with menstrual processes. The condition appears to develop through multiple pathways and is heritable.[13] With no definitively known cause, cure, or prevention, and "[d]espite a high rate of occurrence, endometriosis remains a poorly understood disease that is difficult to diagnose noninvasively or manage appropriately."[14] According to Serdar Bulun, MD, a preeminent specialist, the understanding of endometriosis is "evolving from a local disorder [of the reproductive system] to a complex, chronic systemic disease."[15] A mass of misinformation, taboos, and ignorance surrounding the disease, as well as a long, disturbing history of medical professionals and others blaming patients for their illness and dismissing their symptoms, has contributed to a "sisterhood of pain [that] has extended across millennia."[16]

Prevalence: Who Suffers From Endometriosis?

Endometriosis afflicts 176 million women or an estimated 10% of women worldwide.[17] Prevalence is 35 to 50% among women with pelvic pain and infertility[18] making endometriosis the leading cause of pelvic pain[19] and one of the three primary causes of infertility in women.[20] In North America, 5.5 million women suffer from endometriosis,[21] and in the United States alone, over 50,000 women ages 15 to 64 are hospitalized for the disease annually, making it the third leading cause of gynecological hospitalizations.[22] As endometriosis specialist David B. Redwine, MD, laments, "[b]y any measure, it is one of the most widespread diseases affecting human beings."[23]

While endometriosis primarily occurs in women of childbearing age from menarche through menopause, the disorder has also been found to persist in postmenopausal women, and there are rare occurrences in prepubescent girls and men undergoing estrogen therapy.[24] Women of all ethnicities and socio-economic groups are at risk. According to data collected since the 1980s by the Endometriosis Association, the disorder appears to be occurring in younger women and in more severe forms.[25] First described in the late nineteenth century using microscopic observation, endometriosis is sometimes considered a disease of modern, industrialized society,[26] however, others argue that the disorder has been manifesting in women symptomatically, "called by a variety of names for perhaps thousands of years."[27]

The statistical face of endometriosis outlined above conceals a lamentable history of callous and misogynistic stereotyping of women who suffer from the disease. As recently as the 1980s, endometriosis was characterized as a disease of upper middle-class white women[28] "who wait too long to get pregnant [...and are] too educated for [their] own good."[29] Such attitudes seem to position endometriosis as proof of long held beliefs, even among some physicians, that "emancipation of women would mean the destruction of their menstrual cycles and thus the end of the human race, for woman exists to bear children."[30] While white women with endometriosis have been labeled as "stressed-out, perfectionists [...] who brought it on themselves by postponing childbearing," African American women's symptoms of endometriosis have been dismissed as sexually transmitted disease "based on a racist assumption that black women are sexually promiscuous;" research shows that 40% of African American women diagnosed with sexually transmitted pelvic inflammatory disease had endometriosis instead.[31]

In 1923, Robert Hutchison, MD, wrote in the *The British Medical Journal* about "The Abdominal Woman," whom he describes as "generally a spinster, or, if married, childless and belonging to what are commonly termed rather ironically nowadays the 'comfortable' classes,"[32] with her "incessant demand for sympathy and understanding [...she is] a veritable vampire, sucking the vitality of all who come near her."[33] Hutchison goes on to describe symptoms common to endometriosis followed by his judgment that there is "both a physical and a mental aspect [to chronic abdomen], and that the latter is often the more important."[34] His recommended treatments are distraction and cultivation of a wider perspective by the patient through ill fortune, bereavement, war, the vote, marriage and childbearing, or a sound beating.[35]

Ideas that endometriosis and pelvic pain are primarily manifestations of troubled female minds persist. In 1994 at the Fourth World Congress on Endometriosis, a presentation by a psychologist asserted, without supporting data, that endometriosis is a modern affliction resulting from "woman's conflict over her role in society" and "severe conflict over menstruation and sexuality," which is expressed physically "in the form of endometriosis."[36] This literal, linear causality expressed by someone situated as an expert undermines any functional investigation into the possible relationship between psyche and soma, and, intentional or not, suggests that endometriosis is the unfortunate result of women's liberation. In addition, "the outrageous notion that somehow the woman brought [endometriosis] on herself still exists. [...] All too often [patients] have to overcome the notion that their pain is more psychologically based than physical."[37] There is no scientific evidence to support any of these claims, which are so reminiscent of the rhetoric of the past regarding women's diseases. Yet, the vast majority of women with endometriosis (70 to 75%) report having been told by medical professionals that their symptoms were "psychological in origin."[38]

The continuing thread of women's pelvic and menstrual pain being discounted as mental rather than physical is reflected in the *Diagnostic and Statistical Manual of Mental Disorders (DSM)*, which is used to diagnose psychiatric disorders. Somatization Disorder is identified and described in the *DSM* as a condition suffered primarily by women, which features a list of physical symptoms correlating with those of endometriosis to an uncanny degree.[39] The symptoms of Somatization Disorder are a history of pain including menstrual pain, pain with sex, back pain, headache, rectal pain, and pain with urination, and gastrointestinal symptoms such as nausea, bloating, vomiting, diarrhea, and food sensitivities.[40] All of these symptoms are associated with endometriosis. To make matters worse, despite the fact that the *DSM* concedes that the "symptom picture encountered in Somatization Disorder is frequently nonspecific and can overlap with a multitude of general medical conditions," the three "features" suggested for making a differential diagnosis are the involvement of multiple organ systems, early onset and chronicity with no evident physical signs, and a lack of lab test confirmation.[41] Women with endometriosis very commonly exhibit all of these conditions due to the nature of the disease and the inadequacies of medical treatment. For example, there is still wide-spread physician and patient ignorance of the nature of endometriosis as a multisystem disorder, rather than strictly a gynecological disease. The result is that when women report multisystem symptoms these are frequently not understood as part of a single disorder—endometriosis. Further, symptom onset often begins with menstruation in the early teens; 41 to 66% of women report their first symptoms occurred before age 20.[42, 43] Endometriosis is often chronic with high recurrence rates, even when treated appropriately. The disease has no outward physical signs and, despite the fact that tests such as pelvic ultrasounds are not generally diagnostically effective for endometriosis, they are widely used, resulting in false-negatives that can raise "doubt surrounding the genuineness of symptoms among doctors and the women's social groups," as well as within the women themselves.[44] The possibility of misdiagnosing endometriosis as a psychiatric issue such as Somatization Disorder is likely increased by the conditions upon which differential diagnosis relies. In fact, psychiatrists miss major physical illnesses in 48% of their referrals of patients to outpatient treatment for supposed psychological conditions.[45]

Beyond the Western tendency to assume that the pelvic and menstrual pain of endometriosis is primarily psychosomatic, women in some cultures have gynecological examinations and care withheld due to concerns over preserving virginity or allegiance to other sex norms.[46] Our ability to know the true prevalence of endometriosis is inhibited by such socio-cultural biases, including gender discrimination. Currently, one in 10 women is estimated to suffer from endometriosis, however the actual number is likely higher.

Morphology: What is Endometriosis?

The current understanding of endometriosis is that it is a chronic and likely progressive disease in which endometrial tissue, similar to that lining the uterus, occurs elsewhere in the body as benign (non-cancerous) tumors or implants. It is now known that endometriotic tissue is not identical to the endometrium found within the uterus, however, like the endometrium, endometriosis responds to the hormonal changes of the monthly menstrual cycle by growing, swelling with blood, and then breaking down and bleeding.[47] That is, endometriotic tissue menstruates. Because the blood has no way to exit the body, endometriosis causes internal bleeding, triggering irritation, inflammation, and often scarring of the tissue surrounding the growths. While inflammation is normally a natural and functional immune response, the excessive and chronic inflammation often seen with endometriosis is a primary feature of the disease.[48]

Endometriosis takes several forms depending on its location and severity. Upon microscopic examination, endometriosis consists of two kinds of cells, glands and stroma, occurring together.[49] Visual manifestations including small black, brown, or blue blister-like lesions; nodules; and cysts filled with old blood and surrounded by fibrosis (scarring within muscles or organs) are typical as are red lesions; clear sac-like implants; and white or yellow-brown scars that look like burn marks. Microscopic, essentially invisible, endometriosis is also common.[50] In addition, large ovarian cysts called endometriomas, extensive fibrosis, and adhesions (both filmy and dense) can develop, distorting pelvic organs. Adhesions are bands or networks of tough scar tissue that can literally fuse organs to each other or to the pelvic wall. Endometriomas are filled with thick, tar-like fluid that allows them to adhere to surrounding tissue and organs, encouraging fibrous scar tissue to penetrate deeply and damage organs such as the bowel or fallopian tubes.[51] Endometriosis can also infiltrate the musculature of the uterus creating a condition called adenomyosis in which the womb swells and hardens, losing its ability to contract, resulting in pain and heavy bleeding. In acute cases of endometriosis, endometriotic nodules grow through the peritoneum and invade organs including the uterosacral ligaments, vagina, bowel, bladder, or ureters causing pain and serious damage.[52] In addition, "[s]evere [endometriosis] is frequently associated with significant peritoneal adhesions,"[53] that can fill the pelvis, binding organs together into a stone-like mass, causing a condition known as "frozen pelvis."[54] Other dangerous complications can occur with endometriosis such as bowel or ureter obstruction, peritonitis resulting from ruptured ovarian cysts,[55] and a slightly increased risk of ovarian and other cancers[56] including breast and melanoma.[57]

Location: Where is Endometriosis Found in the Body?

Endometriosis is primarily found in the pelvic cavity and on the organs of the lower abdomen. Common sites include the peritoneum (lining of the pelvic cavity), ovaries, fallopian tubes, cervix, vulva, vagina, and the outside surface of the uterus. Implants have been found on the uterosacral ligaments that support the uterus, the rectouterine pouch between the upper vagina and rectum, and the rectovaginal and vesicovaginal septae that separate the vagina from the rectum and the bladder,[58, 59] as well as on the appendix, bladder and ureters, intestines, colon, and in the rectum. Research that maps the locations of endometriosis reveals a "slight predilection for disease on the left side of the pelvis" as compared to the right.[60] Occasionally, endometriosis is found in abdominal surgical scars.[61] There are also rare instances of endometrial growths occurring in other parts of the body including the "diaphragm, lungs, navel, breasts, arms, legs, groin, nose, and eye,"[62] and in the brain and spine.[63]

Symptoms of Endometriosis

The symptoms of endometriosis tend to be cyclical (relating to the menstrual cycle), increase in severity over time, and are frequently debilitating and chronic. They may vary considerably from one woman to another and can be similar to those of other conditions such as irritable bowel syndrome, appendicitis, ovarian cysts, or cancer.[64] On rare occasions, a woman with endometriosis will be asymptomatic so that the disease is only discovered when she undergoes surgery for infertility or some other abdominal surgical procedure.[65] And, while the disease usually appears to be progressive, sometimes, for unknown reasons, painful symptoms spontaneously resolve without treatment;[66] although cessation of pain may not indicate disease resolution.

Generally, the two most common symptoms of endometriosis are severe pelvic pain and diminished fertility.[67] While infertility affects approximately 38% of women with endometriosis,[68] the primary symptom indicating the disease is pain—acute, chronic, and cyclic; pain that interferes with daily functioning and can come to dominate a woman's life. Ninety-six percent of women with endometriosis report suffering dysmenorrhea, or painful periods[69] and 80% of women have pain sufficient to keep them from their regular activities one to three days per month.[70]

Pain symptoms

Painful menstrual periods (dysmenorrhea), pain during and after sexual intercourse (dyspareunia), pelvic pain, pain during ovulation, lower back pain, pain with bowel movements, and painful urination are all typical with endometriosis.[71] Discomfort associated with heavy menstrual bleeding, abdominal bloating, bouts of constipation and diarrhea, urinary dysfunction, and fatigue are also common.[72] Nearly 80% of patients report bowel symptoms and endometriosis occurs on or in the large intestine, particularly the sigmoid colon, rectovaginal septum, and rectum, in approximately 10 to 15%t of patients, with some estimates as high as 37%.[73] The intestines and their function can be affected by the biochemicals produced by endometriosis sharing the peritoneal cavity with the colon as well as by inflammatory chemokines (a type of cytokine or immune cell) produced by the body in response to the disease.[74] Urinary tract endometriosis may include implants on the ureters (tubes connecting the kidneys to the bladder), which can lead to kidney failure.[75]

While the pain associated with endometriosis has multiple sources, including "chemical and mechanical interference with pain receptors (nerve endings),"[76] inflammation appears to be a central mechanism. Inflammation is triggered by the presence of refluxed menstrual blood and also by abnormally high levels of inflammatory biochemicals, including cytokines, prostaglandins, and histamines produced by the immune system and the endometriosis lesions themselves.[77, 78, 79] Nerve pain receptors are irritated by these biochemicals and respond with pain sensations. Cyclical and self-perpetuating, "inflammation can cause tissue damage [and ...t]issue damage can also cause inflammation"[80] resulting in chronic pain that becomes progressively worse.

In addition to chemically induced inflammatory pain, tenderness, pressure, swelling, and stretching caused by organs stuck to each other or to the peritoneum by adhesions can cause pain during menses and with movement, including exercise, bladder or bowel activity, and sexual intercourse.[81] Research indicates that adhesions and fibrotic scarring may also cause pain by limiting blood supply to nerves, resulting in oxygen deprivation and trapped "aggravating metabolic waste products."[82, 83] The endometrial lesions themselves are like "inflamed blisters," causing pain when they come into contact with other tissue and when they burst, spreading "even more inflammatory chemicals which further [irritate] the pain receptors."[84] Prostaglandins, not only contribute to pain by causing inflammation, but also cause strong muscle contractions resulting in cramping.[85] Additionally, endometriosis appears to generate its own nerve fibers, perhaps in conjunction with its development of blood vessels (angiogenesis), and these pain receptors can communicate directly with the central nervous system[86] creating yet another pain pathway. According to David Olive, MD, the intensity of pain seems to be related to the location of the endometriosis in the body and the depth of penetration of lesions rather than simply to the number of lesions and adhesions.[87] When endometriosis invades surrounding tissues, as it does in severe disease, the pain becomes excruciating.

Chronically inflamed and irritated, pain receptors, whether via mechanical or chemical stimulation, may become hyper-sensitive and dysfunctionally reactive.[88] When the pain from endometriosis becomes chronic, the nature of the pain experienced may change from nociceptive pain—the normal, acute sensation in response to a particular stimulus at a specific site—to neuropathic or even centralized pain, thus complicating treatment.[89] Neuropathic pain, a result of chronicity, is not restricted to the site of injury, but rather involves the peripheral and central nervous systems so that pain may be present without a specific stimulus.[90] In cases of centralized pain, the "system itself starts acting like a nerve ending" resulting in exaggerated pain responses to even slight stimuli.[91] Any or all of these pain mechanisms can be involved in women's physical experiences of endometriosis.

Many pain symptoms of endometriosis are exacerbated by non-physical factors. For example, women who experience dyspareunia may be accused of having intimacy problems or of using disease—

feigned or real—as an excuse to avoid sex. When medical professionals erroneously believe that endometriosis pain is psychological, they contribute to the stress a woman and her partner contend with regarding sexual intercourse. In an effort to help male partners understand the intensity and reality of dyspareunia, endometriosis specialist Andrew S. Cook, MD, describes it as "pain so severe [the man would feel] as if his testicles were being hit repeatedly."[92]

Social taboos about menstruation that limit open discussion about the process also normalize and minimize dysmenorrhea, isolating women and reinforcing self-doubt regarding the severity and legitimacy of their pain.[93] Having their dysmenorrhea minimized, normalized, or dismissed as unreal by gynecologists—as is reported by near 70% of endometriosis patients[94]—contributes to guilt and self-blame in women, as well as undermining their social support. Women may feel doubly victimized; once by endometriosis and again by the medical establishment.

Menstrual taboos reflect fear, disgust, and shame around the menses—attitudes still prevalent in women and men for "[m]enstrual taboos are among the most inviolate in many societies."[95] In the United States, menstruation is being more openly discussed now than in the past. However, comprehensive research on attitudes is scarce. According to an atypically large nationwide research project done in 1981, two-thirds of Americans believed that menstruation should not be discussed directly or indirectly, while more than one-third "thought women should conceal the fact that they're menstruating from their families," and 50% believed women should not have sexual intercourse during menses.[96] Generally women and men had "negative" attitudes and "confused" understanding about menstruation.[97] A third of women had not known "what menstruation was the first time they got their periods" and 43% reported feeling "scared, confused, terrible, panicky, or ill" in response to the onset of their menses.[98] Other taboos and norms reflected in the research included the beliefs that women "should make an effort to stay away from others when they're having their periods," suffered menstrual cognitive and functional impairment, should limit physical exercise—especially swimming, and smelled and looked different during menstruation.[99]

Researcher Emily Martin concludes that, in the modern West, menstruation is "consistently seen as pathological"[100] in part because it is conceptualized using the language of failure, a *"lack* of production: the disused factory, the failed business, the idle machine."[101] In our capitalist reverence for growth and production, menstruation has the "connotation of a productive system that has failed to produce [...], gone awry," or produced only waste.[102] Menstruation as lack and failure situates an essentially female process as counter to a primary cultural value—orderly growth and continual productivity are positive and necessary. Menstruating women "are in some sinister sense out of control [...]. They are not reproducing, not continuing the species, not preparing to stay at home with the baby, not providing a safe, warm womb to nurture a man's sperm."[103] Menstrual pain becomes further proof of the pathological nature of menstruation's grossly "unproductive" nature. The pain of endometriosis plays into this aspect of menstrual taboo as does the disease's connection to infertility.

Infertility symptoms

Infertility is defined as being unable to conceive despite one year of unprotected sexual intercourse or experiencing two or more spontaneous miscarriages.[104] Approximately one third of women with endometriosis suffer diminished fertility.[105] In addition, higher rates of miscarriage, ectopic pregnancies, and premature birthing have been reported.[106, 107] Generally, the exact relationship between infertility and endometriosis is not known. Sometimes infertility results when the reproductive or pelvic organs are sufficiently damaged by endometriosis[108] or when adhesions distort the anatomy of the pelvis enough to interfere with conception and successful pregnancy.[109] In addition, the pelvic inflammation caused by endometriosis can "impair the function of uterine tubes, decrease receptivity of the endometrium, and hinder development of the oocyte [immature ovum] and embryo."[110] In some cases, the fallopian tubes are obstructed by endometriosis resulting in infertility.[111] Other disease-related mechanisms that may contribute to infertility include immune system dysfunctions, "hormone and ovulation abnormalities," and exposure to "environmental contaminants such as dioxin."[112] Additional agents that are as yet unknown may contribute to infertility as well.

Infertility and other reproductive complications affect women, their partners, and families profoundly. A woman's capacity to become pregnant and deliver a healthy child is a fundamental part of her biological, psychological, and social identity, whether or not she chooses to become a mother. Women who suffer infertility, miscarriage, stillbirth, or other birthing complications contend with feelings of grief, fear, anger, guilt, shame, inadequacy, and "impaired self-image."[113] Even in the West, where women enjoy relative reproductive control and freedom, the cultural valuation of women's worth as directly related to motherhood underlies biases in the medical diagnosis and treatment of endometriosis and the seriousness with which specific symptoms may be addressed by doctors and others.

Theories of Pathogenesis: What Causes Endometriosis?

The cause of endometriosis is not known.[114] While it has been traditionally thought of as a gynecological disease, it is more likely a complex, multifactorial disorder in which dysfunctions in the immune and endocrine systems, genetic and epigenetic predispositions, and environmental factors all play significant roles.[115] (Epigenetics is the study of biochemical and environmental factors affecting gene expression.) There are multiple and evolving hypotheses about the pathogenesis of endometriosis and uncertainties about what aspects of the disease are causes versus effects or symptoms. Endometriosis is not contagious and is not caused by inanimate objects such as tampons.[116]

There are many misconceptions about the cause of endometriosis that have roots in outdated and sometimes prejudicial theories. These include the disease resulting from female sexual promiscuity[117] and nymphomania,[118] sexually transmitted diseases,[119] too little sex (with one's husband) or intercourse during menstruation,[120] childbirth or postponing childbearing, over-education of women, women's innate nervous temperament and "inbred weakness,"[121] hysteria, hypochondria, female moral weakness and inferiority to men,[122] not marrying,[123] and abortion or using contraception.[124] God's vengeance for female disobedience is cited as the cause of menstrual, pelvic, and other female pain.[125] According to a respected physician and teacher from the mid nineteenth century, symptoms of what is now recognized as endometriosis are caused by:

Child-bearing, unrestrained sexual intercourse, abortions, precocious nervous excitement from the perusal of prurient books, the lascivious polka, and the various exciting scenes of city life. [...] The lady, who revels in luxury, and has around her, even to satiety, all the comforts and pleasures which opulence can secure, would gladly, whilst writhing under the agonizing pain incident to some formidable affliction of the womb, surrender all these comforts to regain the health which, it too often happens, she has sacrificed by her own folly and imprudence![126]

These supposed causes reflect the enigmatic nature of endometriosis, but are also informed by menstrual and other taboos and biases surrounding women's bodies and reproductive power.

There exists a long tradition of characterizing the uterus as innately "mischievous" or misbehaving; the uterus is "the primitive Seat of the Evil (hysteric fits)."[127] Negative attitudes toward the uterus are often linked to aversion toward menstruation. For Aristotle, the menses demonstrated woman's inferiority to man and the "female state as being as it were a deformity."[128] The eleventh century physician Avicenna proclaimed that "menstrual blood is eliminated through the womb because that organ is the weakest and the last formed."[129] And in the seventeenth century, Regnier de Graaf, the physician and anatomist for whom the ovarian follicles are named, asserted that "the uterus is the weak point of the female and hence the outlet for menses."[130] In the tradition of Western culture, woman is equated with the womb and its functions, which are characterized as inherently inferior and troublesome.[131]

Another misconception is that stress causes endometriosis. However, "there is no scientific evidence of a link between stress or any one life event and the onset of endometriosis."[132] As with other issues of mind-body-environment interaction, understanding about how stress affects the body and disease is emerging through research in epigenetics and molecular biology. What is relevant here is that the development or cure of endometriosis is not under the conscious control of an individual and the paradigm of blaming the victim is a distortion of reality. Direct, linear causation is not supported by research and such explanations oversimplify complex, subtle interactions and correlations.

In 1991, a widely circulated women's health publication asserted that the chronic pelvic pain of endometriosis is caused by "psychological factors" linked to a history of major physical and sexual abuse.[133] However, research indicates that the "majority of those with endometriosis or adhesions or chronic pelvic pain are *not* found to have had prior sexual or physical abuse."[134] While physical and sexual abuse of women is widespread, a causal link to endometriosis has not been proved despite some pressure to validate the assertion; regardless of "widespread belief" to the contrary, a history of sexual abuse does not cause endometriosis.[135] The misguided "science" supporting claims of sexual abuse as a cause of endometriosis notwithstanding, both the urge to connect women's chronic pelvic pain with traumatic abuse and the vehement disavowal of the hypothesis stimulate reflection. The association of abuse and disease can endorse the cause to combat abuse, and yet, there is an echo of the dismissal—"it's all in her head"—connected to the argument.

Another common psychological profile assigned to the woman with endometriosis, and characterized as a cause of the disease, is that she has deep-seated resentment about being female, ambivalence about her sexuality, and hostility toward men and that her inner conflict causes "the organic disease."[136] While women may be negatively affected by and experience anger regarding gender injustice and the low status of women in patriarchal culture, this sort of literalism reflected in supposed explanations of female disease is a profound obstacle to both a functional scientific understanding of the disease—a *concrete* understanding—and an efficacious mythopoetic apprehension of endometriosis.

Beyond the misconceptions, current scientific theories of the development of endometriosis—each of which contributes to an understanding of the disease, but none of which provides a definitive explanation—include retrograde menstruation/implantation, coelomic metaplasia, embryonic rests, lymphovascular metastasis, and accidental transplantation. In addition to these theories, ongoing research in areas including stem cells, immunological and endocrine anomalies, genetics, and environmental toxin exposure is challenging outdated, unproven ideas and leading to a clearer understanding of the nature and complexity of endometriosis, its cause, and possible treatment.

Medical science categorizes endometriosis as the "dominant member of five closely related benign müllerian diseases" affecting various female reproductive organs.[137] The condition of being benign simply indicates that endometriotic tumors or lesions are not cancerous. The characterization of endometriosis as a müllerian disease means that the cells making up the lesions originate from fetal cells of the mesoderm, or middle layer, of embryonic cells that differentiate into "the müllerian ducts and the urogenital ridge" in utero.[138] In other words, endometriotic cells come from the fetal precursor cells that differentiate into the female reproductive organs, as well as other tissues. This does not mean that the "mesoderm that forms the urogenital ridge and the müllerian ducts is [...] the cause of endometriosis, [rather] it is the final common pathway for multifactorial causation."[139] The various theories of cause address the source of endometriotic tissue and the mechanisms by which endometrial cells occur ectopically (outside of the uterus) and proliferate into disease.

The theories of retrograde menstruation/implantation, lymphovascular metastasis, and accidental transplantation generally assume the primary source of endometrial cells is the uterus. The theories of coelomic metaplasia and embryonic rests focus on the observation that under the influence of biochemical stimuli (such as hormones or inflammation), certain cells retain the ability, like embryonic cells, to transform from one type to another and that some of these cells become invasive after transformation. It is thought that endometriotic tissue arises from these embryonic cells at the location they occur. In other words, they did not implant, but are congenital.

Regardless of the source of the endometrial cells, the disease occurs when the cells attach to and invade the pelvic peritoneum or other host tissue; avoid identification and eradication by the immune system and the normal process of apoptosis (biologically programmed cell death); chemically "counter-attack" the "host" immune system; establish a blood supply (angiogenesis); and apparently use the body's natural inflammation responses to "promote their [...] invasion and persistent growth."[140] In addition, establishment and growth of endometrial implants requires estrogen; estrogen that is produced primarily by the ovaries, but also by the endometriosis itself.[141] It is possible that given the complexity of the process of proliferation, the "defining" endometrial lesions may turn out to be a symptom, rather than the cause of endometriosis.[142]

Theory of retrograde menstruation and implantation

A widely accepted theory of the primary cause of endometriosis, put forth in the 1920s by John A. Sampson, MD, is implantation via retrograde menstruation.[143] During menstruation, under the force of uterine contractions, some menstrual fluid containing endometrial cells from the uterus flows backward through the fallopian tubes and out into the pelvic cavity. Normally, the immune system isolates and removes misplaced endometrial cells. If not eradicated, refluxed endometrial cells are theorized to implant onto the peritoneum and pelvic organs and develop into endometriosis.

The vast majority of menstruating women—up to 90%—experience retrograde flow and women with endometriosis have greater amounts of menstrual reflux.[144] However, while most women appear to experience retrograde menstruation, only about 10% develop endometriosis.[145] This disparity has spurred investigation into contributing factors that might explain how retrograde menstruation could develop into endometriosis in some women, including the identification of "molecular defects or immunologic abnormalities (or both)."[146] Other issues not resolved by retrograde menstruation theory include the disease's appearance outside of the peritoneal cavity and its rare but observed development in women post-hysterectomy or tubal ligation, and in men treated with estrogen and prepubescent girls.[147,148] Sampson himself recognized that his "implantation theory does not account for all instances of ectopic endometrium-like tissue in the pelvis and that menstruation is only one means of disseminating that tissue."[149] However, his theory of the uterine origin of endometriotic tissue prevailed when in 1925, his name for the disease, "endometriosis," was widely accepted, turning the scientific conceptualization of the disease away from embryological origins to the uterus.[150] Despite the theory's limitations, it is still generally accepted that retrograde menstruation plays a key role in the pathogenesis of endometriosis. However, specialists speak of "multiple pathways" of development[151] and some vehemently challenge the theory as "mythic and incorrect;" a misdirected theory that predicts "100% failure for any treatment method because the disease will simply be re-established with the next menstrual flow."[152]

Theories of coelomic metaplasia and embryonic rests

In contrast to Sampson's hypothesis of retrograde menstruation/implantation as the origin of endometriosis, are theories of the "embryonic origin" of the disease.[153] Embryonic origin asserts that endometriosis is congenital, developing from embryonic precursor cells in utero or via coelomic metaplasia (cell transformation) after birth.[154] Theories of embryonic origin set forth in the early twentieth century were supported by the fact that pathologists had demonstrated metaplasia in many tissues in the human body."[155] "[A]nyone skilled in microscopy could see the transition from normal germinal layer to endometriosis and back to normal ovarian germinal epithelium [...and] they could see also invasion of normal endometrium into underlying [muscular wall of the uterus]."[156] The existence of cell transformation in the body and the invasion of normal tissue by transformed tissue were established, even if the precise biochemical stimulus was undetermined.

Simply stated, the theory of coelomic metaplasia suggests that peritoneal cells can transform into endometrial tissue.[157] Both peritoneal and endometrial cells arise from the same embryonic origins—the coelomic epithelium—during the prenatal stage of development. Three possible catalysts hypothesized to cause the transformation of peritoneal cells include "chronic inflammation or chemical irritation from refluxed menstrual blood";[158] some mechanism related to estrogen production;[159] or response to infectious or environmental stimuli.[160]

The embryonic rests theory suggests that remnants of the embryonic precursor to parts of the reproductive system, so-called müllerian ducts, may "differentiate into endometrial tissue" by an unknown mechanism.[161] Whatever the specific triggers for cell transformation, the basic idea of both coelomic metaplasia and embryonic rests is that some adult cells—which like embryonic tissue are capable of transforming into reproductive tissue—or certain remnant embryonic cells are chemically influenced to turn into endometriosis.[162] Because embryonic cell transformation theories assert a congenital pathogenesis of endometriosis, such theories may explain the appearance of ectopic endometrial cells where menstrual reflux is not likely to be their source, such as in premenstrual girls or males undergoing estrogen therapy, as well as other unusual presentations.[163] However, the theories have yet to be proved and require further exploration.[164]

Lymphovascular metastasis theory

This theory attempts to address cases where endometriosis appears in remote parts of the body, such as the brain, lung, lymph nodes, extremities, or spine. The exact mechanism is not known, but, endometrial cells are thought to be transported via the lymph and/or blood systems to distant locations where they implant and grow into endometriosis. This hypothesis may provide insight into the spread of endometriosis, but does not contribute to understanding its primary cause. In addition, these presentations are rare.[165]

Accidental transplantation theory

Endometriosis is sometimes found in abdominal surgical scars. In these particular cases, it is believed that endometrial tissue has been inadvertently deposited during gynecological surgeries, such as cesarean sections or even during the delivery of a baby. The misplaced cells then implant and grow into endometriosis. Accidental transplantation theory has limited application, but it may explain this particular presentation of the disease and indicates the need for surgeons to take precautions and to guard against adhesion formation during procedures.

Areas of ongoing research

Stem cells and the pathogenesis of endometriosis

According to endometriosis researchers, Isaac E. Sasson and Hugh S. Taylor, "several lines of experimental evidence suggest that endometrial stem/progenitor cells function in the development of endometriosis;" these stem cells "could account for the observations that drive all of the other hypotheses" of the origin of endometriosis. Stem cells, the precursors of all other cell types, are undifferentiated cells that can self-renew and produce differentiated daughter cells.[166] (Daughter cells result from simple cell division, or mitosis, and are genetically identical to the parent cell.) Endometrial stem/progenitor cells have been identified in the uterus and also as possibly being generated by the bone marrow.[167] It is thought that these stem cells may be the mechanism by which the endometrium regenerates following menses and that endometrial stem/progenitor cells are present in menstrual blood.[168] If so, then stem cells from the uterine endometrium refluxed into the peritoneum could be the source of endometriosis as hypothesized by the retrograde menstruation theory.[169] In addition, the existence of endometrial stem/progenitor cells from the endometrium, marrow, or other sources may help explain the cell transformation speculated by coelomic metaplasia and the embryonic rests theories, as well as observations of remote endometriosis facilitated by lymphovascular transport. Despite the progress represented by the identification of endometrial stem/progenitor cells, these stem cells have not been proven to be the cause of endometriosis and further study is warranted.

Genetic, immunological, and endocrine connections

As mentioned previously, through investigations into the molecular mechanisms of the disease, a picture of endometriosis is emerging as a complicated condition involving numerous biological and environmental processes within multiple physiological systems.[170] The implications are that endometriosis is likely caused by alterations in a woman's genes, hormones, and immune response triggered by the biochemical compounds and reactions that control gene expression and environmental influences, including "[s]tress, diet, behavior, toxins, and other factors."[171, 172]

This re-conceptualization of endometriosis arises from a host of research findings. For example, endometriosis runs in families, through the mother,[173] and having a first degree relative—a mother or sister—with endometriosis is a significant risk factor for developing the disease.[174] According to Harvard researcher Rose Frisch, PhD, carrying the gene for red hair is shown to be a risk factor for developing endometriosis because of biochemical differences that effect allergic reactions and menstruation.[175] Genetic anomalies have been found in the endometrial tissue of women with endometriosis; differences exist between tissue located within and outside of the uterus and compared to women without the disorder.[176] Some abnormalities in the endometrial cells have been found to over-stimulate or disrupt immune response.[177] Multiple immune system abnormalities have been observed, including elevated levels of various types of immune cells and atypically high levels of inflammatory agents in the peritoneal fluid; the production of immune-function-disrupting chemicals by endometriotic lesions; over, under, and non-reactivity on the part of immune cells; autoimmune reactions that produce antibodies to attack endometrial cells or cell components as if they were foreign bodies rather than simply misplaced tissue; and generally chaotic and confused immune responses to stimuli.[178]

Researchers are investigating how the immune, endocrine, and female reproductive systems interact and how these complex interactions are disrupted by endometriosis. Estrogen and progesterone communicate with the immune system via chemical messengers called cytokines to maintain a healthy, functioning reproductive tract.[179] Estrogen stimulates immune function while progesterone is immunosuppressive or quiets immune activity. With endometriosis, the hormone balance is disturbed, demonstrating estrogen dominance and decreased progesterone sensitivity; this imbalance disrupts the "endocrine-immune communication pathways" in the endometrium, negatively affecting menstruation, reproduction, and immune function.[180] Reduced progesterone responsiveness in the endometrium (both within the uterus and outside of it) is now widely recognized as a primary condition of endometriosis,[181] allowing lesions to establish and grow. Additional anomalies have been identified in the endometrium, hormones, and immune activity of women with endometriosis who suffer from diminished fertility.[182] These hormone/immune disruptions may contribute to infertility by causing alterations in the uterine lining that inhibit embryo implantation or by contributing to a pelvic cavity environment invaded by excessive amounts of cytokines, and other immune biochemicals, that are toxic to sperm and damage ovaries and/or ova.[183]

Women with endometriosis appear to suffer from other immune and endocrine-related disorders at higher rates than the general population. These comorbidities include irritable bowel syndrome, interstitial cystitis, allergies, asthma,[184] insulin resistance, food and environmental sensitivities, fibromyalgia, chronic fatigue syndrome, eczema, vaginal yeast infections, migraine, rheumatoid arthritis, autoimmune diseases, Hashimoto's thyroiditis/hypothyroidism,[185] and multiple sclerosis.[186]

The precise mechanisms and implications of many of the above findings are still under investigation. However, whether immunological aspects of endometriosis are causal or symptomatic, "it's very obvious that the immune system is a key player" in the disorder.[187] If findings with regards to the interaction of hormones and the immune system within the reproductive tracts of women with endometriosis are proved fundamental to disease pathogenesis, researchers will need to "determine whether the initial trigger for the development of endometriosis comes from the endocrine system, the immune system or both."[188]

Environmental toxin exposure

There is epigenetic evidence that environmental exposure to toxins and processes that influence gene expression, such as radiation, trigger endometriosis and perhaps explain observations that the disorder's severity may be increasing.[189] In 1991, studies by the National Aeronautics and Space Administration and the United States Air Force on the effects of long term radiation exposure found that 53% of the exposed rhesus monkeys developed endometriosis—more than double to control rate of incidence.[190] The elevated level of endometriosis was "conclusively linked" to the radiation, and recommendations specifically addressed women's exposure to "doses of protons or x-rays" as a factor increasing risk for the disorder.[191]

Women exposed in utero to "environmental toxins or potent estrogens such as diethylstilbestrol [or DES]" have higher rates of endometriosis.[192] Between 1940 and 1971, five to 10 million pregnant women were prescribed the synthetic estrogen product DES, which, in addition to its connection with endometriosis and cancer in the patients, is linked to cancer, endocrine disruption, infertility, and possible immune problems in the daughters of medicated women.[193] The granddaughters of women given DES suffer menstrual abnormalities as well as possible infertility.[194]

In addition, evidence is mounting linking the development of endometriosis with exposure to a group of environmental toxins called organochlorines commonly referred to as dioxins (dioxin, PCBs, TCDD, PCDD, etc.).[195, 196] In the 1980s, studies suggested that rhesus monkeys exposed to PCBs developed endometriosis and exhibited excessive inflammation and reproduction problems including miscarriages and stillbirths.[197] Further experiments on monkeys in the early 1990s linked dioxin exposure directly to endometriosis,[198] even at very low doses—five parts per trillion of

TCDD.[199] Seventy-nine percent of exposed subjects developed the disease; the greater the dioxin exposure the more severe the endometriosis.[200] Findings proving causation in humans have been mixed; some demonstrate a direct connection, while others are less conclusive.[201] However, dioxin's disruption of the endocrine and immune systems is confirmed: "TCDD [...] clearly act[s] as an endocrine disrupting chemical in several systems affecting both estrogen and progesterone action" and "TCDD and PCBs can cause chemotoxic disruption of cytokine-mediated communication among immune cells [...that] can impair immune response" in ways exhibited in several diseases including endometriosis.[202] The World Health Organization documents immune, endocrine, and reproductive disorders due to environmental exposure to dioxin.[203]

From an epigenetic view of endometriosis, "dioxins seem to turn on genes that promote inflammation" and disrupt estrogen metabolization contributing to a functional imbalance between estrogen and progesterone.[204] Effects of different compounds vary, but generally they mimic the actions of hormones by "recognizing their binding sites;" counteracting the effects of the hormones by "blocking their interaction with their binding sites;" interacting with the hormones and altering their synthesis; and causing changes in the levels of hormone receptors.[205] However, while it is known that dioxins disrupt the endocrine-immune interface, it has not been determined how, which is essential if treatment interventions are to be produced.[206]

Given their links with disease, concerns over exposure to dioxins and other organochlorines seem well founded as these highly toxic chemicals are "ubiquitous in soil, sediment and air;" present in foods, especially meat, dairy products, and fish; and found in human beings in body fat, mother's milk, blood, semen, and respiration.[207, 208] Dioxins, PCBs and other organochlorines result from industrial and natural processes when chlorine combines with organic compounds, mainly petrochemicals. Dioxins can occur from natural incineration sources like forest fires, but are more typically byproducts of waste incineration, metal processing, production of some herbicides and pesticides, and paper bleaching.[209] Dioxins do not easily break down and so persist environmentally, bioaccumulating and biomagnifying through the food chain such that concentrations in human beings continually increase over time. In addition to being carcinogenic and disruptors of the immune, reproductive, and endocrine systems, dioxins and PCBs are linked to developmental problems including learning disabilities, IQ deficits, and psychomotor and neurological delays; hyperactivity and other behavioral issues; the development of diabetes and endometriosis;[210] and alterations in thyroid function, and glucose and hormone metabolism.[211]

While some organochlorines have been banned in the United States, including PCBs and DDT, many dioxins continue to be produced and those already in the environment will remain for a very long time, continuing to contaminate humans and other species.[212] Based on contamination levels of women living near the Great Lakes in the Midwestern United States, and without additional exposure, it "may take six generations before PCBs are cleared from our bodies."[213] Environmental exposure to organochlorines like dioxin and its link to the development of endometriosis is a critical area of research for prevention and treatment.

Diagnosing Endometriosis

There is no lab test to diagnose endometriosis and it cannot be accurately identified using CT, MRI, or ultrasound technologies.[214] Transvaginal ultrasound may reveal large endometriomas (ovarian endometriosis) or help to rule out other conditions that cause pelvic pain and infertility,[215] but cannot detect the peritoneal lesions characteristic of endometriosis or the amount of disease present.[216] Unfortunately, "nondiscriminatory" tests, such as transvaginal ultrasounds are frequently used by doctors in the attempt to diagnose endometriosis, which leads to misdiagnoses and/or delays in diagnosis that undermine the patient's ability to get proper care and support and contributes to the common belief that pelvic pain is psychological in origin.[217]

Pelvic and rectal examinations can sometimes suggest the presence of endometriosis either because the doctor can feel nodules in the rectouterine pouch, an enlarged ovary or other anomalies, or the examination itself causes the patient pain.[218, 219] If such examinations strongly indicate endometriosis, surgical confirmation is necessary for proper treatment. Diagnosis is further complicated because the symptoms of endometriosis overlap with other conditions, endometriotic lesions may be clear or microscopic and therefore virtually invisible to the surgeon's eye, and some women with the disease are asymptomatic. Currently, the only conclusive way to diagnose endometriosis is through abdominal laparoscopic surgery wherein, under general anesthesia, the abdomen is distended with carbon dioxide and a tiny, lighted camera and other surgical tools are inserted into the abdomen so that the physician can identify lesions and adhesions and take samples to be confirmed for pathology.[220] Both glands and stroma cells must be identified by microscopic examination in order for endometriosis to be confirmed—a "lack of microscopic confirmation [...] remains today one of the underlying problems with clinical management of the disease" since proper treatment requires accurate diagnosis.[221]

As with other diseases such as diabetes or cancer, diagnosis of endometriosis includes an assessment of the stage of the disease; stages I through IV are characterized as minimal, mild, moderate, and severe. Perhaps counter-intuitively, the "stage" does not reflect how symptomatic a woman is, nor does it accurately describe the severity of the disease. Developed by the American Society for Reproductive Medicine, the stages attempt to predict fertility rather than to describe the level of pain or disability, or the likelihood of recurrence after treatment.[222] In fact, the "stages indicate nothing about the level of pain a woman is experiencing" and are not effectively predictive of fertility either.[223] The staging system simply reflects the number, size, and depth of endometriosis lesions and the presence and extent of adhesions.[224] Endometriosis pain does not correlate with the stage or amount of disease, rather, according to Dr. David Olive:

> It seems that the anatomical location and the depth of penetration of endometriosis lesions are the critical factors in determining pain [...as] very superficial lesions tend not to produce much pain unless they are in a crucial anatomic location. Deep, penetrating lesions seem to produce a lot of pain almost no matter where they are located, but if they are at a crucial location, the result can be excruciating pain.[225]

The current staging system reveals an underlying bias toward the validity of infertility symptoms over those of pain, despite the reality that pelvic pain is the most common symptom of endometriosis. Clearly, a more efficacious staging system is needed and others are under investigation.[226]

Delayed diagnosis

Despite the fact that endometriosis can be definitively identified through laparoscopy and microscopic examination of endometriotic tissue, medical diagnoses are frequently complicated and delayed by socio-cultural and psycho-spiritual attitudes. In Western countries, there is an average delay of eight years from the onset of symptoms to the diagnosis of endometriosis.[227] Delays are longer for women seeking care for pelvic pain than for those suffering infertility, "suggesting that there is greater laxity surrounding pelvic pain symptoms" and more urgency when fertility is jeopardized.[228] Diagnostic delays may occur, in part, because surgery is required—a serious prospect for many women. Frequently, however, the issues delaying diagnosis are not medical, but reflect dysfunctional attitudes about women's pain, sexuality, and menstruation.

Delays due to cultural norms and attitudes in patients and society

Women often normalize their menstrual pain even when it is debilitating; dysmenorrhea is perceived of as "'unlucky' rather than ill[ness]"[229] and it is easy to sympathize with not wanting to medicalize a natural process like menstruation. However, suffering in silence is also often validated as strength and "women do not want to appear weak or unable to cope."[230] Menstrual taboos contribute to embarrassment among women so that they lack "comparative evidence from other women" about menstruation.[231] Culturally, "female pain" is seen as normal and possibly a sign of "superior femininity" or "justified pain";[232] "womanly pain" is often considered normal, especially with menstruation and sex.[233] The lower status of women in most societies contributes to diseases such as endometriosis being perceived of as serious only when fertility is jeopardized. Ironically, these same attitudes dismiss the seriousness of female castration (or radical hysterectomy) as compared with male castration or restrict access to health care.[234] Research found that women who lost one to three days per month of work due to pain did not have their symptoms treated aggressively until they suffered infertility, even when they had a diagnosis of endometriosis.[235] The same marginalizing gender biases that undermine assessing the prevalence of endometriosis inhibit timely, accurate diagnosis. The

Endometriosis Association documents personal stories of women who have suffered negative consequences due to delayed diagnoses, including cases of involuntary psychiatric commitment by family, at the behest of physicians.[236] Virginia of Georgia writes, that after 29 months of involuntary commitment, it took her six more years to obtain an accurate diagnosis and appropriate surgery for her endometriosis because of the psychiatric history resulting from her confinement:[237] *"At last after 36 years, I was rid of my physical pain and my complaints were vindicated."*[238] However, even after restoration of her legal competency she continued to suffer appalling social and financial consequences: *"I couldn't live with my children; I couldn't buy real estate. I was limited in other financial transactions. And my former friends and acquaintances shunned me [....]."*[239]

Delays due to norms, attitudes, and biases among medical practitioners

Physicians and other health care providers frequently normalize and minimize pelvic and menstrual pain, delaying diagnosis and causing women to question their experience of their own bodies.[240] Half of women with endometriosis report that their physician did not take their symptoms "very seriously" and 61% were told that there was nothing physically wrong with them—primarily by gynecologists.[241] When pain is the primary symptom, as is most frequently the case with endometriosis, women's complaints are frequently disregarded, resulting in under-diagnosis, under-treatment, and eventually, hysterectomy[242]—nearly three quarters of women with endometriosis have had pain symptoms dismissed by gynecologists as not physically real.[243]

The literature reveals an abundance of tragic anecdotes related to and by physicians as well. Reproductive endocrinologist Michael D. Birnbaum, MD, reflects on a young woman's report that she had hesitated to disclose her dysmenorrhea and dyspareunia to him prior to her diagnosis of endometriosis because of being told by other doctors that it was "all in her head:"

[A]s astonishing as this story may seem, it is, unfortunately [one] that I have heard repeated time and again.... There is a bias that runs through the medical profession. This bias holds that women are neurotic—men are not.... While there is a common belief among some physicians that pelvic pain in women is mainly psychosomatic in origin, my experience is that very little pelvic pain is psychosomatic.[244]

The danger of misdiagnosis is real. Physicians fail to diagnose significant medical conditions in 32% of their referrals to specialists and psychiatrists miss such physical conditions in nearly half their patients.[245] Diagnosis may be delayed due to a tendency to classify symptoms as psychosomatic or even psychopathological; studies reviewed in the *Journal of Women's Health* demonstrate that for similar problems, doctors prescribe tranquilizers and other psychoactive medications two to three times more frequently to female patients than to males.[246] Deeply rooted, perhaps unconscious attitudes toward women's sexuality, menstruation, and power issues around reproduction undermine objective assessment of physical symptoms.[247] In his medical practice focused on endometriosis, Dr. Andrew Cook's experience is that "thousands of women with endometriosis [...] have been misdiagnosed, ignored, treated as hypochondriacs or complainers, sent to psychiatrists instead of to surgeons, and otherwise dismissed."[248]

David Redwine, MD, documents medical attitudes, revealed in texts from multiple traditions and cultures from ancient Egypt (1825 BCE) and Greece (400 BCE) through the turn of the twentieth century in the West, tainted with myriad variations of the idea that women's reproductive diseases are "a pitiful manifestation of [women's] psychological weakness, augmented by God's anger with women and their folly."[249] According to the *Journal of Law, Medicine and Ethics*, "medical professionals take women's reports of pain less seriously than men's and [...] women receive less aggressive treatment."[250] Such studies indicate that too many health care providers assume that women do not or cannot credibly report their own bodily experiences. The relatively recent identification of prostaglandins as a cause of menstrual cramps has helped to legitimize pelvic pain among doctors[251] who have traditionally normalized dysmenorrhea and dyspareunia in part because it was commonly taught that such pain was psychological in origin.[252] Dr. Redwine and Ronald E. Batt, MD, delineate the long, convoluted relationship between social mores, cultural attitudes, magic, scientific inquiry, technology, and suffering women that results in the current understanding of endometriosis; an understanding that is still burdened with cultural taboos, medical misinformation, misogyny, and a genuine lack of scientific consensus that delays diagnosis and hampers the understanding and treatment of the disease. In one study of over 7,000 patients, nearly 50% "had seen at least five different physicians before a diagnosis was made."[253]

In addition, the prescribing of oral contraceptives and other medications, which may help suppress pain, but do not treat endometriosis, and the use of "nondiscriminatory" and ineffective investigation methods, like ultrasound, cause diagnostic delays.[254] While symptom management is important, treatments that may mask underlying disease without a definitive diagnosis imply that endometriosis—or other causes of pelvic pain—is not serious, an assumption that may put patients at risk for requiring major interventions such as hysterectomy. Delay in diagnosis causes women to suffer years of pain; experience "a lack of understanding from others" including doctors, family, friends, employers, and co-workers; diminished self-esteem and increased self-doubt as patients struggle to fulfill their responsibilities; and fear that their symptoms are related to an "ominous condition" such as cancer.[255] Sadly, the long delays in the diagnosis of endometriosis too often appear to be influenced more by psychological factors and socio-cultural norms than sound medical judgment.[256] Ambivalence and taboos regarding female sexuality and menstruation, as well as a lingering perceived inferior otherness of women covertly and overtly conspire against a functional medical response to endometriosis.

Treatment, Remission, and Recurrence

Many treatments for endometriosis currently concentrate on controlling pain and infertility symptoms. This focus is of limited effectiveness since it "merely reacts to and suppresses symptoms as they occur."[257] Treatment results vary widely, disproportionately dependent upon the expertise of the surgeon,[258] the training and experience of the physician, and the woman's ability to tolerate the sometimes serious side effects of potent medications, many of which can only be used for a few months at a time. Many doctors who treat endometriosis patients express dismay at the inadequacy of the care patients typically receive; "the complexity of this disease [...] fully warrants a subspecialty" that includes more in-depth training.[259] In addition, recurrence rates remain high; for all treatments—medical and surgical—the overall recurrence is approximately 20% after 12 months and 50% after five years, while, for half of those treated with drugs alone, endometriosis returns within one year of therapy.[260] Even with surgery, the "gold standard" treatment, recurrence rates for endometriotic implants are 28% within 18 months, 40% after nine years, and up to 50% for adhesions.[261]

In cases of confirmed disease, treatment choices depend upon the severity of symptoms and whether pain or infertility is the primary concern.[262] Treatment of pain can be medical, surgical, or both. Because no available medications have been shown to be effective for the treatment of infertility,[263, 264] intervention consists of surgery and/or assisted reproduction techniques.[265]

Pregnancy and menopause do not cure endometriosis;[266, 267] however, this fallacy is still prevalent among health care providers.[268, 269] Pregnancy, breastfeeding, and menopause alter hormone balance, generally lowering estrogen levels and inhibiting menstruation, and therefore can suppress symptoms.[270] However, following delivery and the cessation of lactation, symptoms tend to recur with the return of menses,[271] and 50 to 60% recurrence rates are found within five years after pregnancy.[272] In some cases of invasive intestinal endometriosis, pregnancy's high levels of estrogen and progesterone may over-stimulate hormone receptors in the endometriotic lesions actually causing proliferation.[273] Other concerns for women considering pregnancy is research that indicates higher rates of complications such as miscarriages and ectopic pregnancy among women with endometriosis and uncertainties about endometriosis being passed on genetically to the child.[274, 275] Research shows that having endometriosis affects women's emotional experience of pregnancy as well. Themes and feelings highlighted include anger and frustration (at oneself and one's body, the medical establishment, and the general situation), fear (of miscarriage or other physical failure of the pregnancy), loss of control, "impaired self-image," guilt, and confusion (over health care, fertility, and endometriosis).[276]

The belief that menopause cures endometriosis is based on the observation that natural menopause results in a decline in ovarian estrogen production. However, it is now known that estrogen is also produced by endometriotic tissue. In addition, hormone replacement regimens may encourage the disease to persist. Hysterectomy with oophorectomy (removal of ovaries) induces medical menopause and eliminates a woman's primary estrogen source, however, surgery also results in a precipitous decline in estrogen with associated symptoms and heightened risks of osteoporosis and heart disease.

Because of the complex, even mysterious nature of endometriosis, the sometimes inadequate response by medical professionals, the failure or cost of traditional Western medical treatments, and psycho-social obstacles that affect women with the disease, myriad alternative treatments are available and frequently sought by patients. According to research by the Endometriosis Association, the top 12 complementary therapies reported yielded relief to between 40 and 65% of women.[277] These therapies include lifestyle changes in diet (including nutritional supplements), exercise, relaxation, and stress management; physical regimens such as neuropathy, acupuncture/acupressure, homeopathy, herbs, immunotherapy, various types of massage, aromatherapy, chiropractic, and yoga; psychological interventions including psychotherapy/counseling, Bach flower remedies, and meditation; and comprehensive systems of healing like Traditional Chinese Medicine[278] and Functional Medicine.[279] Some of these therapies address women's physical needs in dealing with endometriosis, while others, such as psychotherapy provide emotional support, which is efficacious when living with pain, doubt, and worry.

As with other maladies, endometriosis boasts a long and gruesome history of treatments. Even at the end of the nineteenth century, Western physicians, who claimed to base their treatments on the rational, objective principles of science, applied "irritants, counter-irritants, leeches [on the cervix and uterus], bloodletting, and obnoxious items thrust into the vagina, cervix or rectum."[280] "Dilation" of the cervix by means of "mechanical metal dilators, cervical incision, and cervical amputation" which sometimes led to fatal hemorrhaging was common.[281] Intrauterine irrigation with medicinal substances, vaginal baths, abdominal binders,[282] cauterization of the uterus or cervix, packing of the vagina with cotton, clay, or "degreased wool," and vaginal or rectal massage[283] were typical treatments. In addition to these therapies for pelvic pain, intrauterine electrotherapy was introduced in 1887; the remedy was apparently used despite a lack of successful outcomes for the vast majority of patients.[284]

Most physicians and healers practiced their craft with good intentions and according to the knowledge of the day, however flawed or limited those assumptions appear today. What is troubling about the medical history of endometriosis—and many female conditions and diseases—is that treatments often appear based on moral judgments about the innate weakness, irrationality, or evil of women and their sexuality and the malevolent, "bleeding and unpredictably vengeful" nature of the uterus, rather than on objective scientific methods and data.[285] Underlying the treatments, whether efficacious or not, were unscientific beliefs, documented by physicians themselves, about the *"neurotic constitution"* of female patients[286] and the corrupt nature of the uterus: *"Indeed, this organ may almost be considered a center from which the greatest ills for its possessor spring."*[287] The idea that women in pain are neurotic distorts the reality that "the experience of pain includes an emotional response [...]. Pain involves the limbic system of the brain" where survival mechanisms and emotions that underlie our rational centers activate us.[288] Studies of patients with endometriosis demonstrate that psychological profiles indicating psychopathology "return to normal or near normal after patients are successfully cured of their pain."[289] However, as the research demonstrating that generally doctors still do not take the pain of their female patients as seriously as that of their male patients shows, biases about female inferiority and irrationality persist. The pernicious idea that the cure for female diseases, such as endometriosis, is marriage, pregnancy, and retirement from the world of temptation (too overwhelmingly alluring to and stimulating for women) recurs throughout the medical history compiled by Dr. Redwine. The underlying biases toward the proper place for and expression of women's sexuality weakens under the weight of scientific fact and the Women's Liberation Movement, however, it informs lingering prejudices about the cause of endometriosis as postponement of pregnancy and women's striving for power in the wider economic, professional, political, and educational world.

Medical treatments for pain

Generally, medical treatment consists of medications for pain management and pharmaceutical drugs that suppress ovulation, hormonally mimicking pregnancy or menopause. Pain medications do not treat endometriosis, but are used to help control pain and inflammation.[290] These drugs include analgesics, analgesics combined with codeine, non-steroidal anti-inflammatory drugs (NSAIDS), short- and long-acting narcotics, and antidepressants, and are dispensed in regimes specific to the woman's particular pain profile.[291] Chronic pain may be managed using alternative delivery systems for medication such as pain pumps, spinal cord stimulators, nerve blocks, or radiofrequency ablation.[292] Health issues linked to the use of pain medications at high levels and/or for long periods of time vary depending upon the drug and include tolerance and addiction concerns, bleeding, gastrointestinal and liver damage, heart disease, and possibly stroke.[293, 294]

Hormone therapy for treating endometriosis is indicated by the fact that estrogen is required for the development and persistence of the disease. The medical restriction of estrogen synthesis reduces pain, inflammation, and can help control endometriosis.[295] There are several types of hormone medications used to treat endometriosis and each works differently, but the goal of hormonal treatment is to suppress estrogen production and the menstrual cycle.

The most commonly prescribed hormone medications for treating endometriosis are oral contraceptives that combine estrogen and progesterone.[296] Combination oral contraceptives (COCs) limit ovarian estrogen production thereby decreasing the overall level of estrogen in the body and providing some pain relief for 75 to 89% of women who take them.[297] Though they are not without side effects— including blood clots, high blood pressure, nausea, weight gain, headache, irritability, and breakthrough bleeding—COCs are relatively inexpensive and well tolerated by most women.[298] However, these medications do not treat the underlying disease; they do not reduce or eradicate endometriotic tissue, nor do they enhance fertility.[299, 300]

Progestogens are drugs that act like the female hormone progesterone and are prescribed to suppress ovulation,[301] which inhibits endometriotic tissue growth, diminishes lesions, and for many women, reduces pain.[302] However the benefits are temporary, lasting only up to six months after completion of the therapy, which lasts three to 12 months.[303] Progestogens have various side effects including breakthrough bleeding, nausea, fluid retention, weight gain, depression, and a possible increased risk for coronary artery disease.[304, 305]

Danazol is a testosterone derivative that causes a state of pseudomenopause by reducing estrogen production, stopping ovulation and menstruation, and elevating the level of male hormones in the blood, which interferes with the effects of female hormones.[306, 307] Danazol also has effects on the immune system that are beneficial in treating endometriosis.[308] The drug appears to effectively interfere with the processes the allow endometriosis to grow, shrinking lesions and resulting in some pain relief in nearly all patients for up to six months after the three to nine month treatment.[309] Danazol's greatest effect is on mild to moderate endometriotic lesions; it does not affect adhesions or larger cysts and recurrence rates of up to 60% occur within one year of treatment.[310] At typical doses, danazol has "substantial side effects," some of which can be irreversible.[311] A sampling of the side effects include increased body and facial hair, moodiness, weight gain, fluid retention and bloating, acne, increased muscle mass, potentially irreversible deepening of the voice and enlargement of the clitoris, negative effects on HDL cholesterol and carbohydrate metabolism, and occasionally, liver damage and arterial blood clots.[312, 313, 314] Unlike other medications that suppress estrogen, danazol does not cause osteoporosis and may actually add bone mass.[315]

Gonadotropin-releasing hormone agonists (GnRH agonists) suppress ovulation and stop menstruation inducing pseudomenopause.[316] The drugs are effective in temporarily reducing endometriotic lesions and reduce the immune system's over-reactivity to endometriosis caused by estrogen.[317] GnRH agonists do not affect adhesions or other scarring, which may be a source of pain.[318]

A major concern with the use of GnRH agonists is their link to osteoporosis.[319] The length of treatment is limited to six months or less because of associated bone loss[320] and sometimes includes "add-back therapy" of a low-dose combination of female hormones. However, such regimes are expensive and "experimental," and their effectiveness is not confirmed.[321] Other typical side effects include hot flashes, headache, insomnia, vaginal dryness, decreased libido, breast tenderness, depression, irritability, and fatigue.[322, 323] Forty percent of patients experienced short-term memory loss and 10% suffered depression.[324] Recurrence rates five years after treatment are 53 to 74%.[325] GnRH agonists and other hormonal treatments do not cure endometriosis; while the drugs suppress the disease in the short term, they cannot give "long-term relief."[326]

Several other medical therapies are available outside of the United States. Others are being studied or tested in clinical trials. For example, because endometriosis has been found to produce its own estrogen by way of the enzyme aromatase, aromatase enzyme inhibitors, which block all estrogen, may be used as treatment.[327, 328] However, as with GnRH agonists, bone mass loss is a potential problem. Pharmaceutical research is focused on hormonal, immunological, and molecular aspects of the disease.[329]

Surgical treatments

Surgery for pain

Laparoscopic surgery to remove endometriosis and adhesions, with tissue sent for lab pathology confirmation, is currently the most effective treatment for endometriosis.[330, 331] Laparoscopy minimizes adhesion formation and facilitates magnification, which allows for close examination of tissues and organs and excision of all disease possible.[332] Since the mid 1980s, laparoscopy has become the preferred method for endometriosis surgery.[333] However, locating a laparoscopic surgeon with sufficient expertise in endometriosis to ensure desirable surgical outcomes remains difficult.[334] Various studies find that pain relief post-surgery ranges from 61 to 92%[335] with recurrence rates estimated at 15 to 20% after five years.[336] These efficacious results depend upon the expertise of the surgeon, which varies widely due to a lack of specialized training; "it is becoming very clear from recent scientific data that the surgical training doctors receive in residency for even basic laparoscopic procedures is woefully inadequate" for treating endometriosis.[337] Generally excision, or the cutting out, and vaporization of endometriotic tissue is preferable[338] to other surgical techniques such as ablation and cauterization, which do not remove endometrial implants beneath the surface; eliminate only a small proportion of the disease; and cause cell damage, inflammation, and further scarring that can contribute to future pain.[339]

Hysterectomy is sometimes used to treat endometriosis when the disease is severe and other therapies and surgeries have failed to alleviate extreme pain.[340] Despite frequent claims that hysterectomy definitively cures endometriosis, research shows that it does not; 33 to 35% of women do not experience symptom relief or cure and 44% who receive hormone replacement therapy following surgery—a common practice—experience relapse.[341] According to David Redwine, MD, "there is no scientific evidence that endometriosis [lesions are] physically destroyed by either removal of the ovaries or menopausal levels of [estradiol].... In fact, abundant clinical evidence supports the ability of symptomatic endometriosis to exist after menopause [including surgical menopause] without estrogen replacement therapy."[342] This is likely due to the ability of endometriosis to be its own source of estrogen; "endometriotic lesions secrete aromatase enzyme. Androstenedione secreted by the adrenal gland circulates in the blood and is converted by aromatase into estrogen within the endometriosis."[343] However, many women, 60 to 78% in one large survey, gain some relief from surgical intervention.[344]

Hysterectomy is removal of the uterus, and in cases of endometriosis, should include excision and/or vaporization of all endometriotic tissue possible. The most radical form of hysterectomy—removal of the uterus, ovaries, and fallopian tubes (hysterectomy with bilateral salpingo-oophorectomy)—may be necessary depending upon the extent of the disease. Surgical removal of the ovaries, or castration, causes a precipitous loss of estrogen and instant menopause[345] with side effects ranging from hot flashes, night sweats, insomnia, vaginal dryness, decreased libido, mood disturbances, bladder control issues, fatigue, and cognitive effects to osteoporosis and heart disease.[346,347] Because of the severity of the medical effects of total abdominal hysterectomy, there is debate regarding the benefits of preserving at least one ovary, however, for women with stage III or IV endometriosis or with bowel and/or bladder involvement, the recurrence rates with ovary conservation are high—33 to 44%.[348, 349] Hormone replacement therapy is frequently used to ameliorate menopausal symptoms, however it may facilitate return of endometriosis[350, 351]

Intrinsic to discussion of hysterectomy and its efficacy is the underlying cultural attitude about the difference between male and female castration. Male castration is seen as horrific. However, hundreds of thousands of women undergo hysterectomies[352] and the "spaying of women" is normalized and "trivialized";[353] in the words of one physician, "*[a]s to the question of unsexing women, it could not be compared to the unsexing of men.*"[354] In the United States, the general rate of hysterectomies for endometriosis increased 120% between 1977 and 1984.[355] For young women, ages 15 to 24, the rate of increase between 1965 and 1984 was 250% and for women ages 25 to 34, 186%. The use of hysterectomy to treat endometriosis reflects a larger cultural approach to managing menstruation and menopause wherein, according to data collected by the Centers for Disease Control and Prevention between 2000 and 2004, 600,000 American women undergo hysterectomy annually.[356] At any age, hysterectomy has substantial consequences for women. Most women report significant impacts on their sexual experience—often negative.[357] "Symptomatic adhesions" or scar tissue can form following hysterectomy and cause "intermittent bowel obstruction" and other problems, including pain.[358] In addition to significant physical symptoms, women who undergo hysterectomy can experience grief over the loss of their fertility and organs and changes in their experience of their sexual identity.[359]

Surgical procedures are utilized to treat some complications of endometriosis as well as the disease itself. Sometimes endometriosis deeply penetrates the bowel, causing dangerous, even life-threatening blockages that require resection—the surgical removal of the diseased portion of the bowel.[360] Another procedure, used for pain relief, is a presacral or uterosacral neurectomy in which specific uterine nerves are surgically severed.[361]

Surgery for infertility

Currently, laparoscopy and/or use of "assisted reproductive techniques" are the treatments for infertility related to the endometriosis.[362] Surgery removes all of the endometriotic tissue possible along with adhesions and attempts to repair damage to organs.[363] In women with stage I or II endometriosis, surgery nearly doubles fertility rates from 17 to 31% within six months[364] and generally pregnancy success rates improve for six to nine months after surgery.[365]

Advanced reproductive techniques include intrauterine insemination or in vitro fertilization, often in combination with ovarian stimulating medication and/or follicle-stimulating hormones.[366] These procedures result in pregnancy for approximately nine to 18% of women treated, however they are costly[367] and invasive.

Traditional Chinese medicine

Western medicine treats the symptoms of endometriosis by medically interrupting ovulation and the menstrual cycle or surgically removing endometriotic tissue. Because these interventions do not address the root cause, which is still unknown according to the Western medical paradigm, remission may be temporary.[368] In addition, the treatments available are invasive and may cause side effects as disruptive and distressing as the disease itself. The problems encountered in treating endometriosis reflect a tension between the nature of the disease—chronic and multifaceted in terms of cause, biological systems involved, symptoms, and responses to treatment—and the primary strength of the Western approach—responding to immediate, acute physical disease or injury.[369] For the symptoms of extreme endometriosis such as bowel blockage, ureter constriction, or deep penetrating nodules, the West's "extraordinary technological systems [of] diagnosis, surgery and the manipulation of body function" can be life-saving.[370] However, for the intractable, often perplexing symptoms of endometriosis as it is typically experienced, the Western approach is frequently limited, especially long term.

In contrast to the Western model of disease identification and treatment of symptoms through drug therapy and/or surgery, Traditional Chinese Medicine (TCM) takes a more holistic view. According to Daoshing Ni, PhD, Doctor of Oriental Medicine and specialist in Chinese herbology and acupuncture, TCM is based on the understanding that "[o]ur bodies subscribe to the laws of nature, and when there is disease or illness it is because our universe has a certain imbalance," so, the goal of treatment is to restore "homeostasis."[371] *Chi* or *Qi*, "a system of regulating and balancing energy in the body" moves through "pathways called meridians" and animates the body.[372] Disruptions or weaknesses in one's *chi* underlie disease and restoration of *chi*, through the use of acupuncture, herbs, dietary changes, and particular massage techniques, is the focus of cure.[373]

In practice, TCM is based on over 5,000 years of detailed observation, description, and categorization of symptoms, signs, and responses to treatment.[374] It employs more than 5,000 herbs to formulate over 100,000 remedies; 2,000 acupuncture points on the body along 12 primary meridians;[375] and 28 pulses that are interpreted individually and/or in combination.[376] Through close observation of external manifestations of the body—including pulses, appearance of the tongue, pallor, etc.—and bodily responses, TCM focuses on what it theorizes to be the root causes of dysfunction and disease, employing personalized remedies guided by a differential diagnosis process.[377, 378] Treatment is relatively gentle with a "lack of side effects"[379] and, often, results emerge over time. Typically, treatment takes six to 12 months[380] and has been shown to effectively relieve dysmenorrhea in 89% of patients, pelvic pain in 67%, and dyspareunia in 72%.[381]

For the treatment of endometriosis, TCM focuses on what it conceptualizes as the underlying, systemic imbalance or pathology, which Ni describes as "an imbalance of yin and yang, the female and male life forces that run throughout the whole body."[382] Specifically, herbs and acupuncture are prescribed according to the individual woman's primary symptoms and basic constitution, including the patterns of her menstrual cycle.[383] While Western therapies shut down ovulation and menstruation, TCM observes the natural process to identify and treat the underlying imbalance (for example, "Kidney Yang deficiency, Spleen Qi deficiency or Liver Qi stagnation") and the external symptoms ("stagnant Blood and Phlegm-Damp").[384] A detailed explanation of the Chinese system and terminology, and how to understand it from a Western perspective, is beyond this study's parameters. However, what is relevant is that TCM provides an alternative paradigm for understanding endometriosis and its treatment that both complements Western medical approaches[385] and challenges the Western philosophical mind/body split. According to Ni, "the human body does not function on its own; it is a reflection and a coordination of our spirit, mind, emotions, and physical body. No one aspect can function alone […]. Separation of the spirit from the physical body can create or can be seen as a condition of death."[386]

Removing the Medical Mask: Revealing Endometriosis's Archetypal Face

The medical conceptualization of endometriosis is one way to understand the disease; a particular "story" about the experience, constructed by a specific perspective and colored by conscious and unconscious socio-cultural and psycho-spiritual assumptions. Unfortunately, much of medicine's legacy to women encouraged the "lingering concept of doubting a suffering woman's veracity and helped to characterize pelvic pain problems as uncontrollable nervous conditions such as hysteria and hypochondriasis which implied a psychological weakness."[387] As complicated and contentious as the medical story is, it fails to capture the contradictions, frustrations, despair, and rage expressed by many women who suffer from endometriosis. In some ways, the medical story empowers the sufferer by providing concrete facts and objective understanding of the disease. However, the medical perspective also demoralizes because it offers neither solace nor meaning in the face of real suffering and loss.

What is it about endometriosis that makes it a target for controversy? While often debilitating, it is not visible to the eye; it is difficult to diagnose and treat; it has multiple, varied, cyclical, and changing manifestations in the body; its origin and pathogenesis are uncertain; and it affects multiple biological systems often regarded as medically unrelated. But, perhaps most of all, it is a disease tied to female sexuality, menstruation, reproductive power, and feminine identity, which are influenced by taboos, shame, and the low status of women in patriarchal cultures. Taboos reflect "subjects most feared or involved with the power relationships in a society"—women's sexuality including reproduction and menstruation are alien to male experience and therefore a source of threat and potential power.[388] In patriarchy, the power that counts is *power over*. Menstrual taboos are traditionally framed as protection for society, especially its male members, from mysterious female generative powers from which men are excluded.[389] The ambivalent relationship between culture and menstrual processes manifests in dualistic ideas of its sacredness and accursedness, which generalize into contradictory attitudes toward the female body and feminine identity.[390]

Within the literature about endometriosis, deep-seated negative attitudes about women, their inferiority to men, their weakness, untrustworthiness, extreme emotionality, propensity to manipulate and complain, and dire warnings about imagined and real repercussions of their sexuality are explicit and widespread. At the core of these ideas is man's uneasy relationship with the uterus, its blood, "and its capacity to bring both life, suffering and sudden death."[391] A "utero-centric ideology" that sees the womb as "the pathological center of the human female disease universe"[392] contaminates medicine from ancient times into the twenty-first century with ideas such as Hippocrates's "wandering uterus" and the eighteenth and nineteenth century concepts of metritis (inflamed uterus) and hysteria, which was eventually favored by psychoanalytical circles as a frame for understanding physical complaints for which medicine had no effective response, including endometriosis.

Misogyny—fear, hatred, and mistrust of, and prejudice against the so-called feminine and females—including their sexual and reproductive power—underlies utero-centric medicine, many menstrual taboos, and the psychology of "it's all in her head;" a head not to be trusted because it is attached to a female body. Unnecessary suffering results from these attitudes: physical and emotional pain, loss of family and social support, and even incarceration in psychiatric wards. Medical understanding and intervention are hampered as well. In addition, the discussion of any soulful relationship between mind, body, and disease becomes a psycho-social minefield for fear that an imaginal response will be literalized, as psychologist James Hillman warns, and women's experiences will not "signify beyond their literalism";[393] the risk of admitting any nonphysical, psycho-spiritual possibility is the annihilation of one's validity. A danger of linear causality is that it can be used to make the physical literally mental so that we lose the value of the metaphoric relationship between mind, body, and disease as a reality coexisting with the material. As a woman with endometriosis, my character exists in relationship with the disease and yet this does not mean that I am to blame for the disorder's manifestation or that, through my own agency, I cause (or cure) its proliferation. Further, as an endometriosis sufferer who has the capacity to think rationally and scientifically and the ability to intuit, sense, experience, and imagine, I choose to engage all faculties in pursuit of functional, joyful living, even at the risk of marginalization or dismissal.

C.G. Jung proposed that the deities have become our diseases, which means that their visitation is personal and impersonal, particular and universal, and physical and psychological. Research findings that indicate endometriosis is a multisystem disease complex notwithstanding, the disorder's most dramatic manifestations and historical conceptualization tenaciously tie it to menstrual processes and the womb. The uterus, historically "hailed as an organ which commanded obeisance and fear"[394] for its association with death, blood, disease, and female biological generativity, continues to embody polarization as both the cradle of life and a nonessential organ, dispassionately discarded through hysterectomy. The uterus births life and death, perfection and deformity, infant and disease. The dual nature of the womb points to an archetypal energy pattern of which it can be a symbol: the power of female generativity in all its manifestations. Seeing through the medical mask of endometriosis, as a disease most manifest in the female menstrual cycle and reproductive organs, indicates a particular expression or condition of female sexuality and feminine identity to which I turn to the mythology of Medusa to understand.

CHAPTER 3

MEDUSA'S FACE: THE BEAUTY AND THE BEAST

Approaching Medusa

While intended to be scholarly, my exploration is not meant to be an exhaustive study of the mythology of Medusa. I defer to the works I reference throughout this project to provide such comprehensive scholarship. My research is driven by what I intuit to be Medusa's presence in many of the psychological and physical symptoms of endometriosis. I am following inklings, hunches, and associations; searching for a phantom visitor to my imagination and body. I do not call Medusa, she calls me; in some fundamental way, hinted at but not known, Medusa's myth is archetypally my own, lived out in my body through my disease and its effects. I wish to learn what she comes to illuminate in and through me; her persistence dictates that she be my guide.

However, my conjuring of Medusa is grounded in her mythology and iconography; I am not making up my own private Gorgon. As scholar Chris Downing asserts, the deity is revealed through stories: "the god[dess] *is* the stories that are told about [her], the rituals that are celebrated in [her] honor, the temples dedicated to [her]."[395] Therefore the images and narratives associated with the Gorgon are of primary importance, including material that pre-dates her ancient

Greco-Roman manifestations. In addition, "to follow the trail of any one Greek myth is to find oneself engaged with the whole of Greek mythology, all of the stories and all their variants."[396] Obviously, I cannot cast so wide a net; however, I touch upon several other mythic figures as required to more fully constellate Medusa and understand her story. Immersion in the variant myths about and associated with the Gorgon allows the material to "speak for itself," to evoke the mythic Medusa—or more accurately, Medusae.

Finally, I divide my study of Medusa into two parts. In this chapter, I concentrate on the Gorgon's names, image, and origins. In Chapter 4, I examine Medusa's presence in ancient Greek literature. Across the board, I focus my study on her ancient manifestations. I am investigating the primal Medusa as parallel to primal levels of human experience in body and psyche. Therefore, I do not attempt to trace Medusa into modern history, but limit myself to her earliest appearances. My choice does not infer that Medusa's essential, archetypal power has diminished. Despite substantive changes in Medusa's representations, including emergence of the so-called Beautiful Gorgon in fifth century Greece and Ovid's portrayal of her victimization, my sense is that her fundamental potency remains active, though defiled, demonized, and repressed. The explicitly fearsome Medusa reemerged with great vibrancy in the Renaissance,[397] and depictions of her throughout history display a compelling tension between power and pathos. In notable renditions by artists during the fourteenth to seventeenth centuries including Cellini, da Vinci, Rubens, Bernini, Caravaggio, Dante, and Shakespeare, Medusa is "sometimes depicted as horrifyingly ugly, but just as often, beautiful and tragic."[398] In the 19th century she was associated with Jacobinism and emblematic of French liberty. The Gorgon's presence remains vital in modern works by Goethe, Shelley, Rodin, Dali, and Picasso, and in popular culture—where she frequently takes on overtly sexual overtones—in electronic media, film, literature, art, and advertising, including the Versace logo. Even a brief survey of Medusa's potency in stimulating psychological and feminist thought indicates that she still activates the collective imagination, just as she has mine.

What's in a Name?

Erich Neumann observes, the "abundance of manifestations is a characteristic of the archetype, and the plethora of names by which the powers are invoked among peoples is an expression of their numinous ineffability."[399] Medusa's multiple nature is reflected in her stories and also extends to her appellations and their etymologies. She is first a Gorgon, later differentiated from her sister Gorgons as Medusa, the only mortal of the three goddesses. She is also a member of the family Phorkyades. By delving into the meanings of her names and their associations, a fuller understanding of how this goddess constellates in the mythic imagination is uncovered as are clues about how her significance changed through the lenses of time and culture.

"Medusa" as queen

The name Medusa, or Medousa, is Greek for "ruler or queen,"[400] "ruling one,"[401] or "mistress."[402] Ancient legends persisted wherein Medusa was an extraordinarily beautiful, fierce queen or princess who ruled the Libyans (or the Gorgons, in other variations) in her North African domain. Such "rational," historical accounts are recorded by Palaephatus, an Athenian writer from the fourth century BCE; Herodotus, the fifth century BCE "father of history;" Diodorus, a first century CE Sicilian historian; and Pausanias, a Lydian who traveled extensively throughout the ancient Mediterranean in the second century CE.

Palaephatus dismisses the fantastical versions of Medusa the monstrous Gorgon, identifying her instead as one of three Ethiopian princesses who shared rule of their father's kingdom after his death. The greatest treasure of their domain was a golden statue of Athene called the Gorgon, which was the tribal name for the goddess in that region of Libya.[403] The Graiai, who in some mythic accounts are Medusa's sisters and involved in her demise, are absent from Palaephatus's report. However, he offers an interpretation of their single, shared eye as implicated in revealing the Gorgon's secret location: it represented an advisor shared by the sister-rulers. The Eye traveled between the sisters' courts as a trusted counselor. Rather than a great hero, Perseus was a pirate who kidnapped the Eye to extract information about the princesses and their treasures. In order to gain possession of the golden Gorgon, Perseus threatened the princesses and only Medusa refused to cooperate, so he killed her. Her sisters' divulged the Gorgon's location and Perseus made off with the statue. He cut off its head to adorn his ship, which he renamed the Gorgon and used to terrorize and pillage throughout the area, demanding tribute from the islanders. Palaephatus explains that the Gorgon's reported ability to turn people to stone arose from an episode wherein a group of islanders set up decoys—men of stone— in their marketplace in order to escape from Perseus and the Gorgon's tyranny.

Herodotus also situates Medusa's historical origins outside of the Aegean in North Africa. He claims that Perseus brought Medusa's head to Greece from Libya near Lake Tritonis. Similarly, Diodorus Siculus connects Medusa with North Africa as Queen of the Gorgons.[404] He describes a war between the Gorgons and Amazons, two races of "women who were famous for valour and warlike exploits" and discloses that the Gorgons "for courage and valour were eminent."[405] Perseus conquered the Gorgons during Medusa's reign and ultimately, both the Gorgon and Amazon tribes were obliterated by Herakles; "For it was a thing intolerable to him, who made it his business to be renowned all the world over, to suffer any nation to be governed any longer by women."[406]

Pausanias "attempts to distinguish between legend and reality" and reports that Medusa was "a Libyan warrior queen" and Perseus, "a Greek prince" of Argos.[407] Again, Medusa's kingdom was located on Lake Tritonis in Libya. Perseus made war on her tribe during which he assassinated her in the night. Struck by her beauty, he removed her head and took it to Greece as a prize. Pausanias's discussion serves to explain a local legend that Medusa's head was buried under a mound in the marketplace of Argos.

What do these historic accounts reveal about Medusa? She was reportedly a powerful ruler from the heroic past reigning over far-off, exotic lands and cultures radically different from Greece, notably for the higher status of women. The stories tied to her queenly name also suggest Medusa's extraordinary allure and battle prowess, that is, her potency. Her queenship appears to have been an abomination to the Greek patriarchal ideals of heroism embodied in Perseus and Herakles. A cultural and political struggle against neighboring gynocentric cultures echoes through the historical accounts, suggesting that Medusa's identity as a monster reflects a distortion or constriction since she was, as a supreme female ruler, anathema to patriarchy. In addition, the contradiction between the monstrosity of a female ruling over men and Medusa's reported allure and renown is echoed in later tales where she is conversely negative and positive, terrible and lovely. Further, that the accounts situate Medusa's origins outside of Greece, particularly in Northern Africa, or Libya, suggests that she represents very ancient, alien values. The stories firmly position Medusa and the feminine values she embodies as "other," therefore inherently threatening to the later Greek worldview.

Medusa as "ruling one" also resonates with the findings of Marija Gimbutas and Miriam Robbins Dexter that support the goddess's emergence out of the Gorgon of the Bronze Age and the Bird/Snake Goddesses of earlier Neolithic traditions in which great goddesses appeared to be vital. It is significant that Medusa and Athene are connected in the historic narratives and that the two figures are enmeshed in time, place, and identity as Gimbutas' work hypothesizes common origins for the two goddesses. I examine her findings more thoroughly later in this book. In regards to Medusa's queenly name, Gimbutas asserts that the "usage of the term *queen*" for virgin goddesses "who continued to be powerful in their own right" rather than ceding or modulating power through marriage to the male gods of the Olympian pantheon, is a vestige of the Great Goddesses' ruling power.[408] And in fact, in later Greek myth, through the unity of Athene Gorgopis (Athene with Medusa's head upon her breastplate), the feminine divinity retains much of her potency as a "ruling one," despite her inescapable adaptation to Apollonian realities and values.

"Medusa" and connotations of water, the underworld, and the unconscious

The scholar Karl Kerényi observes that while Medusa means "ruleress," the name also pertains to the sea as the masculine version was used to refer to the sea gods Phorkys (Medusa's father) and Poseidon (her consort/father of her children).[409] Mythically, water is also associated with the feminine and its symbolic meanings can be generalized into three categories: "it is a source of life, a vehicle of cleansing and a centre of regeneration."[410] In the *Theogony*, Hesiod distinguishes the ocean as masculine and fresh water as feminine[411] and describes Medusa's birthplace as "the *pegai*" or springs.[412] When feminine, water is linked with the Earth, the Moon, menstrual blood,[413] and mother/fertility goddesses such that Medusa's name ties her to a long tradition of goddesses of life, death, regeneration, and fertility.

The link between the name Medusa and water also infers her connection to water creatures. Not surprising, Medusa's mother Keto is goddess of the monsters of the sea, including whales and sharks.[414] The Medusa (subphylum Medusozoa) is another "monster" of the deep—the formidable adult stage of a stinging, carnivorous jellyfish found in all of the world's oceans. Horses and snakes, also symbolic water creatures, are frequent animal doubles for Medusa. Mythically, the horse comes from the primordial waters and is "the mysterious child of darkness and carrier both of death and of life"[415] and serpents emerge from and embody water as the primordial source of life and regeneration.[416] Medusa is depicted with horse features, births the flying horse, Pegasos, and couples with Poseidon, the "dark-blue-maned" one who also rapes other goddesses in the form of a stallion.[417] Medusa's horse associations link her with the Mother Goddess as primordial source of life; the archetypal feminine in her fertility, death, and rebirth aspects; a symbol of sacrifice and apotropaic powers; and as associated with shamanic powers of sight and the ability to cross boundaries.[418] Like the horse, the serpent, Medusa's most iconic animal familiar, has meaningful associations with not only water, but the archetypal feminine as source and embodiment of the life force.

Medusa's identification with water, its deities, and creatures indicates lower world qualities in contrast to solar aspects embodied by upper world and heavenly deities. In depth psychological terms, Medusa's name, with its watery, otherworldly implications, situates her as a specter of the unconscious; an aspect of feminine shadow values. This realm of the unconscious includes not only the personal shadow—populated with the rejected, unlived aspects of any one individual—but also archetypal energies subordinated by whole cultures.

Along these lines, Dexter compares Medusa to underworld and death goddesses such as Ereshkigal, Hecate, Persephone, and "Varvakeion Athena," as well as "female monsters" like the Furies, Erinyes, Harpies, and Sirens" all of whom signify the death and regenerative aspects of the Great Goddess traditions pre-dating ancient Greece.[419] Kerényi mentions that the name Medusa appears in reference to one of the Hesperides who live at the ends of the

Earth, where the sun sets and night comes;[420] the place of death and essentially, where the Gorgons live as well. Deities are often conflated, but what is relevant here is that Medusa's name connects her with archetypal energies from the edge or below the edge of normal consciousness.

Robert Graves observes that Medusa means "cunning one"—an epitaph of the Moon-goddess.[421] The Moon-goddess is equivalent to the "Goddess of Regeneration" who gives life and fertility, but is also responsible for the "destructive powers of nature" including death.[422] In its Moon-goddess connotations, the name Medusa implies intelligence, complexity, and unpredictability, but also the psychological recognition that "the dark side is what redeems."[423] Medusa's name indicates that her complexity is both contradictory and complementary and depends upon one's perspective. That she is both "dark" and redemptive is revealed not only in her name, but in the contradiction of her watery, underworld connotations juxtaposed with the solar disc representation of her sundered head. The fact that Medusa's name evokes powers of the underworld or otherworld is not surprising given her pre-Greek lineage out of chthonic goddesses (which I discuss later in this book); her connections with terror and death in Greco-Roman mythology; and her continued links to horror today. However, it is in her appellation "Gorgon" that terror truly resides.

Gorgon

Medusa is, first and foremost, the Gorgon, which serves as both a description and an identity. In Greek, *Gorgó* means "'monster' or 'monstrous situation.'"[424] Joseph Campbell describes a monster as "some horrendous presence or apparition that explodes all of your standards for harmony, order, and ethical conduct" and that elicits the "sublime."[425] The sense of the sublime as that which fascinates and terrifies is reflected in the Latin wherein Gorgon means fierce, terrible,[426] or frightful,[427] and is associated with "the moon as it is terrible to behold."[428] The Gorgon epithet unambiguously makes Medusa the face of fear, though not necessarily its source. Cambridge scholar Jean Ellen Harrison discerns, the "Gorgon was made out of the terror, not the terror out of the Gorgon" for the Gorgon is the face, not the essence of the archetypal energy she reveals.[429] The monstrosity of the Gorgon expresses a human response to the overwhelming experience of the numinous as *tremendum*.

Kerényi expands the meaning of Gorgon by pointing out that "Gorgides and Gorgades were names for sea-goddesses."[430] The Gorgon identifier continues Medusa's connection with water and all that that implies, including death and the unconscious, as discussed above. Kerényi likens the Gorgon to various "dark," monstrous, or death-related female spirits and concludes that "appellations such as Erinyes, Gorgo and Harpyia all mean much the same thing";[431] they signify the monstrous feminine; polluter, death-dealer.

Harrison also equates Gorgons with Erinyes and Harpies,[432] all of whom she sees as manifestations of the idea of the *Ker*, which, because of its multiplicity is "perhaps the most untranslatable of all Greek words."[433] Harrison outlines the etymology of the term including approximations such as "[g]host, bacillus, disease, death-angel, death-fate, fate, bogey, [and] magician."[434] Further, *Ker* has a linguistic connection with the name for women whose job it was to collect "things polluted" and dispose of those things in the sea.[435] We see here the close association of magic and mystery with illness, contamination, and death—all tied to the female through the *Ker* exemplified in the Gorgon, Erinyes, and Harpy. Conversely, Harrison explores another variation of *Ker* that means "messengers, ministers, [or] a priestly race descended from Hermes."[436] Finally, *Ker* is the term applied to the "insects that impregnate the wild fig," a connection which causes Harrison to conclude: "Here are bacilli indeed, but for life not for death."[437] This linguistic web captures the sense of the contagion of taboo that is manifest in female monsters including the Gorgon, but also hints at a sacred regenerative quality. Further, it raises questions about the Gorgon's connections to menstruation as the possible source of "things polluted" returned to the sea by the *Ker*.

The relationship between contagion and the Gorgon is evident in the noxious aspect of her blood, stories of which I examine in Chapter 4. Simply put, the Gorgon's blood can spawn monsters and be deadly. Within the highly patriarchal culture of ancient Greece, the terror of the feminine, female power, and contamination were linked to menstruation. Recall the connection of the name Gorgon with the "terrible" face of the moon, the Moon-goddess of fertility, and by extension woman's moon cycle and moon blood. Menstruation taboos, confinement, and the control of women and their sexuality—all of which were common practices in Greece—relate not only to control of paternity, but to the supposed need for protection from menstruating females, so it is conceivable that "Medusa's terrible mask [or Gorgoneion] was a reflection of menstrual taboos."[438]

To return to the confluence of Medusa with the Erinyes through the Gorgon, it is instructive to note that the Erinyes or Furies were extremely ancient spirits that visited revenge upon those who committed crimes against kinship, the mother, or the maternal order. However, the Erinyes were not the only spirits to exact divine or cosmic revenge. In contemplating the Gorgon, Harrison compares her with particular manifestations of the goddesses Demeter and "Praxidike, Exactress of Vengeance," both of whom, like Medusa, appeared as stone masks or faces that were used to enforce proper behavior, keep chaos at bay, and "were part of the apparatus of a religion of terror among the Greeks."[439] Further, "Demeter [... as] 'Bringer of the Law'" was identified with Themis, the Titan Goddess of Justice.[440] What emerges is an idea of cosmic enforcement imposed upon humans by some aspect of the sacred feminine. Marie-Louise von Franz defines the mythological differentiation of feminine justice (as opposed to masculine justice) as a "feminine principle of revenge;" or more precisely, the justice of "natural consequences—wrong behavior is followed by bad luck or illness."[441] The Gorgon designation links Medusa to this idea of feminine justice.

A quick divergence is helpful here because, when literalized, the idea that illness arises as punishment contributes to misunderstandings about endometriosis (and other diseases), leading to victimization of sufferers; the "blame the victim" or self-blame phenomena discussed in Chapter 2. While the link between goddesses of vengeance such as Medusa and the psychological experience of a disease like endometriosis can arouse feelings of inflated personal responsibility and shame, it also has the potential to engender a sense of divine context, a sort of karmic or sacred reframing of suffering. I revisit the experience of disease as repercussion—deserved and meaningless or meaningful divine visitation—in Chapter 6.

To return to Medusa's Gorgon designation and what it reveals about the goddess's identity, as with "Medusa," particular animal features and familiars are identified with and define the Gorgon, populating her iconography. As Greek culture evolved, its goddesses and gods became more anthropomorphic; however, they remained associated with their earlier animal manifestations in art and narrative.

While Medusa may have the face and body of a woman, the Gorgon has the eyes of a bird of prey, owl, or snake; serpentine hair and accessories; bird or bee wings; boar's tusks; and sometimes the body or head of a horse.[442] In addition, her distinguishing associates are serpentine, canine, porcine, and equine.

The Gorgon's animal qualities reflect particular traits—intense, piercing, and mesmerizing owl or serpent eyes express the uncanny; great, protruding boar's tusks convey fierceness; and wings suggest divinity. In addition, animal forms identify the Gorgon as an incarnation of a larger category of goddesses called the Lady of the Beasts[443] or Mistress of Wild Things.[444] Beyond being simply a "monster" which terrifies humans through her animal signifiers the Gorgon connotes a greater archetypal complexity, a deeper and broader power. The Gorgon's familiars—the snake, bird, horse, swine, dog, and bee—are associated with the ancient goddesses of creation, life, birth, death, and regeneration from the Upper Paleolithic into the Neolithic, who are likely her forbearers.[445]

Finally, the Gorgon appellation unites Medusa with Athene, perhaps most obviously through the Gorgoneion worn upon Athene's aegis, but also as one of Athene's surnames, "Gorgopis," the "Grim-eyed or the Gorgon-faced."[446] Athene's Gorgopis epithet is echoed in Homer's "fire-eyed" Athene[447] and in "Varvakeion Athena"—the goddess "fully armed, wearing an Attic gown girded with a serpent," the Medusa-headed aegis upon her breast.[448] Recall that some of the historical accounts connect the Gorgon with Athene, even equating the two in some cases. Both Medusa and Athene emerge from "pre-patriarchal" traditions associated with the "uncanny and the magical—all those dark, chthonic, and 'disorderly' elements abandoned by the archaic and classical Greeks, who assigned supreme value to reason and order."[449] The Gorgon may be seen as Athene's "shadow" double, mirroring her and "confounding impiety and piety, savageness and civilization, monstrosity and divinity."[450, 451]

Phorkyades

Medusa is one of the Phorkyades, that is, a child of the "Greybeard of the Sea, Phorkys" and his wife, Keto.[452] Medusa shares this moniker with her sister Gorgons, Sthenno (strong) and Euryale (wide-roaming, wide-stepping, or pertaining to the sea), as well as with the Graiai, Echidna, and, according to some accounts, the three Hesperides, and the serpent Ladon.[453, 454, 455] The connections with water inherent in Medusa as daughter of Phorkys and Keto have been fairly thoroughly examined above and will not be repeated here. However, the Phorkyades designation has additional relevant connotations.

In Greek, Phorkys or Phorcys is "a masculine form of Phorcis, the Goddess or Sow [...] who devours corpses."[456] In Latin, as *Orcus*, the name is a title for Hades, god of the underworld, and connected to *"porcus* [or] hog."[457] Swine were sacred to the Great Goddess and were part of her mysteries. Gimbutas estimates that pigs were considered sacred as early as 6000 BCE in the cults of the Vegetation Goddesses[458] and in Greece, swine were associated with the goddesses Demeter and Persephone and the sacred festivals of the *Thesmophoria* and the Eleusinian Mysteries.[459] Medusa's Phorkyades denotation, along with her boar's tusks, further strengthens her connection to death and regeneration and extremely ancient (pre-Greek) mother goddesses.

Reflections on Medusa's names

Medusa's names, beyond evoking the terror of mortality so potent in patriarchy with its conceptions of individualism and linear time, also point to a natural, ruling power over which humanity has no control—the mystery of inviolable death and its reciprocity with life. Her names paradoxically encompass the moon's stony solidity and watery dissolution. Death—including the petrifaction of rigor mortis followed by fluid decomposition—also unites these qualities, as does a woman's monthly cycle with its transformation of the endometrium into menstrual flow. In her monikers, the Gorgon Medusa indicates the primal and primordial, reaching back into the Neolithic Age to a time when the goddess had her body intact and female blood was sacred.[460]

Pre-Greek Images of Medusa

Medusa, as she is generally known, reflects her Greco-Roman mythological manifestation as a snaky-haired woman-monster decapitated by the hero Perseus; a silently shrieking head with glaring eyes. In fact, Medusa—as Medusa—first appears during the Greek archaic period, named in the literature of Hesiod in the mid-eighth century BCE. However, the image of the Gorgon as a "greater undifferentiated genus of which the Gorgon Medusa is a particular member, reaches back seven thousand years or more into Neolithic prehistory.[461] Dexter reflects:

> It is likely that [Medusa's] tapestry weaves together threads which stretch back in time to European and Near Eastern Neolithic cultures, and which are reflected both in the earliest Neolithic shamanic figures and in early historic demon and death figures throughout Europe, the Near East, and elsewhere in the ancient world.[462]

While scholars generally agree that the Gorgon is rooted in traditions preceding ancient Greece, theories and speculation abound as to "which mythical figures were antecedents to Medusa."[463] Gimbutas situates the Gorgon in the Great Goddess traditions of the Neolithic and asserts that the "early Gorgon was a potent Goddess dealing with life and death, not the later Indo-European monster to be slain by heroes such as Perseus."[464] Joseph Campbell posits an even more ancient and universal origin for the Gorgon, connecting her Aegean and Near Eastern iconography with an "early Neolithic— perhaps even Mesolithic—lunar-serpent-pig context that is represented in the myths of Melanesia and the Pacific and also Celtic Ireland."[465] Harrison, despite espousing that the Gorgoneion (or Gorgon mask) is Medusa's primary form, also describes the early Gorgon as "the ugly bogey-, Erinyes-side of the Great Mother; she is a potent goddess, not as in later days a monster to be slain by heroes."[466]

From a depth psychological view, deities like Medusa are primarily expressions of archetypal energy patterns; they constellate and morph, consolidate and differentiate so that myth, in all its forms, serves as a sort of genealogy by which to trace divine roots in the psyche. Despite their protean nature, archetypal images are essentially conservative such that a persistence of imagery can be discerned over time; as Gimbutas observes: "what is striking is not the metamorphosis of the symbols over the millennia but rather the continuity from Paleolithic times on."[467] These symbols are the threads with which we weave an image of Medusa's foremothers.

Medusa's Ancestry

That Medusa was "originally a Great Goddess," with a body and head, is supported by iconographic evidence such as the full-body representation of the goddess that appears on the western pediment of Artemis's temple at Corfu from the late sixth century BCE.[468] While later, Medusa was represented mainly as "a terror mask," Gimbutas asserts that the "earliest Greek gorgons, [...] are not terrifying symbols that turn humans into stones. They are portrayed as having the wings of a bee and snakes as antennae and are decorated with a honeycomb design," all motifs of regeneration not fear.[469] The Gorgon shares these symbolic features, along with her exaggerated eyes, with much earlier goddesses from the Bronze and Iron Ages worshipped throughout the Mediterranean region, as well as into Northern Europe.[470] Such goddesses were central to the Minoan civilization of Crete (c. 3650-1450 BCE), which Gimbutas theorizes emerged from the gynocentric Neolithic cultures of Old Europe.[471]

Graves cites evidence that Minoan culture was shaped by Libyans from North Africa when large numbers of "goddess-worshipping" immigrants arrived in Crete around 4000 BCE.[472] It is notable that Medusa and Athene have historic and mythic origin stories situating their roots in Libya. Archeological evidence suggests that the Minoan culture can be characterized as one in which the feminine was highly valued: Minoan religion was goddess-centered, the cities relatively unfortified, and the arts elevated without the usual depictions of war and violence typical of the period.[473] After two millennia, Crete was invaded by the Mycenaeans, known to Homer as the Achaeans, who, despite being more warlike retained much of Minoan culture, blending the two religions. I revisit this transformation when I address Athene's relationship with Medusa in Chapter 5. What is relevant here is that the Minoan culture shaped the Mycenaean civilization, which strongly influenced ancient Greek culture in turn. It is highly probable that the Gorgon Medusa was inherited by the archaic Greeks from the Bronze Age Mycenaean culture by way of the Minoans and earlier gynocentric civilizations.[474, 475]

It remains open to speculation precisely how matriarchal the prehistoric cultures of Old Europe and the Aegean actually were. Some scholars assert that Gimbutas overreached the evidence in her interpretations of the many thousands of objects she catalogued from the multiple digs she supervised and studied. For those who criticize Gimbutas' work, her concept of the "Great Goddess" is controversial. However, from a depth psychological perspective, the Great Goddess is a functional conceptualization unifying the multiplicity of the archetypal feminine. Traditions that revere goddesses as fundamental do not necessarily denote literal monotheistic matriarchy. In fact, the so-called Great Goddess appeared in diverse forms and identities—bird, snake, sow, birth, death and regeneration, fertility, grain, and so on. Further, the evidence suggests that Great Goddess traditions in which female deities were central are not simply wishful-thinking on the part of modern feminist scholars. Reverence for feminine power is reflected iconographically in thousands of representations of female genitalia and in ancient "agricultural rituals of fecundity" surrounding the use of menstrual blood as sacred.[476] Artifacts from Neolithic Europe and the Near East, including masks and carved figurines, depict females with avian, serpent, or combined bird/snake iconography, which scholars, including Gimbutas and Dexter, interpret as signifying the Great Goddess who was many goddesses and signified "the continuum of life, death, and rebirth."[477] Gimbutas classifies some representations of the Great Goddess as Bird Goddesses, associated with death and regeneration[478] or Snake Goddesses, signifying "life creation, [...] fertility and increase, and particularly in the regeneration of dying life energy."[479] Actually, there is a good deal of overlap between the two representations and this "intimate relation between [...] Bird Goddess and Snake Goddess continued throughout prehistory and into historic times."[480] This intermingling may indicate the underlying wholeness of the feminine archetype— whether she be the Great Goddess, Great Mother, Moon Goddess, or Snake/Bird Goddess—from which many incarnations emerge, including Medusa. It also speaks to the interconnection of Medusa and Athene as having a sort of archetypal logic.

Artifacts such as Great Goddess masks—with their "owlish" or "snake" faces, large eyes, gaping mouths, lolling tongues, and fangs[481]—are essentially Gorgoneia, and evoke Medusa in all their details, so that one senses the archetypal nature of the life-death mystery she signifies. Intriguingly, Edelman observes "the very direct and immediate link between death and the rictus and protruding tongue of the Gorgon mask. Facial muscles after death rigidify until the mouth is opened as in a grin, and the tongue extends."[482] Add to this the uncanny stare of the dead. These physiological expressions, compounded by the very real sense of a profound, irreversible, and total loss of animating energy in the deceased are "enough to account for the pancultural appearance of the 'death bogey' and to be the basis of the Gorgon's archetypal nature."[483] Hence, iconography and mythology recapitulate physiology, supporting Gimbutas' conjecture that the Gorgon probably emerged "from the death aspect of the Snake/Bird Goddess."[484]

However, it is also critical to contextualize Medusa's association with death by noting that in pre-patriarchal Snake/Bird Goddess-worshiping cultures "there is much more emphasis on regeneration than death in [the] iconography," and that only later were death and terror primary foci.[485] Dexter indicates that while Medusa "likely reflects the range of spheres of the Neolithic Goddesses of birth, death, and regeneration," emphasis on her negative attributes in the written narratives of Greece attests to a bias against the "Goddesses of death by early Western writers, who viewed death as an end of existence rather than as part of a Great Round."[486] The less individualistic, cyclical context of birth-death-regeneration repositions death as life's regenerative partner and the chthonic feminine divinity as more than simply monstrous.

In fact, prehistoric goddess traditions are thought to have been chthonic, magical, and shamanic in nature. A defining feature of reality was its cyclicality; life, time, and creation were likely not expressed as linear. As a "ritual place for rebirth: the tomb could also represent the womb."[487] These shamanic traditions valued descent into the underworld as regenerative; death was the source of new life and descent yielded new wisdom. That the Gorgon has roots in such worldviews is suggested in her imagery, as already discussed. But it is also indicated by the dual nature of her blood—representing both death and regeneration—as shamanic.[488] The menstrual processes of women were once held to be sacred and moon blood was likely part of ancient shamanic "agricultural rituals of fecundity" and regeneration of plant and human life.[489] Ileen Brennan Root's study of Medusa finds that the Gorgon's history, iconography, and mythology exhibit a "deep entanglement with shamanism" as well as with the later mystery cults of Greece.[490]

In addition to the Gorgon's magical blood, Dexter notes a "shamanic connection" in Medusa's powerful, striding, "bent-knee posture" represented in ancient art; a pose also taken by Indic sky-dancers, Kālī, and the Celtic Sheela na gig.[491] Furthermore, the magical aspects of the Greek Perseus-Medusa myth have shamanic overtones including Athene's "bronze mirror" shield used by Perseus as protection, which is typically the tool of priestess-shamans.[492] Beheading itself is a form of sacrificial dismemberment connected with rituals of death, rebirth, and deification across multiple traditions from prehistory onwards.[493]

Reflections on pre-Greek Medusa

I have focused on Medusa's pre-Greek origins to help free her from the limitations and biases imposed by the patriarchal lens through which we moderns have received and understood her image. Medusa's connection to extremely ancient "magical" traditions later subsumed into Greek culture helps explain her linking with Evil Eye superstitions, which I explore later, and serves to illuminate the evocative effectiveness for ancient audiences of Homer's use of the Gorgoneion as a sort of shorthand for overwhelming terror. The Gorgon's archetypal underpinnings, which are revealed in her association with the Great Goddess and other traditions wherein feminine values were held in high esteem, underscore the unwavering power of her image, even as her meaning fluctuated with cultural norms and projections. The contradiction expressed in Medusa's unrelenting force and suppressed agency can be explained by the likelihood that, despite her fall from apparent Great Goddess status, she continued (and continues) to embody aspects of the archetypal feminine, especially impersonal, mysterious, and difficult energies; forms suppressed by the rise of patriarchy and ascendency of male god(s), but impossible to truly vanquish. As a deity associated with the mysteries of death and life's irrepressible, regenerative vitality, the Gorgon carries the energy of the Death Goddess who "gives birth to life."[494] Archetypally, the suppression of Medusa's powers engenders push back, often in forms ever more compensatory and difficult to apprehend. For me, endometriosis is likely one such form, decipherable through a mythopoetic understanding of the disease.

The Ancient Greco-Roman Medusa

The Gorgoneion

While the Gorgon Medusa is represented mythopoetically and visually as complete, that is, with a body, her most frequent Greco-Roman form (or dominant attribute) is her large, masklike head. Over time, representations of Medusa's decapitated head became somewhat humanized and considerably less fierce. Her wings diminished in size and adorned her head (she no longer had shoulders). In general, Medusa's image evolved through three stages identified by Wilhelm Roscher as the *Archaic Gorgon* (seventh century BCE), the *Transitional Gorgon* (fifth century BCE), and, after the third century BCE, the *Beautiful Gorgon*.[495] In summary:

> The archaic Gorgoneion has a round face, ornate curls, a wide mouth baring teeth and tusks, and a protruding tongue. Snakes and a beard are often apparent. The Gorgoneion of the transitional type retains the round face, formidable teeth, and extended tongue, but these traits are much milder and less repulsive than those of the earlier form. The snakes change into snaky locks, and the beard vanishes. At last, the beautiful Gorgoneion appears. This third type also passes through phases, becoming sinister, sad, and increasingly pathetic, and finally metamorphoses into a calm and dignified death mask.[496]

While there is a trend toward less fierce Medusan imagery through the Greco-Roman period, there is considerable overlap in the styles of the depictions. However, Roscher's observation supports the sense that the Gorgon, while still potent, comes to be more and more under the control of patriarchal power and interpretation. The typical depiction of Medusa's severed head is as a terrible ritualistic mask, or Gorgoneion. I explore this interpretation at length. However, I also consider a less well-known view, that of the vegetation Medusa.

Terrible Gorgoneia and the Evil Eye

The terrible ritual mask or Gorgoneion is ancient and ubiquitous.[497] Frightening Gorgoneia are found around the world as part of ancient and modern religions and folk traditions often in connection with Evil Eye superstitions.[498] Most scholars interpret the Gorgoneion as apotropaic; an evil face that repels and protects against evil. In ancient Greece, the monstrous Gorgoneion Medusa "was regarded as a sort of incarnate Evil Eye. The monster was tricked out with cruel tusks and snakes, but it slew by the eye, it *fascinated*."[499] Harrison tells us that, according to Aeschylus, the Gorgons "slay by a malign effluence, and this effluence, tradition said, came from their eyes."[500]

By virtue of the ancient logic of "like cures like," Medusa's head, as the Evil Eye, was also used as a protective amulet.[501] She was evil, her evil emanated from her eyes, and thereby she defended against the Evil Eye and malignant spirits. The logic echoes in the colloquial "it takes one to know one." In this way, Medusan Gorgoneia were "the natural agents of a religion of fear and 'riddance;'" religious superstitions that lingered among the Greeks despite the elevation of the Olympic Pantheon and rationalism.[502]

Similar to other Gorgoneia, the Greek representations typically had round solar-disk faces surrounded by serpents or serpentine hair and featuring piercing eyes and grimacing mouths. The faces often included large teeth or tusks projecting from the mouth, elongated tongues, bearded chins, and, frequently, combinations of human and animal forms. Gorgoneia occurred throughout the Aegean, adorning architecture, art, and many everyday objects, including clothing, jewelry, tools, coins, roof tiles, armor, sarcophagi, pottery, and pottery ovens.

What accounts for the Gorgoneia's widespread popularity? Whether Medusa's potency arose as a vestige of the mysterious powers of Neolithic Snake/Bird Goddesses or a more primal, instinctual fear of death or blood, the Gorgoneion inherited by the Greeks was imbued with a numinosity that made her indispensable to daily life with its many uncertainties and dangers. From the archaic period forward, Medusa's potency became concentrated in her Gorgoneion form, the primary power of which emanated from the eyes. Graves describes apotropaic Gorgoneia worn by priestesses: "representatives of the Triple-goddess, wearing prophylactic masks—

with scowl, glaring eyes, and protruding tongue between bared teeth—to frighten strangers from her Mysteries."[503] The action of the prophylactic mask is "'to make an ugly face' *at* you if you are doing wrong [...]; *for* you if you are doing right."[504] In other words, the evil one experienced before the Gorgoneion originated in one's own transgression, which may have been as basic as being human in the sight of the divine. Siebers points out that while Medusa petrifies, her mask "has been widely associated with neutralization of fascination," that is, as protection against the overwhelming, daemonic divine.[505] For the Greeks, it was Medusa's essentially evil nature that made her prophylactic against evil. When she is approached through a masculine worldview, the Gorgoneion Medusa is primarily encountered as negative and threatening, and despite artistic renderings to the contrary that echo her more complex identity, Medusa was the Evil Eye.

The Evil Eye, menstruation, and the demonic feminine

Defining the Evil Eye

The Evil Eye superstition is basically a belief that "a person can either cause harm by looking or be physically affected by the object of his or her gaze."[506] As a superstition, the Evil Eye "functions to represent identities as differences" and, in particular, defines these differences as "supernatural" and therefore dangerous.[507] The Evil Eye is a social phenomenon whereby accused individuals or groups are shamed; excluded and persecuted as embodiments of ideas or values rejected by the dominant collective.[508] In depth psychological terms, the dominant cultural projects its shadow—elements that threaten its worldview or primary mythology—onto individuals or groups perceived as carriers of incongruent or challenging archetypal energies. Paradoxically, these shadow carriers serve the primary cultural myth by their presence and are therefore strangely indispensable such that a great deal of ambivalence also surrounds those designated as the Evil Eye; this ambivalence is reflected in their apotropaic function. While not universal, the Evil Eye is pancultural, and likely "one of the oldest continuous religious constructs in the Mediterranean basin."[509]

The Evil Eye and menstruation taboos

In considering the delineation of the Evil Eye superstition proposed by Siebers, Harrison, and others, it strikes me that menstrual taboos can be thought of as a type of Evil Eye superstition. Pancultural phenomena, menstrual taboos are extraordinarily tenacious.[510] Like other forms of the Evil Eye, menstrual taboos are social constructs of identity and containment; beliefs, practices, and norms that serve to discern, separate, exclude, and in their most extreme forms, persecute menstruating women, who are seen as so ambivalently powerful they must be kept separate from others, and in some traditions were reportedly locked up and kept away even from sunlight for months or years.[511] Menstrual taboos, like other forms of the Evil Eye superstition use the evil thing, that is, menstrual processes, to identify women as women and as fundamentally different from mankind by virtue of those processes (menses, ovulation, pregnancy, and menopause). More than simply different, woman is dangerously "other" and not to be trusted with containing or controlling her inherent potency. The menstruating woman and menstrual processes and blood represent "a threatening supernatural power" so that taboos are supposed to protect society and the woman: "The taboos of menstruation are practices that help others to avoid [the menstruating woman] and her dangerous influence and that enable her to get through the menstrual period without succumbing to her own deadly [sacred] power."[512] While these taboos profess to recognize and attempt to contain or channel the implicit otherness and overwhelming power of the sacred *tremendum*, in practice they appear to be less about awe-ful reverence of the divine than fear of females, and many of the resulting practices disempower woman by isolating them as carriers of contagion.

In the ancient world (and today) taboos surrounding menstruation reflected ambivalence; both a fear of pollution and an apprehension of numinosity. On one hand, menstrual taboos alleged "that the look of a menstruating woman can destroy a man, or turn him to stone, or [...] contaminate food and endanger hunting."[513] According to Pliny, the first century CE Roman philosopher, contact with menstrual blood despoiled food and wine; destroyed crops; corroded steel, bronze, and iron; caused rabies in dogs; killed bees; and repelled ants.[514] Conversely, in folk beliefs moon blood was seen as efficacious in curing "leprosy, warts, birthmarks, gout, goiter, hemorrhoids, epilepsy, worms, and headache."[515] Menstrual blood was used in love charms, as an apotropaic amulet, and was "occasionally fit to be an honorific offering to a god."[516] Anthropologist George Thomson notes in *Studies in Ancient Greek Society,* that the menstruating woman was considered both "inviolable, holy" and "polluted, unclean;" she was "*sacra,* sacred and accursed."[517] Aristotle believed that menstrual fluid was an inert substance while semen carried the life force and that being female meant being less than male, having a malformed body and soul, and a defective psyche or intellect.[518] And yet women possessed powers necessary to procreation, powers that were paradoxically conceptualized as inferior and yet required vigilant control by men.

The defining feature of the Evil Eye superstition is that the magic to fascinate or kill emanates from the eyes—as with Medusa's mesmerizing gaze. It may seem strange to connect aversion to menstrual bleeding with superstitions about the power of evil emanating from the eyes, however, recall that Medusa petrified by way of a "malign effluence" from her eyes. I return to Medusa as the link between the Evil Eye and menstrual taboos below. However, before I explore the convergence of Medusa, the Evil Eye superstition, and menstrual taboos, it is first enlightening to study the deeper meaning of the Evil Eye.

The Evil Eye and the daemonic sacred

One way to comprehend the Evil Eye is in terms of the mystery of the archetypal "other," both sacred and profane, and human fear of it. The "other" is ultimately an unknown and unknowable enigma. In the spiritual realm, Edelman, recalling Jane Ellen Harrison and Paul Ricoeur, reminds us that this extreme other-ness is the sacred as daemonic, which, although now equated with evil, originally expressed the aspect of the divine that is pure potency, undifferentiated power, and which cannot be represented anthropomorphically.[519] In other words, it is the taboo: "Whether in the archaic or later mind, it is the daemonic sacred, the unknowable, which is *tremendum* and which becomes the taboo area of the sacred."[520] In ancient Greece, the term *aidos* expressed, among other things, the feeling of shame engendered in humans when encountering the overwhelming potency of the sacred—a taboo experience.[521] I revisit the concept of *aidos* when I explore Athene in

Chapter 5. However, with regards to Medusa as conveyor of the Evil Eye, the Gorgon embodies the shame-provoking, taboo aspect of the sacred—awesome and impossible to depict as *anthropo*, that is, a force that can be signified only as wholly other; apparently, female.

The daemonic sacred as feminine/female

Edelman poses the possibility that the daemonic sacred is aptly depicted as female; that, for humans, "the daemonic sacred is *au fond* feminine."[522] Basically a psychological argument, Edelman's assertion relies on the observation from biology that "ontogeny recapitulat[es] phylogeny;" the development of the individual mirrors the evolution of the race.[523] Physiologically and psychologically, in our individual and collective maturity, we carry all previous stages of development within in at least some lingering way, and these previous conditions continue to exert their influence. This is precisely what occurs in the human brain, where the limbic or "reptilian" brain, our first brain, continues to control fundamental processes and, yet, operates outside normal consciousness.

In terms of the feminine nature of the daemonic sacred, Edelman's assertion rests upon archetypal, primal, and natal experiences of being human. Because this idea, under the influence of patriarchal values and psycho-spiritual literalism, can be distorted to equate woman with evil, I quote the points of her supporting argument at length:

> [T]hat nature itself has from time immemorial been perceived as feminine; that the earliest religions were matrifocal or at least included female deities as an element at least as important as the male; the obvious archetypal centrality and potency of the mother, stemming in no small part from the human mother's physiological centrality;[and] the fact that in the infant psyche the importance of the mother predates that of the father by several weeks, even to the point of experiencing the mother as *all* of reality, from which the father is excluded completely.[524]

To these assertions, Edelman adds an observation by psychoanalyst Nini Herman, which is remarkably reminiscent of Siebers's definition of the supernatural power of the Evil Eye cited earlier. Herman states that contents from the unconscious psyches of mother and child interact without conscious mediation.[525] Further, Herman contends that this phenomenon is "a specific function of maternal reverie," contained in the mother's gaze, and, though males are likely affected, "woman's susceptibilities to this phenomenon are considerably greater—a positive liability—and operate to a degree where it can deal life or death to so forceful an extent that it belongs to the uncanny...."[526] In other words, the archetype of the daemonic sacred—the unknowable, essentially other numinous in its undifferentiated omnipotence—exists in the unconscious psyche of the infant with the potential to constellate in its Gorgon form. Because the mother serves as the first totality, "the infant's experience of chaos, of the daemonic will necessarily be assigned the feminine gender;" hence, the Gorgon and other dark goddesses such as the Erinyes.[527] While the human mother may mediate the terrifying archetypal content for the infant to some degree, the Gorgon's presence in the woman's psyche, as well as her personal shadow material, strengthens rather than mitigates the archetype, despite her outward behavior. The process of archetypal constellation appears to be influenced by maternal attunement and its limitations and the Gorgon lingers in the mother's gaze.

However, as Edelman points out, "the gaze of the Gorgon may be *in* the personal mother but (unless the mother is entirely psychotic) it is not the gaze *of* the mother."[528] Recall Harrison's assertion that the Gorgon was made from the terror but not the terror from the Gorgon. The potency of attachment and maternal reverie notwithstanding, Edelman also argues, based on the work of Jungian Michael Fordham and psychoanalyst Heinz Kohut, that "the primary relationship of the infant is to the infant's inner world, not to the mother."[529] That is, the Gorgon is an archetypal energy pattern within the human psyche and as such is larger and more primal than the individual child's experience of the personal mother, regardless of how mitigating that experience may or may not be.

The archetypal Gorgon *in potentia* is presumably stimulated by the characterization of the feminine as inherently other, flawed, and evil within the patriarchal milieu, and it is conceivable that every daughter (and son) of patriarchy carries this Gorgon wound to some degree. The archetypal content of maternal reverie only exacerbates rather than creates the dilemma of how the human psyche can contend with such raw, numinous power as the daemonic sacred represents.

However, without an equally potent generative, creatrix goddess to compensate and complete the feminine archetypally—and under the influence of worldviews that literalize the archetypal—feminine power remains associated with chaos and females with evil. As a result, both goddesses and women must be pressed into service to the masculine principle. This dynamic is evident in Greek culture and the Olympian Pantheon, where men and gods co-opt creativity and life-giving energy, and it is a misogynistic legacy of the Greek origins of modern Western civilization.

The Medusan Evil Eye, menstrual taboos, and endometriosis

I contend that one way in which misogynistic scorn plays out psycho-spiritually is through the experience of the endometriotic body and other disturbances in the menstrual process. Endometriosis amplifies menstrual taboos in ways that mirror the concentration of Medusan power in the terrible Gorgoneion. The symptoms of the disease exaggerate and complicate the normal processes of menstruation, which are already demonized or medicalized and unmentionable, isolating the sufferer even more than normal menstruation does by seemingly confirming that her cycle really is a disease. Although endometriosis has multiple vectors of cause and effect, it is experienced primarily as a disorder of menstrual processes in the form of heavy, unpredictable bleeding, dysmenorrheal, dyspareunia, and infertility. Menstrual taboos are supposedly in place to protect against exposure to the numinous power of the bleeding woman; however, in practice they reflect fear of her power and assumptions about her untrustworthy, dangerous character and her polluted, contagious nature. Menstrual taboos often function more like punishment than protection. The reciprocal relationship between being a bleeding woman and punishment is exacerbated by disorders like endometriosis, which, for many women, add a sense that their bodies are at fault, flawed, or vengeful. Personal psychology, culture, and even medical science remain vulnerable to the idea that "evil and misfortune" are causally related: "[P]unishment falls on man in the guise of misfortune and transforms all possible sufferings, all diseases, all death, all failure into a sign of defilement."[530] Menstruation, "the Curse" in Western parlance, is not only framed as such a deserved misfortune, but also as a testament of defilement;

woman is not man and this is her great sin, proved more abominable
by the potent mysteries of her menstruation by which she bleeds like
a mortal and yet lives like a deity. Medusa, an archetypal face of
"feminine justice" becomes the mask of shame, blame, and horror.

Whether any individual woman feels "cursed" or not is not the
issue, as Karen Houppert chronicles in her book on the subject; the
reality is that menstruation remains an "unmentionable taboo." A
large study conducted in the United States in the 1980s and cited in
Chapter 1, shows that 67% of those surveyed thought women should
never mention their periods, overtly or in "veiled references to
cramps or headaches."[531] More than one-third expressed that women
should "conceal the fact that they're menstruating from their families
(for example, by hiding sanitary products)" and nearly 10%, that
represents 14 million respondents, said that "women should make an
effort to stay away from others when they're having their periods."[532]
These shame- and fear-laden norms reflect the menstrual taboos still
shaping women's lives and attitudes towards their bodies and power;
attitudes that have permeated Western civilization for some
thousands of years. Is it surprising that in the purportedly civilized
West "up to 90% of women suffer from some form of
'dysmenorrhea'" with or without an identified physiological cause?[533]
When menstruation is complicated by the symptoms of disorders
such as endometriosis, menstrual taboos can be experienced as
embodied misogyny. The Gorgoneion Medusa is incarnated and
literalized as the face of the ravaged womb.

In fact, Medusa's bleeding head, exemplar of the Evil Eye, is
repeatedly equated with women's genitalia and, either overtly or
covertly, with menstruation; Freud and many others have made the
connection. Does the abhorrence Medusa engenders reflect
patriarchal terror and envy of "the first 'magic,'" the blood magic of
fertility "exercised by the women, who had, and have, the original
power as priests, magicians, prophets and shamans[?]"[534] According
to Gimbutas, the large eyes and open mouth of the Great Goddesses
were originally sources and symbols of moisture and "the Divine
Source."[535] Later, these became the source of the "foul ooze,"[536] the
poisonous "breath" emanating from the Evil Eye by which the
female monster petrified and annihilated all who beheld her or whom
she beheld. This maligned effluence, which contains the death-
dealing and regenerative power of the feminine and streams from the
goddess's body petrifying men, is reminiscent of menstrual blood,

which, taboos warn, can turn a man to stone and despoil all it touches.[537, 538] It is also an image of Medusa's mythic blood with its deadly and resurrective qualities. In addition to Edelman's psychological hypothesis about the source of the daemonic sacred as *au fond* feminine, I add the fact that the original blood sacrifice—absolutely essential to human life, death, and renewal—is women's menstrual blood. The raw power, the uncontrollable, explicit human expression of the numinous *tremendum* is menstrual blood and the embodiment of that power is the menstruating woman. When culture fears that power, the face of the Great Mother's mysterious death and renewal aspects turns monstrous; the appalling face of the Gorgon whether Medusa, Fury, Demeter Erinyes, or some other manifestation.

For the ancient Greeks, Medusa's identity and power became concentrated in her head, the terrible Gorgoneion. Gimbutas, despite her conceptualization of Medusa as a descendent of the Great Goddess, recognizes the classical Greek Gorgon as essentially a frightening, prophylactic mask with "glaring eyes, [… and] hideous features—lolling tongue, projecting teeth, and writhing snakes for hair."[539] Harrison insists that "in her essence Medusa is a head and nothing more; her potency only begins when her head is severed, and that potency resides in the head; she is in a word a mask with a body later appended."[540] Such a claim begs for examination.

There is no doubt that Medusa's deadly power emanates from her head—particularly from her eyes, but also from her bleeding severed neck. However, the Gorgon's lethality precedes her beheading as illustrated in tales of those petrified by her before her execution by Perseus.[541] In addition, if power is defined as other than lethality, then Medusa's generative power, demonstrated by her lovemaking with Poseidon and the conception and birthing of her children in Hesiod's *Theogony* and her erotic power to attract suitors in Ovid, reveals Medusa's embodied sexual potency. These stories emphasize Medusa's mortal womanliness as a fertile (menstruating) female rather than her immortal nature. While her full-body representations display such power as to elicit claims by scholars that Medusa was first a potent goddess before she was demoted to hero-fodder, the Gorgon's power also lies in her fertile female humanity. As Medusa came to be equated almost exclusively with her severed head, her connections with what she had been—the full embodiment of the feminine power of generativity—was veiled and distorted by the ever-growing dominance of patriarchal interpretations. It seems apparent that womankind, as the revered embodiment of the bleeding goddess, suffered a similar fate; their female genitalia reduced to either "their horrifying effects" or "pleasure-giving ones" according to a one-sided male idea of sexuality.[542] This reality notwithstanding, something more symbolically generative may have been happening as well.

In ancient Greece, it was the head, not the genitals that was considered the seat of the life-force required for reproduction.[543] Furthermore, males had the exclusive claim to the life spark, for only the male head contained a fully potent and animating psyche. It was thought that menstrual blood was inert matter that must be animated by the power of life-creating semen in order to generate a human being.[544] Woman was not only separate from the true human spark (that is, the masculine psyche), but subordinate to man even in procreation, her *raison d'être* in Greek culture: "The mother is no parent of that which is called her child [....] The parent is he who mounts. A stranger she preserves a stranger's seed."[545] Perhaps Medusa's head, as a remnant of the potency of pre-Greek goddess traditions, presents an exception to this male claim. In exploring this possibility Edelman compares Perseus's taking of Medusa's head to Prometheus's theft of Olympian fire; both are acts of transgression against the dominant male power:

> [F]or Athene to have retained and worn the head was to have reclaimed and deployed the life-seed of a highly potent form of the primordial and the chthonic. [...] Perseus released, or stole back, the power of the fire-eyed, fiercely apotropaic, chthonic feminine. The act may be the only tacit admission in Greek myth that a mortal woman, as Medousa was, is more than matter and that the psyche does not reside exclusively in the male head.[546]

It seems that the Gorgoneion Medusa consolidates the feminine mystery of generation into a bleeding head; an image of menstruating female genitalia, source of life, death, and regeneration. However, her power is polarized as negative by equating it and her with the evil of the Evil Eye. The apotropaic nature of the Gorgoneion Evil Eye reflects the same ambiguous superstitions surrounding menstrual blood: sacred, taboo, magical, contaminant. I will return to the peculiarity of the demonized, bleeding genitals of womanhood being worn upon the breast of the great goddess Athene. For now, I turn to the regenerative vegetation Gorgoneion, which seems to demonstrate that the Perseus myth may not be the only "tacit admission" of the life-giving feminine in ancient Greece.

The vegetation Gorgoneia

In contrast to the focus on Medusa as embodiment of the Evil Eye in ancient Greece, A. L. Frothingham vehemently challenges "the delusion that Medusa's fundamental characteristic was apotropaic."[547] Frothingham insists that if we actually look at the iconography of funerary Gorgoneia, a different Medusa is revealed. He sees the Gorgon as protective, however proclaims that she "protected not negatively but positively."[548]

By the third century BCE (with at least one example dating from the late fifth century BCE) the "vegetation gorgoneion" is ubiquitous on funerary architecture and art including tombs, sarcophagi, and sepulchral urns.[549] An abundant and rich category of Gorgons, these represent a more serene or beautiful Medusa. The so-called beautiful or pathetic Medusa occurs in Greco-Roman and later representations and often seems to depotentiate the goddess. However, the vegetation Gorgoneia, primarily from the Hellenistic and Greco-Roman periods, are consistently linked with empowering motifs of renewal.[550] While some of the vegetation Medusas exhibit the round, masklike head and characteristic scowl of other Gorgons, many have a composed, calm, and even lovely countenance. Commonly two serpents twine around the face forming a lose knot on top of the head and under the chin, or are arranged in "heraldic fashion above the head."[551] The Gorgon's hair, while serpentine, is not usually composed of snakes and the face shape is more typically human. Wings of varying size and composition—sometimes of feathers, sometimes leaves—emerge from Medusa's head. And most significantly, she is always surrounded by foliage, radiating like a halo about her face, garlanded under her chin, or sometimes growing out of her severed neck.[552] In addition, the vegetation Gorgoneion is accompanied by bowls, baskets, garlands, or cornucopias of fruit or flowers; representatives of Apollo including dolphins, swans, and griffins; winged Victories and Erotes; centaurs and satyrs; Cupids; the doves of Aphrodite; and the god Eros.[553] Inextricably connected to images of life and rebirth, the vegetation Medusas share the regenerative quality claimed by Gimbutas and Dexter as essential to the Gorgon's identity as a vestige of the Great Goddess traditions.

In his analysis of ancient Greek, Roman, and Etruscan funerary objects and tombs Frothingham finds a ubiquitous integration of vegetation symbols of regeneration with the Gorgoneion, indicating that Medusa was not exclusively an "emblem of suffering and death."[554] Rather, Frothingham concludes, Medusa was the primary "Hellenic emblem for life-force and immortality" that was also embraced by the Etruscans and Romans in their art as symbolic of the "resurgence of life" from death and dormancy.[555] This connection between Medusa and the regenerative power of life is reminiscent of her association with the regenerative aspects of the Great Goddess traditions of ancient Europe and the Near East. It is not congruent with the position that Medusa protects against evil simply by embodying it. Frothingham argues:

> These theories are that the Gorgon was used as an emblem of death or of pain, or as a protective evil bogey. But if preconceptions are laid aside, and if the plain evidence of the monuments is alone admitted, the law of the association of ideas would seem to lead inevitably to just the contrary conclusion. Eros, the god of life, the dove of fertility, the Victories, the eagle and griffin of apotheosis, the first fruits of the earth in the sacred basket or the horn of plenty; these and the rest all point to the Gorgon as the emblem of life, of victory over death, and of a renewed life beyond the grave.[556]

Medusa, as essentially irredeemable evil and paralyzing despair, is simply not borne out by her actual appearance on funerary objects. Frothingham's finding that vegetation Medusa's funerary symbolism is not negative or evil, but somehow reassuring by its connection with other emblems of life and rebirth, seems to position the Gorgon as a figure of hope and renewed vitality, akin to the Great Goddess's regenerative function. Frothingham reframes Medusa and her undeniable association with death, reconnecting her with a more holistic view that is lost when the primary focus is on her as a meaningless horror.

That Medusa retains a positive function despite her terrible aspect echoes the contradiction that, despite their predominantly low status and restricted freedom, Greek women participated in great festivals like the *Thesmophoria*. Kerényi, Burkert, and others speculate that the *Thesmophoria* was a menstruation ritual; "nothing else but the periods of the Greek women elevated to an annual festival."[557] If this is the case, then menstrual processes may have provoked a similar accommodation as that represented by vegetation Gorgoneia; an outlet for the positive expression of feminine regenerative power. While Medusa may not have been explicitly associated with the *Thesmophoria*, her archetypal presence is implied by her strong connection to Demeter Erinyes. Beyond speculations about the menstrual foundations of the *Thesmophoria* is the fact that Medusa's closest divine associate, Athene—"the root meaning of whose name is 'vulva' or 'lap' or 'womb'"—was the center of the menstrual cult in Athens.[558]

Beyond the Gorgoneion

While the Gorgoneion appears to have been the primary artistic representation of Medusa in ancient Greece, the goddess was also portrayed with a body. When her body is rendered, Medusa is often depicted as a larger-than-life human female, waist girded by serpents, muscular, and frequently in a powerful striding pose, suggesting a great deal of movement and agency. She typically has two or four wings, may hold snakes in her hands, and wear huntress boots.[559] She is sometimes flanked by her children, Chrysaor and Pegasos or by cranes and lions or shown "holding cranes and geese in her hands."[560] In visual depictions focusing on the story of her beheading by Perseus and/or Athene, Medusa's body is present, collapsing, bleeding, and sometimes birthing winged Pegasus. Even in these full-body depictions of Medusa, the defining trait that commands attention is her large masklike head with its distinctive features. She shares some characteristics, such as her wings, with other deities, but what sets the Gorgon apart is her head.

The Gorgon's distinctive head also dominates her first literary references. However, ancient narratives describe not only a head, but a body and other essential details that complement the visual representations of Medusa from the pre-historic and Greco-Roman periods. I now examine Medusa's written stories.

CHAPTER 4

WRITING MEDUSA: MYTHOS, HISTORY, AND PROPAGANDA

Ancient Greek and Roman Narratives

Most of us know one story about Medusa: that of her rape, transformation, and beheading. But the Gorgon appears in many myths and it is through the nuances and details—shared or unique—that she is revealed and substantiated. For this reason I include several renditions and fragments despite some repetition. In fact, repetitions, singular details, and changes over time combine to express Medusa's identity.

Homer

Medusa first appears in Greek literature in Homer's *The Iliad* and *The Odyssey*; accredited to "Homer," these works emerged from a long oral tradition and are thought to have been written down beginning around 750 BCE. In *The Iliad*, Medusa appears simply as the terrifying Gorgoneion upon Athene's aegis or breastplate: the "Gorgon's monstrous head, that rippling dragon horror."[561] The Gorgoneion is also described on the shield of King Agamemnon: "the Gorgon's grim mask—the burning eyes, the stark, transfixing horror."[562] Medusa's visage endows these warriors with the power to overwhelm enemies in battle. Homer also describes the Trojan hero, Hektor, in battle with "eyes glaring bright as a Gorgon's eyes."[563] No specific details beyond the terrible power of her eyes are provided, but the efficacy of the Gorgon's appearance to evoke petrifying terror and death is clear; and her eyes as the source of that power is established.

In *The Odyssey*, Homer tells us that while traversing the underworld, Odysseus feared "lest noble Persephone send the Gorgon head / Of the dread monster from the hall of Hades against me."[564] Medusa herself is not specifically named or given a back story in Homer's references. She is simply a mask—worn or embodied in the eyes—that evokes terror, the power of which is brandished by and for the benefit of others.

Dexter concludes that at the time that *The Iliad* and *The Odyssey* were written down (750-725 BCE), "it is likely that the story of Medusa and Perseus was not known" since Perseus appears in *The Iliad* along with elements of his story, but without any reference to Medusa's beheading.[565] Beginning around 800 BCE, Greek civilization was just starting to coalesce out of the chaos of the Greek Dark Age, which followed the collapse of the Minoan-Mycenaean culture around 1100 BCE. This Dark Age is "referred to consistently as bleak, hard, and poverty-stricken," characterized by illiteracy, the disappearance of large-scale building and plastic arts, and disintegration of the socio-political structure into small, warring tribal/familial groups wherein the father "was the supreme authority."[566] As Edelman despairs: "We can imagine that people in such conditions would place little value on literacy, the arts, diplomacy—that it was a time when only brute male force guaranteed survival and a maternal deity was cast out in favor of a cosmology which reflected the tenor of the social environment."[567] Whether or not the demise of more gynocentric religions was as precipitous as Edelman imagines, it seems likely that this "cultural vacuum became the crucible for the formation of the patriarchal world view and the domination of the Father principle" that engendered the patriarchal Olympian religion of the later Greeks, which tended to associate evil with the dark feminine.[568] The disembodied, terror-inspiring Gorgon of archaic Greece may have arisen, as Edelman muses, out of the "imagination of the Dark Age"[569] or, as Gimbutas asserts, as a distortion and demonization of the goddesses of death and regeneration reflected in the transition to patriarchal values from earlier goddess-revering cultures; a fearful remnant of powerful female priestess magicians. Or, as Harrison concludes, Medusa may simply represent the ubiquitous bogey or Evil Eye so deeply rooted in the human psyche. However, a bogey is never just a bogey, being enlivened and energized by our human psyches in response to mystery and taboo. Whatever the factors that contributed to Homer's characterization, the first literary glimpses of Medusa are perhaps the more potent because she is portrayed solely as the Gorgoneion, a monstrous force of mayhem—impersonal and trans-human, or in Hillman's language, dehumanized and archetypal.

Hesiod

Around 700 BCE, the Greek poet Hesiod connects the two mythic figures of Perseus and Medusa in his *Theogony*. The poet also identifies Medusa by name, delineates her family (including her ancestors and offspring), locates her home, and provides her with other attributes, including a body from which her head is removed.

According to the *Theogony*, Medusa's parents are Keto and Phorkys. Medusa's sisters include the other two Gorgons, Sthenno and Euryale, and the grey-haired Graiai, who were old from birth. The great dragon-serpent, Ladon, guardian of the golden apples of the Hesperides in Hera's garden and gifted with human speech, is also Medusa's sibling. Predating the gods of Olympus—except for Aphrodite—the Gorgons represent the fourth generation of deities born after the creation of the world. In other words, they are ancient even to the ancient Greeks; their grandparents are Gaia, the Earth, and Pontos, the Sea. Born "beyond the famous stream of the Ocean," a river which the Greeks imagined encircled the world, the *Theogony* claims that the Gorgons live at the end of the Earth in the West—"the utmost place toward night, by the singing Hesperides."[570] This mythical location is likely referring to an area called Libya by the Greeks and is thought to have been near the Atlas Mountains in northwestern Africa around modern-day Morocco.[571]

While Medusa's physical description is not given, in the *Theogony* Hesiod tells us that of her sisters, she was the only mortal, had a sexual liaison with Poseidon "in a soft meadow and among spring flowers,"[572] and was beheaded by Perseus. The poet also describes the births of Pegasos and Chrysaor from Medusa's blood and delineates episodes from their futures. Pegasos, named for the place of Medusa's birth, "the *pegai*, the springs of the Ocean,"[573] is destined to live among the Immortals, carrying Zeus's thunderbolts. Chrysaor, who is named for his golden sword or *aör,* fathers a line of monstrous liminal creatures, true heirs to Medusa's terrible aspect. With his wife Kallirhoe he sires triple-headed Geryon and Echidna, half beautiful nymph and half monstrous serpent. Echidna births Orthos, Geryon's herding dog; Kerberos, the ferocious, triple-headed hound of Hades; and the formidable Hydra. With her son Orthos, Echidna produces the Sphinx and the Nemeian Lion. Hydra births the Chimera, whose three heads include that of a lion, a goat, and a fire-breathing dragon. Like their foremother Medusa, many of these creatures are slain by Golden Age heroes. Herakles dispatches Geryon, Orthos, Hydra, and the Nemeian Lion and Bellerophon, upon Pegasos, destroys the Chimera.

In another interweaving of stories, Hesiod associates Medusa's descendants, the Hydra, the Nemeian Lion, and the serpent Ladon, with Hera as servants of her will and accessories to her schemes. In *The Shield of Herakles*, the mythic image of Perseus's post-beheading escape from the horrifying Sthenno and Euryale is described. Medusa's sisters are "unapproachable, indescribable" with angry serpents at their waists.[574] Upon the back of the flying hero, is Medusa's head, huge within his magical *kibisis*: "all his back was covered with the head of the monster."[575]

Through Hesiod's narrative, Medusa begins to come to life. She is primordial and pre-Olympian, which indicates her roots in chthonic traditions preceding archaic Greece. Further, as discussed earlier, the name Hesiod assigns her, "Medusa," means "queen," which implies her mythic connection to ruling goddesses of old and, psychologically, to ruling feminine principles. This queenly connection is echoed in her association with Hera, Queen of Olympus. Medusa is born of the "ancient sea god of the hidden dangers of the deep" and the goddess of "sea monsters,"[576, 577] and therefore, of the waters, the primal birthplace of all life. These watery ties are suggested by her name, as discussed in the previous chapter. The ocean depths—awesome in their mysteriousness— connote the dangers of the unknown, but also allude to riches from the deep. From a depth psychological point of view, the water signifies the unconscious, also a source of fearful and fruitful gifts. Medusa's watery birthplace and home in the West, at the end of the world—the very edge of what can be known only by heroic effort, divine intervention, and trickery—equates with the mysteries of death and the unconscious.

Medusa's family amplifies the sense of apprehension with their potent, exotic combinations of human and dangerous animal forms: serpents, ferocious canines, and sea monsters. The Gorgon shares these animal doubles with other goddesses so that the creatures serve to express Medusa's particular qualities, but also characteristics of the greater feminine archetype of which she is an aspect.

Medusa, like many goddesses, is part of a divine triplet, but uniquely she is both immortal and mortal. As an unmarried human woman capable of sexual reproduction, that is, menstruating, Medusa is a *parthenos*, which, as I discuss later in this chapter and extensively in Chapter 5, is an extremely troublesome condition for Greek culture.

Unlike other variations, Hesiod's version of Medusa's encounter with Poseidon is no rape scene, but rather, evokes the sense of divine Spring renewal in the form of sexual union of the Great Goddess with her consort. Pegasos, as one of the offspring of Medusa's consensual sexual liaison with Poseidon, extends the magic and mystery of the union. Recall that horses are associated with water deities. In addition, Pegasos's liminal form unites all realms: water, earth, and sky.

Chrysaor, as heir to Medusa's chthonic nature, fathers her legacy of monster-fodder for Greek heroes, perhaps reinforcing through repetition the patriarchy's imperative to vanquish mystery, animal-nature, and the dark feminine once and for all. However, these monsters also reflect the tenacity and uncontrollable aspects of life, even as humankind strives to conquer inner and outer wild nature. Finally, Hesiod provides a glimpse of Medusa's fate as Perseus's prey and her head's utility to its bearer—a head which carries apotropaic power and the life seed.

Apollodorus

In *The Library of Greek Mythology*, a second century BCE compendium of Greek mythology credited to the Athenian scholar Apollodorus, details of Perseus and his decapitation of Medusa are provided—particulars that illuminate the Hellenistic version of Medusa's story. Apollodorus, like Homer, depicts Medusa as a threatening phantom in Hades encountered, and obviously well known, by Herakles during his twelfth labor: approached by the ghostly Medusa, Herakles "drew his sword against the Gorgon as if she were still alive, but learned from Hermes that she was an empty phantom."[578]

In Perseus's narrative, Apollodorus sketches the Gorgons' deadly, monstrous appearance: "heads with scaly serpents coiled around them, and large tusks like those of swine, and hands of bronze, and wings of gold which gave them the power of flight; and they turned all who beheld them to stone."[579] The poet reports that Perseus receives a good deal of divine help, both willing and coerced, in his endeavor against Medusa. Athene, Hermes, the Graiai, and a group of nymphs all assist. Hermes and Athene guide Perseus to the Graiai, Medusa's sisters, who share among them one eye and one tooth. The hero steals the eye and tooth, forcing the Graiai to reveal the location of the nymphs who possess three essential items: winged sandals, Hades' cap (which renders the wearer invisible), and the *kibisis*, or magical bag in which to carry Medusa's severed head. Once Perseus obtains these tools of his trade, and armed with an indestructible sickle from Hermes, the hero flies to Medusa's home at the ends of the Earth. There he locates the three Gorgons asleep and using Athene's shiny shield to safely spy his prey, he approaches and beheads Medusa. Specifically, "Perseus stood over them as they slept, and while Athene guided his hand, he turned aside, and looking into a bronze shield in which he could see the reflection of the Gorgon, he cut off her head."[580] In this story, Athene's participation in Medusa's death is explicit and primary. Upon Medusa's beheading, Pegasos and Chrysaor, her children by Poseidon, spring from her body. Perseus places the severed head into the *kibisis* and flees, with Sthenno and Euryale attempting to pursue their invisible foe.

Apollodorus goes on to describe how Perseus wins Andromeda's hand by slaying a sea monster and using Medusa's head to turn the Ethiopian princess's jealous uncle-suitor, Phineus, and his followers to stone. Next, Perseus travels to Seriphos where he rescues his mother and foster father, Danae and Dictys, from King Polydectes, again using Medusa's head as a lethal weapon. Perseus then returns the flying sandals, *kibisis*, and cap to Hermes and presents Medusa's head to Athene, who places it in the middle of her aegis.

Apollodorus suggests that Medusa was killed on behalf of Athene because "the Gorgon had claimed to rival the goddess in beauty."[581] Given the poet's earlier description of the monstrous Gorgons, his comment about Medusa's beauty seems incongruent. However, it recalls references such as that of the poet Pindar to Medusa-of-the-lovely-cheek and contributes, along with Apollodorus's rendering of Athene as Medusa's co-executioner, to a sense of a singular connection between the two goddesses.

Apollodorus also recounts two incidences where Athene gifts the power of Medusa through relics of the Gorgon. Herakles "acquired from Athene a lock of the Gorgon's hair in a bronze jar,"[582] which he provides as protection to the princess of an ally city, telling her that "if an army attacked, she should hold up the lock three times from the ramparts, without looking at it herself and the enemy would turn and flee."[583] Additionally, Apollodorus recounts the story of Athene providing Medusa's blood to Asklepios, God of Healing. In *The Library*, it explains that Asklepios "had received from Athene blood that had flowed from the veins of the Gorgon; and he used the blood that had flowed from the veins on the left side to put people to death, and that which had flowed from the right, to save them—and it was by this means that he raised the dead."[584]

Apollodorus's stories link Medusa and Athene repeatedly: Medusa's visage upon Athene's aegis; the reported rivalry between the goddesses; Athene's gifting of Medusan relics, including hair and blood, to others; and Athene's direct implication in Medusa's beheading all excite curiosity as to the nature of the relationship between the two goddesses. Medusa's physical appearance, provided in more graphic detail than in previous accounts, is reminiscent of bogeys in general, but also of artifacts representing the Great Goddess mysteries, particularly the snake and avian forms commonly found on Neolithic art objects.[585] Significantly, Athene also has roots in Snake/Bird Goddesses, particularly those of the Minoan civilization, which deeply influenced later Greek culture.

The potency of Medusan relics—especially the ultimate power over life, death, and resurrection of the dead engendered in her blood —"alludes to a cosmic force much greater than the familiar image of the hideous Gorgon would suggest"[586] and points to Medusa's Great Goddess ancestry. In addition, the peculiar nature of Medusa's blood as both creative and pathogenic is integral to my intuition of her as a Goddess of Endometriosis. Recall that with endometriosis, tissue, like that within the uterus, called endometrium occurs ectopically, that is, outside of the uterus. In the disease process, the blood of endometrial tissue is both generative—when located within the uterus where it supports fetal development and the monthly renewal of the uterine lining—*and* extremely destructive when ectopic. Like the Gorgon's blood, a woman's endometrial blood is both the basis of life for the growing fetus and the defining symptom of the disease, a disorder that petrifies the reproductive organs and, for women like me, is life-threatening.

One additional comment on Medusa's blood regards Athene's gift to Asklepios. Just drops of Medusa's potent lifeblood provide the male god of healing his *pharmakon*. I cannot help but note how the story mirrors the eventual domination of the medical mindset, establishment, and practice by masculine values and men wielding the wisdom of Nature.

In his telling of Herakles's encounter with Medusa, Apollodorus associates Medusa with death and the fear of death as the terrible end of life, with no sense of the Great Round. However, while she still evokes his fear, Medusa's power to actually harm Herakles has apparently been undone, presumably by her decapitation. This tale implies that, despite the Gorgon's suppression and apparent depotentiation by the patriarchal worldview, the heroic ego remains threatened by encounters with chthonic forces. In contrast to the idea that the Gorgon's deadly power is diminished is Perseus's wielding of Medusa's visage to great effect. Given divine access to chthonic power by way of the Gorgoneion, he employs it according to his power motives and desires for personal gain, defense, and revenge, until at last presenting the head to Athene. In this way, Medusa becomes a tool for amplifying Perseus's own destructive emotions, functioning apotropaically for the hero.

The story of Medusa's beheading by Perseus in Apollodorus's account is fascinating in its detail and in the centrality of divine intervention and trickery. The level of involvement by Athene, and, to a lesser extent Hermes, sets Medusa apart as a mighty foe indeed; at a glance it is difficult to reconcile the causes given with the actions taken. However, understood psychologically, it appears that potent archetypal forces are required for the integration of Medusa's chthonic feminine powers within the personality. Perseus, as a human ego, serves this integration by accessing the wisdom signified by Athene, wisdom that includes Hermetic trickery. In addition, Perseus's use of Hermes's magical sickle to harvest Medusa's head (a head that carries the "life-seed") for Athene positions the story within the agricultural domain of the Great Goddess, accentuating Athene's subversive challenge of the prevailing Greek assumptions about reproduction, human essence, and sexual power.[587]

The idea that the head contains the seed of life provides a way to understand the narrative momentum of Medusa's transformations first from beauty to monster and then from whole-bodied to a dismembered head. Rather than representing depotentiation, it is as if her power is being distilled to its essential seed-form. From this perspective Athene's repeated interventions in Medusa's story appear less like divine retribution or jealousy and more conservative in nature; an effort to preserve the chthonic, sacred feminine in response to the growing power of one-sided masculine political, social, and spiritual power. In addition to the significance of the use of the sickle to behead Medusa, Dexter notes that the brazen or "bronze mirror" shield lent to Perseus by Athene to reflect, or deflect, Medusa's gaze "is historically the priestess/shaman's tool, rather than the tool of the young male hero."[588] Perseus has his own sword and shield, and yet he uses the tools of the Great Mother to cut off her own head.

Apollodorus highlights the theme of female beauty and its dangerous consequences, including envy and retribution, by identifying the dynamic as engendering Medusa's sin against Athene. The theme is also present in Ovid's variation of Medusa's story, in which Athene essentially punishes Medusa for attracting Poseidon's lust. There are various ways to understand these stories. They can be read as examples of the danger of *hybris* (that is, hubris or human arrogance), which results in *phronos* (retribution by vengeful gods).[589] However, beyond the moral imperative of recognizing one's human limitations, in the context of my work, the allusion to beauty implies fascination as the ambivalent, overwhelming power of the Gorgon. In particular, the essential power of the feminine to fascinate and the reactive, defensive postures of envy and retribution which motivate superstitions such as the Evil Eye and menstrual taboos.

Ovid

Despite positioning her within Perseus's narrative, the Roman poet Ovid (43 BCE - 17 CE) grants Medusa a relatively complete and personal narrative in his *Metamorphoses*. She is first mentioned only as Perseus's "famous trophy, the head of the snake-headed Gorgon"[590] who's dripping blood, spilled as the hero flies over the desert, is the source of the poisonous snakes of Libya. Continuing his narration of Perseus's tale, Ovid describes how the hero uses the Gorgon head to turn the suspicious and inhospitable Atlas to stone. After leaving Atlas, Perseus encounters Andromeda, naked and bound to a rock as an offering to a sea monster in order to appease divine wrath over her mother's boasts of beauty. Ovid describes Andromeda as seeming to be "merely a marble statue"[591] and so beautiful that Perseus is stunned and nearly petrified by the effect. (This paralleling of the effect of beholding Andromeda with that of espying Medusa—especially tied to the female beauty taboos implicated in both women's punishment—is striking. The feminine power to fascinate comes at a high price.) Regaining his composure, Perseus ascertains the situation, dispatches the sea monster with his borrowed scimitar, and claims Andromeda, to her parents' great relief and satisfaction, at least in Ovid's version.

Ovid includes a lovely passage in his tale wherein the hero, needing to wash after his labors, tenderly places Medusa's head on a soft bed of seaweed to protect it from the hard ground. The power of the Gorgon causes the seaweed to solidify into coral. Nearby sea-nymphs play with this Medusan magic, spreading it and Ovid tells us that this is the source of coral's peculiar quality of being pliable under water and rocklike above. The story reunites Medusa's cosmic, transformational power with nature, where it creates beauty rather than mayhem.

During the wedding celebration for Perseus and Andromeda, the hero is asked to tell how he acquired Medusa's head. Perseus recounts a story similar to that related in Apollodorus's account with slight variations. Perseus chronicles how he stole the Graiai's eye and forced them to reveal the location of the Gorgon's home. Upon his approach, Perseus claims that he encountered men and beasts turned to stone "at the sight of Medusa."[592] Perseus describes how, using the reflective quality of the bronze shield, he beheaded the sleeping Medusa whereupon Pegasos and Chrysaor sprang forth from her blood. Urged on by the captivated wedding guests, Perseus next recounts Medusa's back story.

Through this biography, Ovid gives Medusa the pathos of being an unwilling monster, apparently transformed by an angry goddess following violation by a lustful god. Medusa is described as a maiden of extraordinary loveliness whose glory of glories is her hair, a symbol of sexual potency. Many suitors vie for her favor, but to no avail. Unfortunately, she catches the eye of Poseidon who rapes her in Athene's temple, to the horror of Zeus's daughter, who "screened her virginal eyes with her aegis."[593] Athene responds by transforming the young woman's hair into serpents and wearing Medusa's snake-wreathed head upon her aegis to terrify enemies.

Although Ovid proclaims Athene the architect of the transforming curse affecting Medusa, he does not directly connect Zeus's daughter with Perseus's beheading of the Gorgon. The tale is told from Perseus's perspective and he takes full credit for the deed. However, in a separate story, Ovid tells that Athene visits the muses at Mount Helicon to see a miraculous fountain created when Pegasos struck the ground with his hoof. Explaining her curiosity to view the fountain, Athene places herself at the scene of Medusa's death by claiming, "I wanted to see this amazing spring, as I witnessed the horse's birth from the blood of his Gorgon mother."[594] So, once again, Athene is in fact present at Medusa's decapitation.

From a depth psychological standpoint, it seems that Perseus-as-ego suffers inflation in the face of collective admiration of his heroism; a real danger for an ego that encounters numinous power from the unconscious and then attempts to wield it for personal gain. Athene's story compensates for Perseus's omissions and points to the efficacy of her ultimate possession of the Gorgoneion. The power over life and death appears to be dangerously destructive in human hands without the divine wisdom and strategies of the goddess.

As if to drive the point home, Ovid retains Medusa's presence in Perseus's story for three additional bloody adventures, starting with the hero's merciless destruction of Phineus, Andromeda's uncle-suitor, in an extended and graphic depiction. Next, Perseus returns home to Argos where he petrifies his Great Uncle Proetus, who has usurped power from Perseus's grandfather. Finally, Perseus wields Medusa's head against the tyrant Polydectes for denying Perseus's glory and success in slaying the Gorgon. Presumably, Perseus can settle down now, having cleaned his house, and so returns the Gorgon head to Athene, its rightful and more prudent keeper.

A curious observation inspired by Ovid's tale is that Medusa is so often the object rather than the subject of her story. In the surviving narratives about Medusa from ancient Greece and Rome written down from the eighth century BCE to the second century CE, she tends not to be the protagonist in her own story. Reading Homer, the impression is that the Gorgoneion was so iconic a symbol of terror for ancient audiences that her mere mention was adequate to communicate a complexity of horror and evil. Though she appears frequently in narratives, with a few exceptions, she is mentioned as a monster; seen as a ghostly emissary of Persephone in Hades; portrayed as passive or victimized; or presented simply as a masklike severed head. Even in her potent Gorgoneion form as a petrifying, dismembered head, Medusa does not have agency; her power is wielded as a weapon by champions such as Perseus or Agamemnon. Despite Medusa's fearsome reputation, in the heroic epics, she often appears not as predator but prey; the monster to be hunted and destroyed so that her power can be transferred to another. This trend likely reflects tension between the cultural devaluation of the sacred feminine and her lingering archetypal potential in the unconscious, a tension which demands that her powers be controlled. Ancient Greek civilization was patriarchal and one function of mythology is to "give divine sanction to the social patterns of a culture."[595]

Ovid provides vivid and expansive reports of Perseus's use of Medusa's head as a weapon. However, he also shares the detail of the hero's tender care of the head epitomized in the story-within-the-story of coral's creation. Viewed archetypally, the tale constellates the feminine power to bring up, from the watery depths of the unconscious into solid form that which remains insubstantial without her mediation. That the process is expedited by the play of the sea nymphs implies a natural, spontaneous quality to such creativity. The story also speaks to the way in which the Medusan quality of endometriosis solidifies soft tissues of the female body within the watery peritoneal environment. I return to these reveries in Chapter 6.

Ovid gives a nod to Medusa's generative powers—though more of evil than good—both in reference to the serpents of Libya and the births of Pegasos and Chrysaor. In the details of his telling, Ovid also raises issues of the dangers and pleasures of seeing and being seen, the safety engendered in reflection, and the connection between female beauty and violation or punishment. And, perhaps most crucial, he solidifies Medusa's identity as victim—of divine rape and wrath. His *explicit* linking of female sexuality with monstrosity is like a stone dropped into a still pool, sending ripples of meaning in all directions: issues of othering and identity, superstition, menstrual taboos, women's rights, and distorted attitudes about the female body, its processes, and sexuality, which are amplified by Freud's equating of Medusa with the mutilated female genitalia of the mother.

Lucan

A first century Roman, Lucan, discloses what he considered the "delusive but widespread legend of Medusa, daughter of Phorcys" in his larger work *Pharsalia*.[596] Lucan tells a tale very similar in plot to those of Hesiod, Apollodorus, and Ovid, but embellishes it with evocative and even gruesome details: "Medusa's features must have worn a ghastly grimace in the moment of her decapitation—I have no doubt that the mouth belched poison and the eyes flashed instant death."[597] Describing how the Gorgon's blood created the snakes of the Libyan desert, he delights in lurid touches: "The first snake to spring from the ground after this rain of Gorgon's blood was the deadly asp with its puffed neck; and since the blood happened to be particularly abundant at this point, and mixed with clotted venom, it proved to be the most deadly of all the Libyan varieties."[598]

Exaggerating earlier depictions of Medusa's power to petrify, he declares it unique to her, claiming she "was dreaded by her own father Phorcys [... and] by her mother Ceto, and even by her sister-Gorgons."[599] According to Lucan, Medusa's gaze was a threat to all living creatures, including the serpents upon her head; to the land itself; and to deities—"Athene herself could not look at those eyes."[600] Even death was somehow suspended by Medusa for we could not "describe what happened [...] as death, for being prevented from gasping out his spirit, this became petrified with his body."[601]

Lucan's special contribution to my understanding of Medusa is his obscene relish and sensual articulation of the Gorgon's evil and power. His Medusa is no sad victim of fate: "Medusa loved to feel the serpents which served for her hair curled close to her neck and dangling down her back."[602] However, there is something unsettlingly misogynistic and salacious in his fascination with Medusa that feels analogous to renditions of Medusa (and other goddesses and females) wherein her extreme sexualized sensuality is essential to her dangerous allure. Like Ovid's story, Lucan links female sexuality with monstrosity. However, while Ovid portrays Medusa as an unwilling victim, Lucan depicts willful, sensual evil. By virtue of her powers, Medusa is so completely other that she is a threat to her family, nature, the gods, and herself; even her snaky hair must fear her. In addition, Medusa's blood, which previously had healing and regenerative powers, is thoroughly malignant, mingled with "clotted venom" and producing supremely dangerous offspring. The grotesque fertility of Medusa's harvested head echoes the likelihood that she was the exception to the rule that only the male head contained the seed of life. However, Medusa's head breeds monstrosity, evil, and death rather than human children. Blood from the woman's reproductive organs is menstrual blood, the evils of which are graphically, though not explicitly evoked by Lucan.

Furthermore, Lucan endows Medusa with abominable, exaggerated lethality. For example, the inability of mortals to withstand direct sight of a deity is a commonplace taboo and was part of the Olympian tradition as evidenced by the story of Zeus and Semele. Lucan's overstatement of Medusa's ability to annihilate as unique elevates her to supreme deity status, however, in her case, it is a capital offense. Could it be that Medusa's co-condition as a mortal woman is at issue? A supreme deity has the power to give life and take it away, a power shared by females in their reproductive processes. This is the very power that menstrual taboos and the patriarchal worldview strive to control and appropriate.

One other detail of interest is Lucan's insistence that the penalty exacted for both Medusa's gaze and the glimpsing of her was a sort of spiritual death that was worse than physical annihilation. This claim epitomizes an extreme demonization of Medusa as an especially unnatural abomination, a quintessential monster. However, Lucan's description also resonates with the psychological experience of encountering the Gorgon as face of the daemonic sacred; an experience of ontic or primal shame as self-defilement that engenders deep dread making one "feel frozen, paralyzed, turned to stone."[603]

Lucian

The Greek Lucian (120-80 CE) opines, perhaps satirically, that "the power of the tongue is no match for the eyes."[604] To prove his point he recounts what he claims is a story that "everyone says" is true: "the beauty of the Gorgons, being extremely powerful and affecting the very vitals of the soul, stunned its beholders and made them speechless, so that, as the story has it and everyone says, they turned to stone in wonder."[605] Here it is the Gorgon's arresting beauty that is the source of her great and petrifying power. Though Medusa's overwhelming capacity to fascinate is born of beauty rather than terror, it is no less dangerous and Lucian echoes the necessity of not gazing upon her directly, describing Athene shielding Perseus, as the hero, looking only at the Gorgon's reflection, decapitates Medusa.

Identifying Medusa's beauty as the source of her power to petrify is not unique to Lucian. Such stories highlight ambivalence about and fear of the power of fascination—particularly for men—apparently emanating from a beautiful woman. The idea that females in particular and the eye generally can fascinate to the point of bewitching, emasculating, or even killing is fundamental to menstrual taboos and ideas of the Evil Eye. The need for protective deflection, reflection, and/or isolation is a basic mechanism of dealing with such taboos. Similar techniques are employed psychologically when approaching shadow aspects of the unconscious through reflection rather than direct confrontation.

Pindar, Aeschylus, and Euripides

In addition to more expansive narratives about Medusa, brief mentions and descriptions appear throughout mythopoetic texts including those of Pindar, Aeschylus, Euripides, and others. These allusions both reflect and add to the picture of Medusa provided by the more complete stories. For example, in his *Pythian 12* (490 BCE), the lyric poet Pindar offers a contradictory glimpse of Medusa-the-terrible calling her "the fair-cheeked Medusa."[606] In addition to his reference to Medusa's beauty, Pindar describes the creation of the funeral song by Athene based upon the enraged and mournful cries of Medusa's Gorgon sisters as they pursued Perseus after the beheading.

In the fifth century BCE tragedy *Prometheus Bound*, attributed to Aeschylus, the three Gorgons are described as being deadly to look upon with wings and serpentine hair. Aeschylus also describes the Gorgonean plane, home of the Graiai and the Gorgons, as a desolate place where the light of the sun and moon are never seen. In his tragedy, *The Eumenides,* Aeschylus, in attempting to visually evoke the Erinyes, likens them first to Gorgons and then Harpies.[607] In each case the creatures lack a defining feature—the masklike face or the wings. However, the three categories of demons are equated in their loathsomeness and, even more, in their femaleness. The removal of the supernatural features typically used to make bogeys monstrous ironically humanizes them and makes them more abominable, in Harrison's words, a "wholly human horror."[608] I return to *The*

Eumenides in my discussion of Athene in Chapter 5 for what it reveals about the relationship between Zeus's daughter and Medusa.

Euripides's fifth century play *Ion* also highlights Medusa's connection to Athene as well as the Gorgon's dual nature through the peculiar power of her harvested blood. In the tragedy, Euripides describes Athene wearing the hideous Gorgon head on her aegis and credits Athene with killing Medusa; there is no mention of Perseus. In a crucial scene, Creusa, the Queen of Athens, describes an heirloom bracelet she wears containing a drop of Medusa's blood that cures—"Medicinal, of sovereign use to life"—and separately, a drop which kills.[609] The blood was gifted by Athene to Erichthonios, an early King of Athens and the Olympian goddess's foster son, born of the soil and Hephaistos's seed.

Repeated themes of Medusa's contradictory appearance as lovely and hideous, her association with death and the other/underworld, and the dual nature of her blood recur in the above narratives, highlighting the Gorgon's continued mythic presence in Greek literature over time. However, it is Aeschylus's innovative depiction of the Erinyes in *The Eumenides* that catches my attention because of what it implies about the negative nature of females and female sexuality. The Erinyes or Furies are frequently equated with Gorgons and Harpies[610, 611] and so Aeschylus's treatment can be applied to female bogeys in general, rather than simply to Furies. Harrison emphasizes, that the poet makes the Erinyes more disgusting by making them more womanly. By first associating Furies verbally with Gorgons and Harpies, but then removing mask and wing, Aeschylus transforms "the Erinyes from the region of grotesque impossible bogeydom to a lower and more loathsome, because wholly human horror."[612] In her footnote, Harrison bemoans the fact that Aeschylus blackened the faces of the Erinyes on stage, thereby "half alienat[ing] our sympathies."[613] Her point is well taken, however, she completely overlooks the fact that monstrosity has taken the guise of human woman, now devoid of any real supernatural designation to distinguish the evil, disgusting, and abhorrent from womankind.

Of course, the tangling of females, female sexuality, and demonic monstrosity appears not only in Aeschylus but elsewhere in ancient Greek (and other) mythology as well. Three hundred years before Aeschylus's time, Hesiod depicts the creation of woman as an eternal punishment suffered by man for receiving the gift of stolen fire from Prometheus. The mother of womankind is a "beautiful evil thing,

[...] a sheer deception" [614]and women are a "great sorrow" to men, demanding luxury, breeding "cantankerous children," and sapping men of all their strength in service to female supposed sexual and other appetites.[615]

Mythological misogyny is reciprocal with the repression of women and coincides with what author Eva Keuls calls the rise of the "phallocracy," which was well established by fifth century classical Greece.[616] Medusa's loss of agency and demonization from Hesiod's *Theogony*, where she is a beautiful maiden-goddess who has consensual sexual intercourse with Poseidon in the meadow, to Apollodorus's account of rape, victimization, and female jealousy six centuries later serves as a mythic reflection of a socio-political reality. Lubell points to the interplay between representations of the sacred and cultural attitudes:

> By the fifth century BCE in Greece, Medusa's mask was isolated as the quintessential icon of *aideomai*, of fear and shame, [.... for] Greek women had by this time come to be regarded as inherently flawed beings, obviously inferior to men, and Medusa had come to represent the sum total of male fears about the power and dangers of female sexuality.[617]

In fact, what we find in ancient Greek social norms and practices reveals that feminine power apparently posed a great threat to masculinized civilization and needed to be controlled. Greek cultural characterization of females as "potentially threatening to the male sex" was exemplified in myth and custom.[618] Women and girls were associated with animals because of their supposed uncivilized, "unruly nature" and were generally believed to be "prone to excessive and uncontrolled behavior, and [...] in need of male guidance, provided first by their fathers and later by their husbands."[619] Girls were not allowed to attend school and had no formal education as boys did. Women did not participate in Greek democracy or have political rights, and were legal minors under male guardianship their entire lives.[620] By law, females could not inherit property or spend money beyond "the price of a few basic household provisions."[621] Women of the upper class could not leave their homes unless escorted by a male relative, and then only for certain festivals or under other limited circumstances. Slaves and peasant women appeared to have more freedom of movement as was necessary for their work, but they too were property of men like their more privileged sisters. Marriage was an arrangement between a girl's father and future husband and occurred shortly after menarche with brides typically being 14 to 18 years old while grooms were closer to 30.[622] The production of children, especially boys, was the primary function of females and marriage; menstruation was a condition to be cured by pregnancy and was surrounded by "a variety of pollution rules and taboos."[623, 624] Generally the sexes moved in separate social spheres.

Because the primary purpose of women was to birth offspring, much of female power coalesced around menstruation and its procreative associations, which, though misunderstood by the ancient Greeks, were recognized as essential. The physician Hippocrates (400 BCE) wrote extensively on reproduction and gynecological disorders and offers a portal through which to understand the Greek mind with regards to the female body. Although he laid the foundation for the science of modern medicine by seeking "natural origins for disease," the Hippocratic gynecological corpus was limited by its own empiricism and an understandingly primitive grasp of human physiology.[625] These limitations resulted in seemingly bizarre, but wholly embraced ideas such as the wandering uterus. It also appears that some of the notions espoused relied more on philosophical ideas of women's inherent inferiority to men than on scientific observation. As Aristotle asserts in his *Generation of Animals*, "a woman is, as it were, an infertile male. She is female, in fact, on account of a kind of inadequacy."[626] Given scientific advancements, it is tempting to criticize ancient medicine. However, misogynistic ideas based in Greek medical concepts tenaciously linger into the twenty-first century as demonstrated in my research on endometriosis in Chapter 2.

Classical scholar and feminist Barbara Smith opines that the Hippocratic gynecological corpus appears "almost wholly concerned with the male regulation of female menstrual blood," and menstruation itself appeared to be "viewed as a pathological condition the best cure for which was sexual intercourse [within marriage] followed by pregnancy."[627] Pregnancy was a risky treatment since "as many as one birth in five may have resulted in the death of the mother."[628] Smith argues that in ancient Greece, female identity and status was, "unlike that of males, [...] based on biology—their sexuality and fertility—and the various statuses seem to have been determined by a flow of blood: menarche, defloration and parturition

[....] and [the females'] social kinship relation to men," father, husband, or son.[629] A pre-menses girl, or *kore*, was identified with her father's hearth and home. A married woman, *gune*, or a mother, *meter*, was under the control of her husband. An unmarried female past menarche was identified as a *parthenos*, which, according to Smith appears to have been "an ambivalent sociopathological condition to be 'cured' by [....] the spilling of her blood (menarche, defloration, parturition)."[630]

Language of sociopathology might seem extreme. However, Smith supports her assertion by observing that when Greek myth is classified by biosocial grouping, "by far the majority is about *parthenoi*, reflecting the extreme sexual anxiety of ancient Greek men and crystallizing their ambivalence towards women out of male control."[631] In fact, within myth, the menstruating maiden or *parthenos* is consistently "transformed or destroyed," perhaps reflecting the social norm that the only good menstruating human is a married, pregnant one.[632] While other virgin goddesses such as Athene and Artemis are exempt from this fate by virtue of their divine virginal status, Medusa is *parthenos par excellence*. Greek sexual anxiety is also evident in ancient medical writings, which characterize *parthenos* as pathology: "at the onset of puberty girls are liable to suffer from hallucinations, brought on when their menstrual blood does not flow out of their bodies but rushes up to their heart and lungs. They become feverish and sometimes suicidally insane."[633]

It is not possible to know what the Greeks understood about endometriosis, since the disease was not described in its particularities in ancient Greece. However, in his extensive writings about menstruation in general, Hippocrates frequently speculates about menstrual disorders, describing symptoms that, according to endometriosis expert Dr. David Redwine are "highly likely" to indicate the disease.[634] Since endometriosis is primarily experienced as a disorder of the menstrual cycle, it is subject to similar assumptions. In addition, attitudes towards females and the norms regulating their behavior and social roles are enmeshed with beliefs about menstruation and menstrual diseases. It is clear that in ancient Greece women were defined by and controlled because of their sex, which was inextricable from menstruation. Underlying the restrictive norms and beliefs that limited women's lives were the philosophies of men such as Aristotle, a contemporary of Hippocrates, which included misogynistic ideas and attitudes.[635] Aristotle is explicit in his arguments proclaiming women's inferiority to men, claiming that the female was "an incomplete male or 'as it were, a deformity.'"[636] As noted, in his *Generation of Animals*, he contends that menstrual blood is an inert substance, matter without form, which must be animated by inspiriting male semen. Hippocrates also espouses the inert nature of menstrual blood, which he understood as an excess of moisture to be flushed from the body or transformed by semen into the fetus's body within the womb.[637] Matter is inferior to spirit as female is inferior to male[638] and the supposed nature of menstrual blood supports the conclusion.

The misogynistic attitudes of ancient Greece matter; in many ways, to criticize ancient Greek culture is to criticize modern Western civilization. Not only is Greece the philosophical progenitor of the modern West, but the Golden Age of Greece continues to be glorified: "So strong is this ideal image [of Greece's Golden Age] that it persists, even as part of our own myth, despite our knowledge that Greek 'democracy' did not extend to women" and others.[639] The misogynistic attitudes represented in Aeschylus's woman-Furies, Aristotle's philosophy, Hippocrates's medicine and elsewhere in ancient Greek myth and culture continue to shape and limit the lives of women, creating suffering and unfulfilled potential.

Conclusion: Medusa and Endometriosis

Medusa is a multivalent goddess of contradiction as her severed head—eyes wide, mouth gaping, snaky hair erect—is widely recognized and iconic for strikingly disparate concepts. She represents, in turn, male depotentiation and castration; the power to vanquish enemies; the psycho-spiritually terrifying daemonic feminine; female disempowerment and silencing; female empowerment and rage; revolution and political liberty; petrifaction and death; and the life-giving, regenerative Great Goddess. Medusa signifies the archetype of the Terrible Mother; a female monster; woman as monstrous; a social scapegoat; the Evil Eye as unredeemable evil and protection from it; menstruation and its taboos; shaman priestesses from the age of the Great Goddess; an expression of phallic energy; frightful female genitalia; the sacred vulva; and the devouring, live-giving womb. Her blood is curative and creative as well as poisonous; capable of producing majestic

Pegasos, monstrous Chrysaor, and Libyan vipers. In the hands of Asklepios it raises the dead. Medusa was reportedly a fiercely powerful African warrior queen, a sensually alluring woman, and a helpless maiden, ravaged and revenged upon. Some insist that she is essentially and only a head or mask. In other potent representations she has a muscular body expressing force and agency. One thing seems clear, what we see when we look at Medusa is a reflection of our own reaction to the unmitigated power she embodies, a power which has constellated in the Western psyche in female form. As with all archetypes, we can only know her by our constructed projection of her and the passionate emotions and behaviors which that projection elicits, individually and collectively.

Regardless of the changes in Medusa's rendering in story and image—expressive of changing socio-cultural norms and psycho-spiritual values through time—her archetypal essence and its inherent tension and polyvalent nature resonate through all expressions: "Rather than 'evolving' over time from one set of interpretations to another, the Medusa myth thus includes, from its very beginnings, all the conflicting elements that have fascinated audiences and readers."[640] Further, scholars Garber and Vickers assert that Medusa's "intrinsic doubleness" accounts for our timeless fascination with her story and image; "at once monster and beauty, disease and cure, threat and protection, poison and remedy," Medusa is both deity—an immortal power—and mortal.[641]

Medusa's dual nature mirrors the dual nature of the womb, cradle of life and death, seat of health and disease, and deliverer of perfection and deformity. Perhaps even more compelling than her duality, is Medusa's polyvalence—image of life *and* death *and* regeneration. This same multiplicity of form and function is found in menstrual blood, which nurtures new life, depotentiates and passes from the body monthly (carrying with it the dead ovum); mysteriously regenerates itself within the uterus; and, when misplaced, is symptomatic of endometriosis. The power of archetypal energy comes through Medusa's image, emanating from the tension of multiple polarities that challenge one-sided ego consciousness and its penchant to isolate, rank, literalize, and suppress what it sees as inferior or threatening to itself.

My wandering through this Medusan study has been an uncovering of soul connections—encounters between my *self* and Medusa's myth, provoking affective and imaginative charges, which engaged through reflection, reveal the Goddess of Endometriosis not as Medusa, but as one face or mask of the great Gorgon. That is, endometriosis as a Gorgoneion worn upon my female sex. My revelation that endometriosis is one mask of Medusa, an embodied manifestation of the misogynistic scorn projected onto the Gorgon, indicates the way in which I have attended her altar. This endometriotic Gorgoneion is the ritual mask which I have unconsciously worn, defending not my face but my sexuality. For attending Medusa's altar means fully inhabiting the female body; experiencing its sensations, attending to its physical and emotional realities—especially those judged as inconvenient, unproductive, disgusting, or even incongruent with life according to the Western ego with its plans, desires, and phallocentric mythology. For me, at this moment, Medusa represents the embodied female in patriarchy, speaking through the body as a physiological and ecological phenomenon. Carrying Medusa in my pelvis, she expresses embodied misogyny. As I have engaged her soulfully through myth she has often taken up residence in my mind and on my tongue, confounding clarity and disorienting my rational functions. I have frequently floundered in my chaotic identification with her, writing in repetitive circles like a wounded creature pacing and pining in agony. I had a dream while writing these chapters on Medusa wherein I encountered the deep and enduring scorn the patriarchal masculine feels toward the archetypal chthonic feminine. This dream demanded recognition of my endometriotic Gorgoneion, pointing me back into the myths where I found myself at Athene's altar, in the very heart of the *phallocracy*—ancient Greek and modern American. Here Medusa's power is luciferian, bringing light out of the dark, or better yet, reconciliation and integration out of suffering.

CHAPTER 5

ATHENE'S REDEMPTION: DIVINE ANDROGYNE AND FEMINIST TRICKSTER

Athene and Medusa

Athene is the goddess of wisdom, war-craft and strategy, weaving, and the work of artisans. Second only to Zeus in the Greek Pantheon, she is "Pallas Athene, the glorious goddess, bright-eyed, inventive, unbending of heart, pure virgin, savior of cities, courageous Tritogeneia."[642] Despite her central position on Olympus, Athene is repeatedly connected with the monstrous outsider Medusa; in ancient Greek mythology and iconography, as well as in the great arc of commentary on the two goddesses, they are inseparable. Athene, as she appears in Homer and onwards, is most frequently represented with the Medusan Gorgoneion upon her aegis or shield. While others, such as Agamemnon, occasionally appear wearing the Gorgoneion into battle, it is consistently associated with Athene; an intrinsic part of her identity as "Gorgopis, 'the Gorgon-faced.'"[643] Mythology claims Athene as Medusa's executioner—either directly or by the guiding of Perseus's hand—and it is Athene who inflicts Medusa's monstrous transformation. There are many interpretations of the nature of the relationship between Medusa and Athene and of

Athene's motivations for her actions regarding Medusa. Since my approach is depth psychological, I seek what is archetypally illuminating in the shared mythology of these two goddesses; truths beyond the heroic vanquishing of a female monster by the patriarchy's shield maiden or her surrogate.

From a depth psychological perspective, deities are constellations of numinous archetypal energy patterns shaped by human apprehension of and associations and experience with the particular pattern. For example, the Great Mother archetype can emerge as the hyper-benevolent Virgin Mary, the fiercest forms of Kālī, or the pervasive Triple Goddess. These manifestations may constellate radically opposing qualities which split or polarize the archetypal energy. However, even between highly differentiated goddesses, iconographic and mythic links, associations, and oddities gently conceal a fundamental interrelatedness and reciprocity intrinsic to what we can call the archetypal feminine. Medusa and Athene are such a pair of goddesses; polarizing and linking the "positive" and "negative" feminine. The material available on Athene is vast, rich, and diverse; well beyond the scope of a single chapter. However, the myths clearly indicate that the only functional approach to Medusa, which is my project, is through Athene. Therefore, the Athene I apprehend here is the one through whom I can understand my embodied experience of endometriosis as Medusan.

I have already laid out various versions of the Greco-Roman Medusa-Athene myths and will not repeat them. It is instructive, however, to examine not only the explicit connections between Medusa and Athene, but also the goddesses' covert associations and mirrorings found in their origins, ancestry, and mythic and iconographic doubling. These connections, as well as Athene herself, including her name, predate Greek stories of the Gorgon's victimization.[644, 645] Older, and sometimes subtler, these affiliations and conjunctions reframe Athene's actions toward Medusa as preservative and reconciliatory rather than as destructive exploitation or jealous revenge. In fact, Athene is much older, more complex, and feminine than the Father's daughter, defender of Greek patriarchy, which she is so often reputed to be.[646]

Athene's Birth

Athene has multiple birth stories. The best known, and also probably the latest version, is judged by Graves,[647] Harrison, and others to be a contrivance of a patriarchal agenda; "a desperate theological expedient to rid an earthborn Kore of her matriarchal conditions."[648] In the common variation of the tale, Athene is the daughter of Zeus, emerging as a fully formed and armed young woman from his head while he walks along the banks of a river or lake called Triton. Zeus, suffering from a horrific headache, is delivered of Athene by the action of Hermes, who calls Hephaistos to cleave the Father God's head open with an axe, releasing the goddess. The typical understanding of this story is that Athene proclaims full and sole allegiance to Zeus and patriarchal principles, denying not only her mother, but feminine values generally. Aeschylus famously gives Athene voice: "There is no mother anywhere who gave me birth, and, but for marriage, I am always for the male with all my heart, and strongly on my father's side."[649]

However, a closer look at additional details of Athene's birth story reveals her matriarchal residue; values that cannot be entirely vanquished, which point to her deeper nature and lineage. The *Homeric Hymn to Athena* describes the awe and turmoil of the entire cosmos at the sight of the newly born goddess Tritogeneia standing before Zeus, brandishing her spear:

> From his awful head wise Zeus himself bare her arrayed in warlike arms of flashing gold, and awe seized all the gods as they gazed. But Athena sprang quickly from the immortal head and stood before Zeus who holds the aegis, shaking a sharp spear: great Olympus began to reel horribly at the might of the bright-eyed goddess, and earth round about cried fearfully, and the sea was moved and tossed with dark waves, while foam burst forth suddenly: the bright Son of Hyperion stopped his swift-footed horses a long while, until the maiden Pallas Athena had stripped the heavenly armor from her immortal shoulders. And wise Zeus was glad.[650]

Hesiod attributes Athene's golden armor to her mother Metis, and it is clearly a gift which bestows horrendous and marvelous power.[651] Athene's flashing eyes recall the death-dealing potency of the Great Goddess's eyes; a power also attributed to the Gorgon. It seems that the patriarchal cosmic order is brought to the brink by Athene's terrible grandeur, when, inexplicably, she shifts from Tritogeneia (chthonic, water-born)[652] to the "maiden Pallas" and removes her armor, to the great relief of the dominant masculine principle. However, we have glimpsed Athene's underlying nature. Her autonomy and power reveal something of the lingering Great Goddess status she inherits through her maternal line.

Metis, Athene's Mother

According to Hesiod, Metis is Zeus's first consort and Athene's mother.[653] A primordial, chthonic goddess, Metis was born of Oceanus, the "stream which girdles the world,"[654] notable also as the birth place of Medusa. Metis is a Titaness, the goddess of good counsel, strategy, wisdom, and supreme knowledge who "knew more than all the gods or mortal people."[655] She is also a shape shifter, a trait retained by her daughter. As Zeus's ally in his war against the Titans, Metis concocts a potion to help him rescue his swallowed siblings and overthrow his father.[656] Her gifts of unsurpassed wisdom and knowledge of good and evil are appropriated by Zeus when he is threatened by her power to generate exceptional children—first, a daughter equaling him in power and wisdom and then a son, eclipsing him. When Metis is about to give birth to Athene, "Zeus, deceiving her perception by treachery / and by slippery speeches, / put her away inside his own belly."[657] From that time onwards, "he claimed [...] that she gave him counsel from inside his belly."[658, 659] In addition to benefiting from Metis's inner guidance, Zeus's devouring of his pregnant wife explains his ability to birth Athene from his brow.

It is noteworthy that in other variations of Athene's paternity she is the daughter of less lofty fathers including the Titan/Giant Pallas, the god Poseidon, Brontes the Kyklopes, and the river-god Triton. These fathers share Metis's chthonic nature, which the tale of Zeus's paternity attempts to sanitize. Regardless of Athene's father's identity, through her maternal ancestral line, her roots and identity emerge out of the Greek cosmic creation myth and link her with powers that pre-date Olympus. Like the Gorgon, Athene arises out of the primordial past and substance; "maiden of the elder stratum"—the most ancient realm of Poseidon[660]—she is Athene Tritogeneia, "born of the water itself,"[661] chthonic and parthenogenetic. The diverse tales of Athene's paternity, which I have only touched upon, link her to chthonic figures and support her complex origins pre-dating the patriarchal, Olympic version.

Pre-Greek Great Goddesses

As with Medusa's pre-Greek roots reviewed previously, a great deal of mythic and historic material indicates Athene's earlier origins outside of archaic Greece. Ancient and modern scholars trace Athene into various cultures and lands reaching back at least into the Bronze Age (c. 3300–600 BCE).

Gimbutas argues that Athene, like Medusa, appears to have developed "as the distant heir" of the Great Goddess traditions of gynocentric Old Europe; particularly from aspects of the deity represented as Bird/Snake Goddesses.[662] Iconographically, Athene shares the avian attributes of the Bird Goddess—features also prominent in Gorgon symbolism—including representations as and connections with uncanny birds.[663, 664] We have Athene as *glaukopis*, the "owl-eyed" and as Aithuia the "sea-bird" or "Diver-Bird," depicted as a "woman-headed bird."[665, 666] In addition, the owl frequently appears with Athene as her animal familiar. Athene and Medusa share the potent avian stare, with its mesmerizing power.

As Gimbutas points out, the Bird/Snake Goddess representations share many commonalities, making the distinction between them somewhat arbitrary. Indeed, Athene's traits and functions are frequently linked to the Snake Goddess, particularly of the Minoan and Minoan-Mycenaean cultures.[667] This association was likely transmitted to ancient Greece where the snake was Athene's "sacred animal [... and] the vehicle of the wrath of the goddess."[668] As part of her role "as an assimilated member of the Greek patriarchy," Athene frequently battles and destroys serpents who threaten the status quo.[669] However, her iconography reflects a close affinity with snakes, despite her later Olympian identity. Athene is often depicted wearing or accompanied by snakes—an obvious example being the Gorgoneion on her aegis. Harrison comments on a vase-painting in which a serpent, "equal in height and majesty" to Athene represents the goddess's double.[670] Dexter notes that on the underside of Athene's Varvakeion shield the "sacred serpent Erichthonios, the guardian of the Acropolis" is coiled.[671] Born of her thwarted sexual encounter with Hephaistos, Erichthonios is Athene's chthonic foster son who "had a snake's tail for feet."[672] Far from rejecting this "monstrous child," (whom Gaia, his "biological" mother, refused to nurture) "Athena took him back and he nestled in her bosom."[673] As the companion of the goddess and protector of the society, this serpent is reminiscent of the snake companion of the Neolithic Goddess of Regeneration.[674]

Plato tracks Athene to matrifocal Libya in North Africa, as does Apollodorus, who claims Athene was born in Libya by Lake Tritonis where she was raised and later came to Greece "by way of Crete."[675] Herodotus reports that the worship of Athene originates in this same region of North Africa: "those who dwell round the lake Tritonis sacrifice most of all to Athene, and next to Triton and Poseidon."[676]

Apollodorus's assertion that Athene came to Greece by way of Crete is supported by iconographic evidence suggesting Athene is a "direct descendant of the Minoan palace" guardian, also known as the Snake Goddess.[677, 678] The Minoan culture of Crete commenced late in the fourth millennium BCE. In 1450 BCE, the Mycenaeans invaded Crete, overthrowing the Minoans. Rather than annihilating the highly advanced Minoan culture, the Mycenaeans integrated many aspects, including the goddess-centered religion with which they enriched their existing pantheon.[679] In Crete, the matrifocal qualities characterizing the Great Goddess traditions propounded by Gimbutas, lingered into the mid-second millennium BCE.[680] Here, Athene likely constellated, first as the Minoan house guardian and then as the palace guardian, who accompanied the king into battle.[681] Ancient tablets include written references to the Mycenaean goddess "Atana" or "Athana," which is "assumed to be a variant or early name for Athene."[682] The Minoan-Mycenaean civilization collapsed around 1100 BCE after which followed the Greek Dark Age discussed earlier, with the robust ascendance of patriarchal gods and values and the repression of the feminine.[683] As archaic Greece emerged out of the Dark Age, it embodied a misogynistic perspective that was normalized and institutionalized in Greek culture and mythology. A revised, overtly patriarchal, Athene—in her Gorgoneion clad armor—appears in Homer in the latter part of the eighth century BCE "on the heels of the full-blown Olympian patriarchy."[684]

It was foretold that Athene was to be "the equal of her father in wise counsel and strength,"[685] but, in the doctrinal myth of her birth from Zeus's head, she appears to veil her true potency after initially asserting it. It seems that what lies dormant within the so-called Father's Daughter, defender of patriarchal civilization, is nothing less than the undying, primordial creatrix. To be honest, part of me is dismayed (and deeply curious) at the goddess's apparent retreat from her cosmic confrontation with Zeus, and I struggle with the turn of events described in the *Homeric Hymn to Athena*. Therefore, it is to Athene's transformation from the awesome "bright-eyed goddess" to maiden that I turn as a possible portal to understanding the significance of the episode for this project.

Athene *Parthenos*, The Maiden

Parthenos denotes a sexually mature—that is, menstruating—virgin or maiden.[686] In Greek myth, Athene is primarily identified as a maiden or virgin: She is *the Parthenos*; her temple is *the* Parthenon.[687] Athene's connection to menstruation is further demonstrated by the fact that she was central to the "menstrual cult of the women" in ancient Athens.[688] The femaleness of Athene's state as *parthenos* indicates that she, like Medusa, is vulnerable to sexual exploitation. In one tale Athene's father, Pallas, attempts to rape her, so she skins him and wears his pelt as her prize and protection, that is, as apotropaic.[689] Several myths match Hephaistos with Athene, however, she does not appear to be a willing partner and whenever he pursues her, she successfully repulses him.[690] Herodotus reports that those living around Lake Tritonis in Libya believed that Poseidon was Athene's father and "that she had some cause of complaint against her father and therefore gave herself to Zeus, and Zeus made her his own daughter."[691] Strikingly, Herodotus connects this report in his narrative with what he describes as the promiscuous sexual customs among the Libyans, who have unrestrained "intercourse like cattle";[692] a reference to coitus outside of marriage and apparent sexual agency exercised by Libyan women. Does this narrative link suggest the possibility of the sexual nature of Poseidon's infraction against Athene as with the Pallas story? If so, it also seems to color the meaning of the goddess's "giving herself" to Zeus. While this can be viewed through a Freudian lens as Oedipal, there is also a mythic interchangeability between Zeus and Poseidon; the father principle split between Heaven and the Deep[693] as is evident in stories about Athene's paternity. Similarly, sometimes Zeus, rather than Poseidon, is identified as Medusa's rapist.[694] Athene and Medusa are linked by their seemingly confounded connections to the underlying principles that they and other deities signify.

In addition to connotations of sexual vulnerability, as *the Parthenos*, Athene especially embodies the Virgin Warrior, exempt from the roles of wife and mother enforced upon Greek females. It is likely that part of Athene's warrior persona came to her from Greece's warlike Mycenaean predecessors. In addition, recall Athene's roots in Libya, a culture which inspired stories of ruling queens and female warriors, including the Amazons. Both Athene's distinctive dress and aegis were reportedly derived by the Greeks from garments worn by Libyan women, as was the word "aegis," which Herodotus contends originates from the goat-skins or "aigeas" worn by the Libyans over their clothes.[695] Graves claims that the aegis was a "goat-skin chastity-tunic worn by Libyan girls" the removal of which, without their consent, was punishable by death[696] and that the aegis "was Athene's long before Zeus claimed to be her father."[697] In addition to the story of Pallas's pelt serving as Athene's aegis, frequently the garment is depicted as being made from Medusa's flayed skin. Harrison likens Athene's aegis, with its Gorgon face, to the apotropaic "head of the slain beast whose skin was the raiment of the primitive goddess" and was worn for protection and to frighten enemies.[698] Clearly, Athene's aegis is fundamental to her identity as *parthenos*-warrior.

Athene's *Aegis*

What are we to make of the connections between Athene's aegis, the chastity belts worn by Libyan maidens who apparently exercised some degree of sexual agency, tales of rape, and Medusa's skin? And why does Athene wear such an aegis upon her breast rather than on her pelvis, as a chastity belt? The Medusan aegis seems to be a symbol that unifies the two aspects of *parthenos*, vulnerability and protection. I am reminded of Ovid's description of Athene covering her eyes with her aegis at the sight of Medusa's rape in the temple. Athene, in the face of the profane violation, preserves her divine intactness behind the Gorgoneion face of sacred outrage and apotropaic magic. How like the paradoxical dissociative state manifest in certain rape traumas wherein the victim's autonomic nervous system functions to obscure her vision of what is happening in a strange experience of suspended animation or disembodiment; the victim herself psychically "protected" or at least distanced, paralyzed by an automatic neurobiological response to an overwhelming experience of violation.

Further, I am drawn to reflect upon Athene's abrupt shift from potent, terrible Tritogeneia to the maiden Pallas, Father's Daughter, in relation to the several tales of rape—Athene's and Medusa's. What engenders Athene's apparent submission to the father principle? Is the answer sexual violence or its threat as recorded in the rape narratives? Sexual violence is a weapon of submission such that archetypally every rape of a woman under the rule of patriarchy might be thought of as the rape of the Daughter by the Father; domination and annihilation of the feminine/maternal principle by the masculine/paternal principal.

Mythologically, chthonic Athene exercises control over her state as *parthenos* and is justified in destroying her attempted assailant, even if he is her own father. The Greek Athene, while retaining in some part her primal fierceness, takes a different strategy; one that appears to be a betrayal of her femaleness and the feminine principles she once represented. But, there is no true protection against sexual violation of the feminine within patriarchy because women's sexuality belongs to men. A female does not have the agency to express her sexual instinct and remain "her own mistress, a virgin in the ancient, original meaning of the word."[699] The chastity belt—concrete or metaphorical—is no longer removed as a prerogative of its wearer, but of her father or husband or some other male. In this world, Athene's integration of Medusa may be seen as an action to reclaim the apotropaic sacredness of her female sex—her archetypal virginity or "one-in-self[ness]"[700]—as the concrete expression of her primordial power of generation and regeneration: a power enslaved by her father when he swallowed her mother. Clearly, the aegis no longer provides female agency or sexual protection in a phallocentric cosmos or civilization. It is no longer the impenetrable "raiment of the primitive goddess," Great Mother, Queen of Heaven and Earth.[701] I begin to comprehend Athene's placement of the Gorgoneion upon her breast, for there, its apotropaic powers may protect the only virginity the patriarchal *parthenos* can hope to retain—that which unites her with the archetypal feminine heart and soul. I return to these reflections in Chapter 6.

Athene as *Meter*

While Athene's strong affiliation with her condition as *parthenos*-warrior is central to her identity, she retains maternal behaviors and attitudes toward her human favorites and is explicitly identified as a Mother Goddess; "invoked as Meter, 'Mother.'"[702] Her maternal nature is a "vestige [...] of her descent from the Great Mother"[703] and her earlier form as the Minoan Snake Goddess, guardian of the house, one of the three primary goddesses in the matrifocal Cretan religion.[704] According to Hesiod, Athene is the mother of humankind; with her consent, Prometheus formed humans in the image of the gods after which she "breathed life into them."[705]

However, Athene, as Mother Goddess, does not give birth; she is "not a goddess of procreation, but of creation."[706] She is "the foster-mother of heroes after the old matriarchal fashion."[707] Athene mothers Dionysos and Erichthonios, but did not birth them. While she is generally shown championing male heroes, including Perseus, Theseus, Herakles, Akhilleus, and Odysseus, Athene is also moved by a just feminine cause, as in her aiding of Penelopeia, and for the common good. In *The Eumenides*, Athene repeatedly acknowledges the Erinyes as ancient goddesses whose sacred nature must not only be contained for the good of Athene's beloved Athens, but appeased as chthonic feminine powers which she invites into her temple and worship, essentially integrating them into herself.

Recall that the Erinyes are equated with Gorgons by Harrison[708] and others, such that Athene's linking herself to the Furies parallels her integration of Medusa. Like Medusa, the Furies enact chthonic, so-called feminine justice, which has more to do with the loyalties of family and blood and natural laws of harmony than manmade law. Edelman argues that Athene's action regarding the Erinyes is protective and "essentially maternal" toward the humans in her domain and reflects her ability to reconcile the old chthonic feminine order with the ascendant Olympian patriarchy without further bloodshed and chaos.[709] Athene's actions, with regards to the Furies and Medusa, also overtly restore that which she denied at birth and in her speech wherein she denounced her mother and proclaimed her allegiance to the masculine. The Erinyes persevere at the center of

Athene's temple and the Gorgon upon her heart center. In this way, Athene embodies the wholeness of her ancestor Great Mother Goddesses, including the daemonic sacred. Like the Moon Goddess, there is a trickster, transgressive quality to Athene; her words and actions do not align and her cunning preserves the chthonic feminine in the midst of patriarchal Greece.

Athene the Trickster

Athene is not traditionally thought of as a trickster, however, her behavior, relationships, and even her "self-protective rhetoric" indicate a mercurial nature under her strategic, wise persona.[710] Clearly, *The Eumenides* reveals Athene's duplicitous aspect. In addition, Athene is connected with Hermes, who is midwife at her birth and co-conspirator in gaining Medusa's head. Further, Hephaistos, the smithy and magician god of fire and craft frees Athene from Zeus's head and is as close to a divine consort as Athene gets—despite his marriage to Aphrodite. While the heroes she champions are cunning, Athene's most beloved Odysseus is perhaps the ultimate human trickster. In addition, Athene is credited with creating the human race with Prometheus and she is implicated in having allowed him to steal the sacred fire for humankind. As the goddess of artisans and craft, Athene's creativity transforms and harnesses nature on behalf of humans; a form of inventiveness associated with the divine and surrounded by taboos and dangerous consequences when displayed by unsanctioned gods or humans. Athene Ergane is "the worker, the maker"[711] and she is credited with inventing the ship, bridle, oxen yoke, plough, flute, trumpet, "mechanical arts," "science of numbers" and the arts of weaving and pottery-making.[712] Athene's inventions endow her human "children" with god-like powers.

 In addition to her transgressive creativity, Athene manipulates identity through her shape-shifting skills. In *The Iliad* she appears as a soldier to Pandoros and Hektor. In *The Odyssey* she comes to Telemachos, Penelopeia, Nausikaa, and Odysseus in disguised forms. She alters the appearance of others as well, as when she enhances Odysseus: "Then Athene poured much beauty upon his head, / Made him bigger to look at and stouter, and made his hair / flow in curls upon his head like the hyacinth flower."[713] Through her shape-shifting, Athene exercises influence and persuasion, guiding circumstances towards her desired outcomes.

Athene's rhetorical prowess also contributes to her trickster identity and its effectiveness in achieving her goals. She can speak convincingly and passionately from both sides of an argument; but, her duplicity is in the service of balance, harmony, and reconciliation, not selfish gain. Even when pushed to the brink by Zeus, she can master and sublimate her rage into mockery and teasing, which disperses tensions. When her father taunts her, siding with the Trojans and Aphrodite against Athene and Hera, the furious daughter is outwardly composed: "True, Athena held her peace and said nothing ... / smoldering at the Father, seized with wild resentment."[714] Yet, after Aphrodite attempts to enter battle on behalf of Troy and flees with a minor wound, Athene takes the opportunity to mock Zeus and his tolerance of Aphrodite's meddling and is met with good natured smiles from her father. And even when Athene provokes Zeus's rage by attempting to enter battle with Hera and the Achaeans against her father's will, she is confident that "the day will come when Father, well I know, calls me his darling gray-eyed girl again."[715] However, Athene's reliance on her trickster skills, and the freedom and protection they engender, has limits.

The father's favor demands and must be granted obedience, and the threat of violence and annihilation in response to disobedience to the patriarch is real even for the goddess Athene. When she plots with Hera, determined to destroy Hektor, Zeus flies into a rage and threatens to attack the rebellious Athene, exclaiming, "[...] not once in the course of ten slow wheeling years / will they [Hera and Athene] heal the wounds my lightning bolt rips open"[716] and never again will they be able to return to Olympus.[717] That Zeus's response to open disobedience in his daughter is *predictably* murderous wrath is reflected in Athene's observation that, "Father rages now, that hard black heart, / always the old outrage, dashing all my plans!"[718] The fate of her mother, Metis, demonstrates that Zeus's threats of violence can be fatal and that sacred feminine agency is perceived as a threat by the patriarch in his quest for absolute power. No wonder Athene engages in subterfuge and rhetoric when exercising her power.

Athene and Aidos

As we have seen, Athene emerges from and surreptitiously continues to honor the archetypal feminine, including its shadowy aspects expressed by the Erinyes and Medusa, and therefore gives the energies of the so-called Great Goddess a central, if covert, position in Greek mythology and the collective psyche. That Athene takes such actions to re-incorporate feminine wholeness can be attributed in part to Metis's invisible influence. But, Athene's sly rebellion may also be tied to her mythic nursemaid Aidos, the Greek Goddess of Shame.[719] Understanding the implications of Athene's association with Aidos reveals the web of chthonic feminine sacred power in the center of which is Athene, weaving in the essential thread represented by the Gorgon.

The goddess Aidos signifies shame, modesty, and self-respect and is best known as a "primary attendant of the love goddess Aphrodite."[720] Like Medusa, Aidos was a divinity who lived on Earth, not in the Heavens.[721] Her altar was in the very heart of Athenian civilization, on the Acropolis near Athene's temple and she had a seat at the Festival of Dionysos.[722] Aidos's close ties to the human world imply that the archetypal energy she represents is particularly relevant to the human condition, the human experience. The concept of *aidos* expressed by the goddess requires a brief explication so that its implications for this project are clear.

Meaning of *aidos*

In Chapter 3, I touched upon *aidos* as the shame connected with Medusa as carrier of the Evil Eye—the gaze of which evokes awe-ful reverence. The ancient idea of *aidos* was subtler and more nuanced than our modern understanding of the term shame. In addition, the definition of *aidos* evolved from the time of Homer through Hellenistic Greece. Edelman, in her fine meditation on shame, explains that early on *aidos* meant one's "sense of duty and honor and respect for public opinion."[723] This was the sort of shame that caused Akhilleus to abandon the Achaeans in response to Agamemnon's dishonoring of him in *The Iliad*. It was an experience of shame that was based on standards of respectful behavior and breeches of those norms, and could be ameliorated by public reparations. However, at its core, *aidos* reflected the respect due one who was exemplary in fulfilling his or her god-given duty; the "powerful person ... is *Aidoios*."[724] Even when individual, *aidos* was grounded in sacred law and transcendent power.

Later, *aidos* became associated with respect for the laws of the polis; human laws were seen as reflections of cosmic law and so reverence for polis reflected piety and right relationship with Olympus.[725] As the Greek conceptualization of the individual came into ascendency in the late classical and Hellenistic periods, the meaning of *aidos* evolved "increasingly as respect (love) for self."[726] While during the archaic period, as represented by Homer, a violation of *aidos* could be repaired through the public restoration of booty or reputation, the implications of such violations became amplified over time so that even an unintentional breech could manifest in one being a "source of contagious pollution" that engendered collective and cosmic disharmony.[727] For instance, in Homer, Oedipus remains king of Thebes while Sophocles's Oedipus "was a reviled exile: his unwitting act had injured the universal order."[728] Edelman reconciles the varied, evolving conceptualizations of *aidos* by recognizing that, though a particular understanding of *aidos* may be shared simultaneously by a group, the locus of experience of both self-reverence and the reverence and awe excited by the numinous is always "deep within the individual psyche and, in the end, wholly independent of collective definitions and norms."[729] Despite collective definitions of shame, the human experience of *aidos* is fundamentally eternal and embodied.

According to renowned philologist Bruno Snell, *aidos* was an incentive to virtue and the divine inhibitor of human impulses that was necessary for civilization; "a mighty pillar in the structure of civilized humanity," *aidos* was "the most powerful agency known in the early age for imposing inhibitions upon an agent."[730] As instrumental to virtue, *aidos* reflected taboos ancient even to the ancient Greeks[731] from a time "when religion was still at its most chthonian, most numinous, when experience of the holy was surrounded with mystery, not with reason or law."[732] *Aidos* was "the feeling of shame, [... that] originates as the reaction which the holy excites" in a human being.[733] *Aidos*, then, is the mythical and religious underpinning of social and legal constructs that dictate and enforce proper behavior. That *aidos* engenders the civilizing force that made the polis possible helps to explain its connection with Athene, as protector of the city and mother of her people. Athene received this civilizing virtue at the breast of its divine embodiment.

The quality of *aidos* is human and sacred, personal and collective, and in its essence transcendent of cultural norms, that is to say, it is archetypal. As an archetypal energy, *aidos* includes its complement—the absence of reverence and self-respect.[734] In fact, while the idea of *aidos* evolved with Greek culture, the understanding of failures of *aidos* known as *aischyne*, remained relatively constant.[735] *Aischyne* more closely aligns with our modern understanding of shame as "disgrace, dishonor, infamy," depravity, indecency, or obscenity; in a word, shamelessness.[736] *Aischyne* also reflects the affect Medusa came to represent; her reverence evokes *aidos* and her desecration *aischyne*, the opposite of *aidos*.

Ana-suromai

The potency of the chthonic goddess inspired *aidos* and one ubiquitous expression of her power was the vulva; recall that "the root meaning of [Athene] is 'vulva' or 'lap' or 'womb.'"[737] *Ana-suromai* was the "ceremonial" exposure of the vulva as an act of transformative power, whether by goddesses or women, which later "acquired both sacred and profane connotations."[738] Mythic examples of *ana-suromai* appear across cultures. It is a well-known part of Demeter's myth wherein Baubo revives the grieving mother-goddess with the gesture. Incidentally, Lubell observes that Baubo had an "ancient, acknowledged kinship" with Medusa and that later "Baubo as Gorgon became one of the many prototypes of the female sexual demon."[739]

Apparently a ritual act and part of ancient religious festivals, which included elements of playful teasing and mockery, *ana-suromai* is reported by Herodotus, Diodorus, and Daniel Marc Fouquet in Egypt[740] and by the Byzantine historian Psellus as part of the Eleusinian rites.[741] The gesture also appears in an ancient Japanese myth where it is employed by Ama-no-Usume, the goddess of dance and mirth, to restore the Sun Goddess Amaterasu after her disrespectful, violent brother causes her withdrawal, plunging the world into darkness.[742] First century CE writer Plutarch recounts incidents wherein fleeing Persian soldiers were shamed into returning to battle by Persian woman who blocked the retreat performing *ana-suromai*.[743] He also tells how the Greek hero Bellerophon was defeated by a group of Lycian women who drove the hero away in shame by exposing their vulvas to him.[744]

This tale is reminiscent of Apollodurus's story of Herakles instructing the princess of an ally city on the use of the Gorgon's hair to protect the city. Recall that Athene gifts the Gorgon lock to Herakles who then teaches the princess to stand upon the rampart and display the hair three times to the enemy so that they will retreat. It is intriguing to find Herakles, who notoriously scorns female agency in worldly matters, plotting with a woman in war. However, the story makes particular sense if it reflects the ancient practice of *ana-suromai* as the princess would be endowed with the essential magic (and anatomy) symbolizing, and symbolized by, the still-potent genitals—or even a remnant thereof—of the chthonic Great Goddess.

Lubell shares an ancient Gaelic legend wherein the hero Cú Chulainn is shamed out of attacking his own people by 150 women exposing their nakedness and boldness through *ana-suromai*: "The boy lowered his gaze away from them/and laid his face/against the chariot."[745] Even the brief survey of the phenomenon of *ana-suromai* offered above indicates its archetypal grounding. Female genitalia boldly exposed is a sacred act that freezes masculine agency gone berserk, that is, it inhibits such behavior through *aidos*. In addition, *ana-suromai* enlivens feminine agency when that power has collapsed, paralyzed by overwhelming *aischyne* under the scorn of the male berserker.

In their earliest representations as the bird/snake aspects of the gynocentric Great Goddess traditions, Medusa and Athene expressed the power of the chthonic feminine, whose potency evoked *aidos*. With the rise of patriarchy, much of the divine feminine was (and is) suppressed and came to evoke, or even be equated with, *aischyne*. As representative of the vestiges of rejected chthonic feminine power, Medusa became the repository for, and face of, shameless/shameful femaleness, including female physiology with its clandestine processes and overtly animal manifestations; woman's biology descended into the collective feminine shadow. The interconnection of shame (*aidos* and *aischyne*), female genitalia, feminine sacred power, and Medusa/Athene is at the crux of embodied misogyny.

Intriguingly, in addition to other implications of *aidos*, *aidoia* "connotes the genital organs."[746] The fuller connotation of the powerful association between reverential awe and genitalia is demonstrated in the tales of apotropaic *ana-suromai*. This understanding, combined with the Greek tradition that the life-seed was carried in the head, helps illuminate the archetypal meaning of Medusa's transformation into the Gorgoneion. Medusa, as the head of the chthonic feminine divine, container of the regenerative life-seed, is simultaneously the representation of sacred female genitalia. However, as noted previously, the ancient Greeks believed females, body and psyche, were inferior to males: the female is "an incomplete male or 'as it were, a deformity'"[747] and the life-spark was a male prerogative. So, Medusa, as the face of feminine power and female genitals is a compound monstrosity.

Freud also proclaims that female genitalia should be understood, at least psychologically, as deformed "castrated" male genitals and that the Medusan Gorgoneion is the horrific and threatening representation of female genitals.[748] Freud's formula eloquently expresses patriarchy's phallocentric worldview and its terror of feminine power: Medusa's head equals female genitals equals the "symbol of horror, [....] the terrifying genitals of the Mother."[749] Females are defined as "[l]ack"[750] and female genitals as either "pleasure-giving" to men or, if not, then "horrifying."[751] Here is the misogynistic heritage of Aristotle and others which endures right up to now. No wonder Medusa's powers are only permitted to exist under the steady hand of Athene, trusted daughter of the Olympian family.

For so long, I resented Athene for what I saw as her complicity. Now, I begin to understand: Athene's engagement of Medusa involving, as it does, the transformative beheading and incorporation of the Gorgoneion aegis preserves the fierce chthonic feminine in a form that is apparently palatable to patriarchy. This compromise is only possible if Athene is truly domesticated and in service of the masculine principle, forsaking her mother, *or* if the goddess is gifted with a uniquely reconciliatory, integrative, and cunning nature.

Athene's Nature: Divine Androgyny

It would be disingenuous to describe Athene without acknowledging the traits she embodies that tend to be characterized as masculine; traits that more often than not dominate her identity, at least as most of us have encountered her in popular myth and art. Athene is the rational, strategy-minded warrior goddess and an emotionally regulated virgin who spends much of her time attending to male heroes and the causes of phallocentric Olympus and Greece. Harrison highlights the price Athene pays for her identification with patriarchal values: "We cannot love a goddess who on principle forgets the Earth from which she sprang."[752] However, potent feminine principles—Aidos, Metis, and Medusa—run in Athene's blood. This truth echoes through her mythology, despite its Apollonian veil; Athene is the *Parthenos*, a quintessentially female state. She is also maternal—a companion, guardian, and protector of humans and gods.[753] She is the Virgin Mother reminiscent of the androgynous creatrix; "the creative power of the feminine spirit, as virgin, [which] antedates or transcends the idea of hierogamy since it approximates the original 'neuter creative wholeness' of the primordial state."[754] In fact, despite Athene's many so-called masculine attributes and allegiances, what is most striking—perhaps her defining quality—is her divine androgyny. Mircea Eliade explains that "androgyny has become a general formula signifying *autonomy*, *strength*, *wholeness*; to say of a divinity that it is androgyne is as much as to say that it is the ultimate being, the ultimate reality."[755] Athene's androgyny indicates that she represents a fundamental archetypal reality, indivisible and transcendent in its underlying nature.

Harrison acknowledges that patriarchy makes Athene a "sexless thing."[756] However, freed from phallocentric distortions, Athene embodies the wholeness of primordial androgyny. Edelman discerns: "[W]here Harrison saw no sexuality, no gender, there may instead be all sexuality, both genders, perfect androgyny."[757] This "sublime androgyny" expresses the inner reality of Jung's transcendent function, the third thing that emerges from the tension of opposites and embodies a new, more whole, adaptive reality or attitude."[758] In this view, Athene has a truly transgressive yet integrative nature. She identified as a woman warrior in a culture with strictly enforced gender roles and rigid concepts of what was properly masculine and feminine with cosmic reprisal for violations. Athene's appearance combines women's garb with men's armor and helm. In addition, her androgyny is reflected in the beautiful duplicity of her actions and thinking. The transgressive nature of her creativity was explored above. I now turn to the way in which Athene's integrated androgyny manifests in her "sense of relatedness" and the quality of her mind.[759]

Athene's *eros*

Athene is a goddess, rather than a god, and therefore signifies a collective experience of qualities and values considered ostensibly feminine. At the heart of the archetypal feminine is the quality of *eros,* frequently represented in psychology and mythology as *the* feminine principle.[760] Jung calls *eros* the "connective quality" within consciousness that is "the function of relationship" in men and "an expression of [women's] true nature."[761] *Eros* is the sense of relatedness that the subject experiences for the beloved object; for a man through his anima and for a woman in her "very being."[762] Traditionally associated with the feminine, feeling, and subjectivity, *eros* has been conceptualized as the opposite, or preferably, the complement of the masculine principle of *logos,* thinking, and objectivity.

However, Athene's *eros* expresses itself in seemingly feminine and masculine ways. She is steadfastly loyal and protective as well as actively directive and decisive in her relationships. Despite her investment in her human devotees, she maintains clear boundaries in her relating[763] and enforces justice even on her favorites as seen in her attack on her beloved Achaeans when they fail to punish Ajax for desecrating her shrine during his rape of Kassandra.[764] Athene balances active paternal involvement with maternal care and yet remains virginal, belonging only to herself; "she is 'one-in-herself.'"[765] While her impulse to relate emerges spontaneously out of her "very being" in response to the objects of her concern, her mythology is punctuated by incidents where she incorporates other females into her identity rather in the way a male projects and then incorporates a female as the image of his anima. There is a myth in which Athene is engaged in mock combat with her dearest friend and foster sister Pallas when Athene accidentally kills the girl. In despair at her deed and the ruptured relationship, Athene takes Pallas as her own name. In this way, she incorporates her outer friend as an inner figure, part and parcel of Athene's feminine identity—for Pallas means maiden. As Downing writes, "Athene *is* Pallas Athene. The double name suggests her two-sidedness: she is a goddess who has her own anima, who is spirit and soul," masculine and feminine.[766] While Medusa may be seen as Athene's shadow, the Gorgon may also be considered as another anima figure. Like Pallas, Medusa is a feminine figure who becomes an inextricable part of Athene and a link to the feminine lineage that was taken from her when Zeus birthed her.

Athene's relatedness is both objective and subjective; she "relate[s] to principles as well as to persons," remaining supremely pragmatic in pursuit of balanced results and the common good, rather than perfection.[767] She can be unapologetically spontaneous in her emotional responses as she demonstrates in her anger at the unfortunate Arachne, whom Athene turns into a spider, or in her frustrated chastisement of Odysseus, when he falters at the thought of destroying Penelopeia's suitors. Yet she is renowned for her capacity for self-regulated clear-sightedness. Aeschylus establishes her as the earthly source of divine judgment: "If it please you, men of Attica, hear my decree now, [...] I [Athene] have judged. For Aegeus' population, this forevermore shall be the ground where justices deliberate."[768] Athene's relational androgyny emanates from her capacity to "yoke[...] feminine and masculine energies" and qualities of mind.[769]

Athene's *logos*

Athene's genius joins the instinctive, intuitive knowing, often depicted as feminine wisdom, with the "strategic, discursive, linear intelligence" typically characterized as masculine *logos*.[770] By reconciling and accessing both qualities of mind, she has the capacity to be discerning, shrewd, and clear-sighted, as well as "vigilant," without being fearful.[771] Athene's intellect is not without affect, but neither does she generally become emotionally dysregulated or reactive. Her responses can be both spontaneous and measured as in her dealings with Teiresias recounted by Apollodorus in *The Library of Greek Mythology*. In the tale, Teiresias is blinded by Athene upon seeing the goddess naked—an instinctual response to such a violation. However, after appeals by his mother to the goddess, Athene endows Teiresias with his power of prophecy—second sight—since she is unable to restore his vision.

Athene's intelligence does not indiscriminately mingle content. Rather, she discerns and relates opposing realities. She is integrative, linking separate, differentiated parts into a functional whole—the definition of integration proposed by the field of interpersonal neurobiology.[772] Through this integrative action, Athene catalyzes reconciliation between opposing and even multiple truths or realities, including the feminine and masculine principles.

Androgyny and the Meaning of Feminine and Masculine

The argument that Athene is androgynous obviously depends upon the notions that masculine and feminine are discernibly different from each other and that males tend to be masculine while females generally exhibit feminine traits. These are ideas that have been and are being vigorously contested, at least in part, because of the tendency to categorize supposed masculine/feminine traits and rank them as superior/inferior to and inherently not feminine/masculine, as well as the real-life consequences this practice has in terms of human rights, identity development, mental health, environmental degradation, spirituality, and so on. In addition, conceptualizations of masculine and feminine are being experienced as incongruent with, and even harmful to, the lived experience of many individuals. Currently, psychology generally recognizes that masculine and feminine traits are observable in female and male psyches and that culture has a great deal to do with how these qualities are categorized and manifest (or not). At first glance, biology may seem to offer a more concrete delineation of feminine and masculine, or at least female and male. However, even in the physical realm objective reality is more subjective than previously imagined and biology may not be destiny.

The shifting nature of feminine and masculine notwithstanding, this book pertains to endometriosis as a disease primarily experienced as a disorder of menstruation and female infertility. That is, the project is deeply invested in specifically female reproductive organs and processes not generally found in or experienced by those humans who are biologically male. For this reason, it is necessary to struggle with the idea and language of feminine and masculine, despite definite difficulties, not the least of which is that the terms and their meanings can become divisive rather than healing. I have the sense that in order to truly apprehend Athene's gifts, it may be helpful to develop a less "loaded" vocabulary so that her qualities, such as active creativity, can be freed from—in Tillie Olsen's words—"the sexist notion that the act of creation is not as inherently natural to a woman as to a man, but rooted instead in unnatural aggression, rivalry, envy, or thwarted sexuality";[773] in other words, in a woman's pathological "gorgonism."

One possible perspective that attempts to free our thinking from the burden of the categories of feminine and masculine while still acknowledging difference is found in Walter Odajnyk's conceptualization of a more "differentiated notion of opposites" wherein "every archetype has a *yin* and *yang* side to it. [... Y]in has both a feminine and a masculine side to it, as does *yang*."[774] Or better yet, *yin* has both *yin* and *yang* aspects as does *yang*. *Yin* is characterized as a "dark, yielding, receptive primal power" associated with nature, earth and matter, spatial reality, and the female-maternal.[775] *Yang* is the creative "primal power, which is light-giving, active, strong, and of the spirit" and is associated with heaven, time, motion, duration, and the male-paternal.[776] *Yin* and *yang* are "complementary, not opposite; they complete each other rather than oppose each other."[777] The quality of *yang* exists in *yin* and vice versa so that an archetypal image, such as Athene, that visibly expresses the *yin*—she is a goddess—can have *yang-yin* and *yin-yin* aspects.[778]

Unfortunately, even with this attempt at a more inclusive paradigm, the female-maternal is still categorized as complementary to the active creative, rather than intrinsically active and creative. Challenging this bias at perhaps the most basic level of biology is medical research supporting "the almost heretical view that sperm and egg are mutually active partners" in fertilization and conception.[779] Duplicated findings since the 1980s indicate that the bold, forceful sperm does not penetrate the passive ovum; rather the egg and sperm mutually activate each other:

> Freshly ejaculated mammalian sperm are not normally able to fertilize eggs [....] They have to become *capacitated*. This capacitation appears to be mediated through secretions of the female genital tract. Furthermore, upon reaching the egg, mammalian sperm release enzymes which digest some of the extracellular vestments which surround the egg. These released enzymes, however, are not active. They become activated by interacting with another secretion of the female reproductive tract. Thus, neither the egg nor the female reproductive tract is a passive element in fertilization.[780]

Further, "the forward thrust of sperm is extremely weak" and "its strongest tendency, by tenfold, is to escape by attempting to pry itself off the egg" to which it has become adhered.[781] This proclivity to *not* be strongly penetrative is necessary so that sperm can make their way successfully to the ovum and not simply burrow into the first tissue they encounter along the way. The ovum "captures and tethers the sperm"[782] after which sperm and egg interlock through the action of a "pair of binding molecules."[783] Both the egg and sperm emit the enzymes involved in facilitating fertilization. Interestingly, it is the sperm which has "pockets" into which the ovum inserts its own "small knobs" or "ligands."[784] In other words, the male-paternal is receptive here while the female-maternal is active. According to researcher Paul Wassarman, the egg's outer layer or coat "screens incoming sperm, selects only those compatible with fertilization and development, prepares sperm for fusion with the egg and later protects the resulting embryo [from destruction from multiple sperm fusing with one egg]."[785]

Even as science acknowledges the active role of the ovum—a direct challenge to ideas about female passivity inherited from Aristotle[786] and elsewhere—conceptualizations slip from one pole of the feminine archetype to the other: from receptive, yielding, inert Great Mother to aggressive, devouring Gorgon. Cultural anthropologist Emily Martin observes that much of the language used by scientists reporting what could be paradigm-shifting observations about the reciprocal nature of fertilization and conception, inadvertently conspires with the "cultural stereotype [of the] woman as a dangerous and aggressive threat," even invoking the dark, devouring specter of the "spider laying in wait in her web."[787] Martin continues: "These images grant the egg an active role but at the cost of appearing disturbingly aggressive."[788] We come full circle to our Gorgon, the demonization of the creative feminine, and Olsen's assertion (recall: "the sexist notion that the act of creation is not as inherently natural to a woman as to a man, but rooted instead in unnatural aggression, rivalry, envy, or thwarted sexuality"). It is not my intention to reduce female creativity to procreation; I turn to biology simply as one example of the lingering tenacity of biased ideas about the nature of female as passive (inferior) and male as active (superior)—even within a scientific paradigm that alleges objectivity. For this reason (science's supposed freedom from subjective influence), the power of the male hero myth underlying theories about sperm highlights just how embedded misogynistic ideas of feminine and masculine are and how unconsciously they create reality. Despite these limitations, because science attempts to discern and describe, to specify and differentiate, for me, it is a fundamental and useful stage for reflecting on and conceptualizing the mysterious natures of feminine and masculine, femaleness and maleness. A primary danger, as we see above, is the literalization of feminine and masculine archetypal energies-turned-concrete in the form of female and male bodies.

Let us return to Odajnyk, whose argument for the use of *yin* and *yang* at least attempts to employ less overtly gendered and, therefore, less literal language to describe differentiation within archetypes. His approach may help to lighten the socio-cultural, personal, and historical burden of the categories of female/feminine and male/masculine, and the groupings and rankings associated with them. For example, this approach does allow active creativity, assertiveness, rational thought, and other so-called masculine qualities natural legitimacy within the female/feminine, even if these traits are still conceptualized as the complementing other, that is, *yang*. While Athene, as a goddess embodies *yin* principles, she is clearly an expression of *yang-yin* and therefore challenges us to consider the reality of the actively creative, objective female—perhaps an image of what a feminine ego, as distinct from a masculine ego, might be. And essential to that depiction of a feminine ego is Athene's Medusan Gorgoneion, face of the female reproductive organs as emblematic of embodied female-ness. Unfortunately, through the lens of patriarchy, the feminine is so easily literalized and reduced to the female genitals, concentrated and objectified as the Terrible Gorgoneion, deeply scorned and enslaved to phallocentric values and desires, her creativity limited to procreativity.

Conclusion

Downing reflects on what her own encounter with Athene demands: "it means looking at the hitherto least explored aspects of my life: the negative side of my love for my father, my ever-repeated tendency to divert energy from my own creative work into relationships, the still present temptation to understand my assertiveness and intellectual acumen as masculine attributes."[789] Like all women who live under patriarchy's rule, Athene exists and functions within a powerfully *yang-yang* oriented cosmos dominated by her father Zeus. Athene "defends against Zeus's potentially overwhelming masculine power by assimilating it in her own being, by being so like him that in many ways she becomes a female Zeus."[790] In order to balance this powerful internalized *yang* Athene requires equally potent *yin* energy. I see her Gorgoneion Medusa providing the *yin-yin* so essential to Athene's balance and efficacy and as necessary to preserving her fundamental *yin* nature, which she, and every female, is in grave danger of rejecting under the weight of misogyny. As a vestige of the Great Goddess in her wholeness as an image of the archetypal feminine, the Gorgoneion Medusa carries the creative seed of death and regeneration, the mysterious sacred *tremendum*. Athene with her Gorgoneion mandala is an image of the androgynous wholeness once attributed to the primordial creatrix. This Athene, "my Athene" becomes a portal out of the suffering engendered by embodying the rejected, despised Medusa—the face of the embodied misogyny of the experience of endometriosis and perhaps other menstrual disorders—without denying her Gorgon nature. Corbett asserts that Medusa is an archetypal manifestation of "a level of evil that is so irredeemable … that (it) has to be killed," that is, psychologically transformed.[791] This stance no longer feels wise. Medusa, like her blood, is both deadly and generative: "Medusa holds […] the function of the prehistoric Goddess of the life continuum: birth, death, and then regeneration. She is multifunctional and multidimensional and should be viewed in all of her complexity, through a nonpatriarchal lens."[792]

For me, this project turns out not to be about transforming Medusa, but rather, loving her, as she truly is: symbolic of my female body and life lived in that body, with its pain and pleasure, loss and creativity. Perhaps it is Medusa who redeems Athene, restoring her from the split engendered in her adaptation to phallocentric demands, reuniting head with body, but not only female body, but the Body, all bodies—female, male, Earth, Nature, matter. The profoundly sacred nature of the Medusan Body, including the daemonic sacred *tremendum*, is reclaimed with a critical piece of instruction, so easily missed: She must be held at the level of the heart, in the field of transpersonal love to be reborn from the heart, fully intact, the virgin birth.

CHAPTER 6

SERVING THE GODDESS: REFLECTIONS AND REVELATIONS

While executing a scholarly examination of endometriosis, Medusa, and Athene in the previous chapters, I have, from another perspective, narrated stories about them. As with all human communications, I have related to, contextualized, interpreted, and shaped the facts into meaningful narratives according to my particular perspective and influenced by my specific motives. In this way, Athene's hermetic nature has guided me and focused my efforts on meaning and the values of relationship. While I am not "more interested in the truth of symbols than the truth of facts," I am compelled by the metaphoric meanings underlying facts.[793] That I have interpreted the facts does not mean that I have changed the data to fit my interpretation. Rather, I have mythologized pieces of information into psychologically meaningful, coherent narratives, which now must be woven together to fulfill the purpose of this project.

Re-storying: My Story and "Mystory"

In order to write a new story, I engage the contexts of the afflicted body and mythic material through a multidisciplinary approach that integrates soma, psyche, and relationship, facilitating meaning-making and incubating a new mythopoetic narrative. This new story transcends victimhood and nourishes psycho-spiritual resilience and the healing of trauma. While overtly personal, the mythic grounding and perspective of my story situates it as potentially healing for the collective as well: "There is a healing of a cultural wound through myth that aids us in repatterning our existence."[794] Peter Levine emphasizes "it is universally true that the renegotiation of trauma is an inherently mythic-poetic-heroic journey;"[795] that is, healing trauma is individual and collective, human and archetypal. My "renegotiation" grows out of the mythopoetic soil of the Gorgon Medusa and employs embodied, psycho-spiritual, imaginal techniques. The essence of any such effort's heroism lies in the collective boon potentiated in the healing mythopoesis of personal psycho-spiritual work. So, I weave my story of endometriosis (as a metaphoric mask of embodied misogyny concretely manifested) with the mythology of Medusa (as an image of an archetypal energy pattern expressing the deeply regenerative, chthonic sacred literalized and scorned as femaleness) and Athene (as an image of the creative reconciliation and integration of feminine spirit with female body) into one expression of the creative imagination or soul, which I see as the energizer of post-traumatic healing and regeneration.

Healing emerges by way of a re-storying that sees through the concrete to the archetypal and reconciles and integrates events into meaningful experience; it is an activity of soul.[796] This sort of reconciliation means the simultaneous acceptance of two or more distinct, seemingly opposing realities as equal in value and archetypally true. Integration can follow with the linking of these differentiated realities, or parts, into a new, functional, interrelating, co-arising whole. Here, I am joining depth psychological concepts with the science of interpersonal neurobiology, thereby employing the inherent gifts of the nervous system overtly into the mythopoetic process. However, even more is required in order to address the traumatic nature of the wounds not only to the feminine, but also to the female. Therefore, I rely upon trauma theory and shamanic-ritual modalities to attend to the body's centrality as a locus of concrete traumatic memory as well as creative mythopoesis, thereby enacting the power of soma as context.

By way of a structure for what may seem an unwieldy multidisciplinary process, I turn to Hillman's method of psychologizing and the practice of dream work because what I truly long to engage is the deeper meaning underlying the manifest. In practical terms, I briefly lay out "my story," a narrative of concrete facts, as accurately as I can recall them. Then I reflect upon the narrative with an attitude of curiosity asking "who" and "what" questions, imagining if this event were a dream what my psyche might be telling me. Like symptoms, thoughts, associations, emotions, and sensations are viewed as valuable information. I also focus on and own my experience as a reflection of me, as in dream work wherein every part of a dream is of the dreamer's psyche; the actions of a "dream" person are not externalized and taken literally, but as metaphor and internal. This is necessary in order to respect the privacy and integrity of other players in my story—recognizing that what I share is my perspective—and to maintain the appropriate tone of the process, which, while therapeutic, is not therapy.

I am guided by Hillman's psychologizing perspective to move into "mystory;" a re-mythologized perspective that sees through, reconciles (discerns and deeply accepts as "true" and of value), and integrates (links in relationship) objective or historic (concrete) facts with subjective, embodied experience, and soulful mystery. The mythic kaleidoscope through which I gaze is Medusa-Athene-ian. To facilitate the personifying, pathologizing, and dehumanizing of experience that Hillman describes, I rely on techniques of Jungian active imagination, shamanic traditions, and tenets of the neurobiology of trauma. I do not assert a monistic interpretation of Medusa, Athene, or endometriosis, but offer one revelation emerging from wounded-ness, recognizing that "it may be a witness to a god or goddess working in the wound."[797] Mine is an inductive process moving from a specific perspective to its potentially universal significance, keeping in mind that the specific, while concrete, is not literal, and that the universal points toward psycho-spiritual meaning not dogmatic truth.

My story

First symptoms, treatment, and diagnosis

With the onset of menstruation I experienced cramps. Over time the intensity of my cyclic pelvic pain increased, as did other symptoms including bowel issues and headaches. By high school, I suffered migraines and sufficiently debilitating menstrual cramps that my physician prescribed oral contraceptives and Darvon (a narcotic painkiller later banned by the FDA due to lethal cardiac side effects). During my twenties, I continued to suffer from acute dysmenorrhea, mild dyspareunia, ovulatory pelvic pain, lower back pain, abdominal bloating, and bowel symptoms. My treatment continued to be focused on suppression through oral contraceptives and pain management with liberal doses of ibuprofen, which became available over the counter in 1984. I accepted my condition as "the way things are" and focused my energy on aggressively attempting to manage the pain so I could live my life, go to school, and work without spending too much time curled around a heating pad in bed.

In my late twenties, during a routine pelvic exam a small tumor or nodule was discovered, and I was referred to a gynecological oncologist. I underwent diagnostics including a biopsy and blood tests for the tumor marker CA 125, a biomarker for ovarian cancer. I was found to have an elevated CA 125 level, which in conjunction with my other symptoms and history indicated that further diagnostic abdominal laparoscopic surgery was appropriate. The fear of cancer upped the emotional ante for me, however, I proceeded with my typical pragmatic, stoic attitude, responsibly managing my job and the medical situation, determined that normal life be minimally disrupted or inconvenienced.

In the mid 1980s, I underwent laparoscopic surgery, which confirmed a diagnosis of endometriosis, rather than ovarian cancer. My genuine relief was overshadowed by a sense of dread brought on by my diagnosis, the implications of which I did not really understand. I was prescribed a six-month round of hormone therapy using the drug danazol. I remember reading the sobering list of potential side effects and collapsing into tears before steeling myself to get through it. The primary goal, according to the doctor, was to suppress the disease and increase my chances of becoming pregnant. I was being married soon and, based on my diagnosis, my ob-gyn recommended that if children were part of the plan we should attempt pregnancy as soon as possible. As I had never tried to become pregnant, there was no evidence of infertility (or fertility). However, danazol treatment was the standard protocol, so we proceeded. In addition to concerns about possible infertility, the doctor believed that pregnancy provided the best hope for disease suppression.

First pregnancy, near-death experiences, and loss

Following the danazol treatment, the side effects of which I tolerated relatively well, I became pregnant with twins. The doctor advised that I could continue to work full time through the end of the second trimester. My husband and I started interviewing nannies as I had no intention of leaving my very demanding job; I had never considered staying home to raise children. The pregnancy progressed relatively normally until the seventh month when I experienced a spontaneous rupture of my uterine artery and catastrophic hemorrhage. The rupture occurred in the evening at home. I was used to "pushing through" terrible pain, but this was a new, overwhelming agony that forced me inward in an effort to simply *exist* in that much pain and panic. I remained at home for a couple of hours during which time we had telephone consultations with my doctor who diligently tried to assess what was occurring and what to do about it.

At one point during this time, I drifted into unconsciousness and upon awaking experienced a remarkably strange encounter with a loving presence which evoked a deep sense of surrender, calm, and clarity in me despite my continued acute pain and distress. Under the influence of this visitation, I told my husband that it was time to go to the hospital. I was admitted through the emergency room and, over the next couple hours, I was examined by several physicians. My symptoms included the sudden onset of excruciating, sharp abdominal pain (pain that caused vomiting and seizures), increasing listlessness, and eventually, referred shoulder pain indicative of internal bleeding.

On the hunch that I had suffered a burst appendix, emergency surgery was initiated which revealed massive abdominal bleeding and the ruptured artery. To minimize the twins' exposure to toxic drugs, I had received a spinal rather than general anesthesia and so was relatively conscious throughout the proceedings. I recall being especially aware of the alarm and dismay expressed by the doctors. The artery was repaired and the hemorrhaging stopped. However, sometime, either during the surgery or shortly thereafter, one of the twins was found to have died. My doctor told my husband and me that the best chance our second son had was to be left in utero with his dead brother for as long as I could carry him. Despite our concern over the effects of this course on our remaining son—a sentient being deeply connected to his now dead brother—we agreed; there was no other choice.

Sometime during the highly disorienting time period shortly after the emergency surgery, the second twin was found to have died. Apparently coinciding with his death, I had an out-of-body experience wherein I was suspended above my body, which lay upon the examination table surrounded by my doctor, husband, and a neonatologist conducting an ultrasound. As I watched and listened from above, with detached clarity and feeling increasingly distant from what was below, my doctor asked the condition of the surviving baby to which the specialist replied that there was no detectable heartbeat. At once I heard the sound of a woman crying loudly, wailing, and I was pulled back into my body such that I was hearing and seeing from inside my skin once more. Strangely, my husband does not recall hearing anything other than the physicians' discussion. To the best of my recollection, there was a great deal of activity for I had begun to labor and the hemorrhaging started again. Since both babies were dead and I was hemorrhaging, an emergency caesarian was done to stop the bleeding, repair the artery, and deliver the stillborn babies. I recall my doctor explaining that typically an epidural was used for such procedures, but, given what I had already been through, they could administer general anesthesia. I chose the general, thinking to myself, "I hope I never wake up." I received six to eight pints of blood during the long night and was moved to intensive care following the caesarian. I remained in the hospital for a couple of weeks until my vitals slowly normalized and the staples were removed from my 18-inch abdominal incision. During that time, my husband and I had the opportunity to hold and name our sons. I also experienced vivid, disturbing, numinous dreams.

Shortly after returning home from the hospital, my husband and I arranged the burial of our sons. The crushing finality of dressing our precious boys, placing them tenderly into their diminutive coffin, turning my back on them, and walking out the door of the private room at the mortuary was almost unbearable. We buried our sons at a graveside service in the chill of March sunshine, nine days after my twenty-ninth birthday. I was emotionally and physically shattered and convalesced at home for three months until returning to work deeply changed and uncertain of the future.

Waking up

Several critical experiences figured into my trajectory following the months of my physical recuperation. First, I began journaling like my life depended upon it. Second, I had a series of profoundly vivid, startlingly archetypal dreams, which I allowed to guide and instruct me. Third, I benefited from a humbling and restorative outpouring of love and support from family, coworkers, friends, and even strangers. Fourth, my estranged father gifted me a copy of *The Power of Myth* by Joseph Campbell and Bill Moyers, which gave me a mythic language with which to begin to understand life. And fifth, I answered a pressing inner call to comprehend the meaning of my losses and my inexplicable "religious" experiences of death by entering psychotherapy with a Jungian analyst. I faced a paradox: the physical and medical realities and demands of endometriosis were objectively outside my control and would continue to shape my life. However, intuitively and psychically, I recognized that my disease and my afflicted body were teaching me. I felt that I must learn to listen to my symptoms as guidance or die.

My extremely shaken physician presented my case at conferences in an effort to research what had occurred and to treat the disease more effectively; however, little changed in practical terms. We now know that, while the hormones of pregnancy can often suppress endometriosis, sometimes they stimulate its growth and this is the most likely explanation for my experience. Endometriotic tissue implanted on the uterine artery likely remained active or was stimulated during pregnancy and compromised the integrity of the artery. Under the strain of gestation, the artery ruptured spontaneously—a rare and bizarre occurrence, which is why it was so difficult to diagnose. With no intervention in the disease process, recuperation meant the return of menstruation and the symptoms of endometriosis as well as the requirement to decide whether or not to attempt another pregnancy.

For me, the fundamental question became whether my life would be motivated by fear and contraction or love and trust. I would not tolerate my sons' deaths as meaningless and therefore I would use every means possible to un-conceal meaning. I had survived and they had not—my life a gift I had been granted by their sacrifice—so I felt compelled to atone for rather than compound the tragic loss. My experience appeared random from a rational perspective, yet I felt the only way to live with, through, and in my losses was to apprehend the meaning of what had occurred and to use that understanding to live intentionally and heal, not just myself, but some greater wound.

Living children, progressing disease

Supported by grief counseling and psychotherapy, I decided, along with my husband, to try again for children. Within two years, our first daughter was born, followed by her sister four years later. Both were delivered caesarian because of extensive scarring from surgery and endometriosis and concern over a recurrence of the rupture or other complications. I recall that after the second delivery, the surgeon commented on the condition of my womb and peritoneal cavity saying that "it was a real mess in there." Being preoccupied with holding my beautiful newborn, I did not ask him to elaborate.

While pregnancy and lactation did not appear to suppress my endometriosis, I did experience the symptoms differently. With breastfeeding, my cyclical pelvic pain was somewhat diminished, but my bowel symptoms and back pain increased and became acute and chronic, and I suffered from headaches. Once I had stopped nursing my children, my dysmenorrhea redoubled as did pain with ovulation, dyspareunia, heavy bleeding, and other symptoms. I lost days to these symptoms, and managed, in part, by attempting to plan around their occurrence when possible. On my physician's advice, I continued on oral contraceptives, though they provided no significant relief. Stoicism and lots of ibuprofen became my primary defenses. My physician offered hysterectomy as the only recourse, which was not an acceptable option to me for many reasons. If she was aware of the other medical or surgical interventions being developed, she did not suggest them.

Busy with raising children, attending graduate school, and working, and unwilling to undergo more surgery and a lifetime of post-hysterectomy adverse effects, I turned to alternative therapies to find what relief they offered for my progressively worsening chronic pain and other symptoms. The devil I knew seemed better than the one I did not, and despite my condition, I remained deeply attached to my female reproductive organs. I could not perceive of hysterectomy as inconsequential and the loss of my ovaries and uterus as insignificant. I also continued to work with the disease and its symptoms psychologically, nurturing my ability to discern meaning in my suffering. Throughout this process, while pain provided motivation, dream work was the guiding source of inspiration. A series of vivid archetypal characters emerged who transcended and reshaped my attitudes and invigorated my psychic life. And then, after several years, I started to dream repeatedly of an encroaching, malevolent, sticky, black tarlike ooze.

Hysterectomy

I began to experience acute bowel pain and bleeding; the specter of cancer arose once again. Recall that the likelihood of some cancers, including ovarian, is increased by endometriosis. Following a series of medical tests over several months, CT and MRI scans finally revealed that my bowel was blocked, likely by invasive endometriosis. The endometriosis had progressed becoming aggressive, invasive stage IV disease that was ultimately found to involve not only my reproductive organs and colon, but other major organs and structures of my pelvis. Surgery was required as soon as possible.

Aware that the medical options available to me close to home were limited, I worked with my gynecological oncologist to arrange for surgery at a leading hospital out of state, with a surgeon specializing in endometriosis. I recall the consultation with the surgeon during which I shared many of the bizarre manifestations of my disease, which he validated, expressing understanding rather than incredulity and dismissal. After the visit, I was overwhelmed by a wave of tearful relief; the epiphanic result of corroboration and hope. In addition to the medical preparations for such extensive surgery, I engaged in a psycho-spiritual process of imaginative, creative, and ritualized "listening" to my womb so that I was able to accept, ritualize, and grieve the surgical intervention that I had long resisted. Within the year I underwent a six hour robotically modified radical hysterectomy including the removal of my uterus, fallopian tubes, ovaries, cervix, appendix, and much of my sigmoid colon. In addition, extensive endometriosis was removed from my bladder and ureters, uterosacral ligament, and peritoneum. The mysterious wisdom of my recurring "black tar" dreams was revealed; invasive endometriosis tumors adhere to surrounding tissue by way of a thick tar-like fluid, encouraging fibrous scar tissue to penetrate deeply and damage organs.[798]

Post-operatively, the surgeon reported to me that he had cut through extensive scar tissue to locate my uterus, which invasive uterine endometriosis (adenomyosis) had caused to swell to three times normal and which was fused with my ovaries, fallopian tubes, and ureters. I had only just escaped kidney damage. Endometriosis had penetrated and was bleeding into my colon in multiple places causing kinks and blockages. However, he believed that the surgery was completely successful and that I would recover well and likely be free of the pain of endometriosis for many years, perhaps the rest of my life. I pressed him about recurrence rates and he contextualized his answer, explaining that it had taken 48 years for the disease to get this bad, so I did not need to worry for another 48. Besides, the disease's primary source of estrogen—my ovaries—was gone; osteoporosis would be a bigger concern. However, he also shared that he had operated on a woman in her eighties because of her recurrent endometriosis. In addition, I was aware that even the most carefully executed surgical intervention generates potentially symptomatic scar tissue, the underlying causes of the disease remain unknown, microscopic endometriosis is sometimes missed during surgery, and my case had been extraordinarily tenacious and unpredictable. What I clearly recall is the word my virtuosic, heroic surgeon used to describe the endometriotic tissue he had toiled for six hours to cut away: "concrete."

Reflections on my story

In relaying the facts of my story, I am aware of their potentially dysregulating effects; a tale of disease, meaningless suffering, and loss, featuring a couple of dissociative experiences likely induced by profound blood loss. The retelling can trigger stress reactions and even become re-traumatizing since it does not provide attuned, embodied, imaginative interaction with the material and the human being who lived it. A critical aspect of healing trauma is attending to its neurobiological foundations and its physiological symptoms. That process is not part of the scope of this project, however, without previously engaging in somatic-based therapies, the mythopoetic restoration I am pursuing would likely be less efficacious. Therefore, I offer a brief overview of neurobiological trauma theory and ritual practice as they apply to trauma treatment.

While depth psychology attends to somatic symptoms as meaningful, its overriding emphases on the psyche, the symbolic, and insight can become mind-focused and imagine the body to be essentially "a magnificent citadel of metaphors."[799] But the conceptualization of body as metaphor, that is, as a revelatory microcosm, while extremely useful, is only part of the story and in the treatment of trauma the demands of physiology often take precedence over those of psyche. Insight and reflection are not possible when the nervous system is overwhelmed by traumatic activation.

Hillman builds on the alchemical tradition to construct a distinction between the "literal" and the "concrete" whereby the literal becomes the "enemy" of psyche because it strips matter of numinous immanence.[800] Concreteness is real in time and space; material objects, living beings, and actions have concrete reality, but one must never "forget that these, too, are always subject to seeing through."[801] Psyche is an expression of the ultimate reality and the material realm, including the body, a legitimate but illusory incarnation of that reality. The body finds its most potent reality here by losing its literalness, becoming a metaphoric "subtle body—a fantasy system of complexes, symptoms, tastes, influences and relations, zones of delight, pathologized images, trapped insights [such that the] body and soul lose their borders, neither more literal or metaphorical than the other."[802] In the effort toward the body not being literalized—stripped of numinosity—it seems that the concrete body becomes a secondary and subordinate reality to that of psyche in this mytho-imaginative language.

In ritual, the body is understood not only as the central, foundational symbol, but also as a definitive, primary reality with a legitimate sensory-led way of knowing and a "medium through which religious states are learned and transmitted."[803] According to Michael Winkelman's research on the universals of shamanism, embodied apprehension can be understood as "neurognostic," that is, based in biological structures and features of the triune brain, its processes and their physiological responses which interact through preverbal perception—and enactment that can be activated through ritual.[804] As a model and source of religious action, the body is both the pathway to and structure of transformation in its ritualized movement through time and space. The ritual action itself is meaningful and potentially transformative because it creates an intentional experience, an encounter with the divine, which can then be symbolized and integrated into insight or not; for the bodily change engendered by the experience (whether or not there is an outward physical change) has definitively, irrevocably occurred. Throughout the text of *The Developing Mind*, Daniel Siegel demonstrates that behavior, especially repeated or highly activating action, actually alters brain structure making new and different behaviors possible and even modifying one's sense of identity.

However, in the attempt to give the body its due, psyche must not be ignored, for as Donald Kalsched argues throughout *The Inner World of Trauma*, the imagination and the archetypal world are integral to healing trauma. Hillman does not conceive of the soul as the opposite of the body, but rather as a sort of encompassing, linking function between matter and spirit: "The body has its home in the soul ...."[805] But, perhaps one can also argue that the soul has its lived experience in the body. The argument begins to sound circular and almost absurd. But, in trauma treatment, the theoretical and literal position of the body is of fundamental concern (for example, when treating early childhood trauma having a client take a prone position in therapy may evoke a re-traumatizing state of helplessness). Insight, reflection, and imagination alone do not appear to heal trauma and its manifestations because post-traumatic stress disorder and other debilitating trauma reactions are wounds of the soul, but are also based in the physiology of the triune brain and the autonomic nervous system.

In simple terms, the triune brain includes the brain stem (or so-called reptilian brain), the limbic area (emotional brain), and the cortex (rational brain). A threat is perceived via the brain stem, which is the center of instinctual survival reactions. The threat is assessed as legitimate by the limbic brain and the alarm signals, releasing neurotransmitters and hormones that trigger the sympathetic branch of the autonomic nervous system. The sympathetic nervous system is the accelerator that prepares the body to fight or flee. One has moved from arousal to hyperarousal through this involuntary biological process. In the face of an overwhelming threat, the sympathetic nervous system, unable to determine whether to fight or flee generates a freeze response resulting in collapse and/or a dissociated state like shock, which is followed by physiological discharge behaviors.[806] When the activated instinctual strategy (fight, flight, or freeze) is successful, the autonomic nervous system, by way of its parasympathetic branch (the brake), returns the individual to a calm and regulated state.[807] Trauma results when the system remains in hyperarousal, that is, the threat cannot be fought or fled from, the instinctual discharge process that completes the freeze response is inhibited, or the threat is chronic. It is as if one has one foot on the accelerator and one foot on the brake simultaneously.[808] The result is a host of disruptive and painful symptoms and behaviors which can appear mysterious, arbitrary, and irresolvable.

The triune brain is implicated in both the biology of trauma and in ritual theory. In his article "Shamanism: A Biogenetic Perspective" Winkelman notes:

> Ritual processes activate connections between the reptilian and paleomammalian [limbic] brains, providing information from these lower systems to the symbolic mechanisms of the frontal brain [cortex]. This engagement permits the symbolic reprogramming of emotional dynamics and behavior repertoires of these lower centers of the brain through the 'language' of ritual and their psychophysiological effects.[809]

That is, ritual integrates physiological experience and perception with the imaginative mind. Trauma is an absence of integration within the triune brain, a misalignment of the inner and outer realities such that long after the threat has passed, the body continues to suffer in a state of hyperarousal. What is required to begin healing is attuned bodily expression of the arousal. Levine repeatedly argues that culture is the primary inhibitor of traumatic discharge behaviors. Culture can also facilitate discharge and healing through ritual, such as shamanic rites,[810] and historically has often done so, resulting in the realignment of bodily and psychic realities.

Likewise, trauma treatment, by attending to actual bodily experience, can facilitate the psychological healing, transformation, and individuation which are the potential boon of depth psychological work. Effective trauma treatment is guided by emotion

and bodily sensation; for the therapist in his or her affective and
sensate attunement to the client and for the client in her or his
learning to identify and connect to feelings, sensations, thoughts, and
images that alternately arouse and calm. What is critical throughout
the process is that the client not move into hyperarousal, and the key
is staying aware of and "in" the immediate, sensational body and
environment. Like an uninitiated shaman pulled into a shamanic
trance, the victim of trauma is prone to leave the body (dissociate)
tumbling into an underworld of devils for which he or she is ill-
prepared. The body, its affect, and sensations are the lifeline to
healing. Through the repetition of intentional, attuned, guided action
of the body and mind—which shares qualities of ritualizing—the
brain develops new, integrative neuropathways that foster a more
creative response to the trauma; a new embodied story.

"Posttraumatic growth" is the paradoxical experience of an
increased sense of vulnerability and personal strength, appreciation,
empathy, and meaning reported by people who have successfully
integrated traumatic loss.[811] The imagining and articulation of a new
self-narrative, or personal myth, which is the purpose of this book, is
a fundamental part and result of healing through grief and loss.
Given the existential nature of the process, depth psychological
conceptions of soul and focus on working with the unconscious and
its manifestation are profoundly helpful in supporting posttraumatic
growth. However, in cases of trauma, access to insight and the
symbol-creating functions of the psyche can be inhibited or
effectively blocked by the body's potent stress reactions. Trauma is a
crisis of the soul to which the psyche responds in deeply symbolic
ways manifested in disturbing and even dangerous raw archetypal
energies or "mythopoetic features."[812] Skillful application of
neurobiological knowledge and ritual wisdom about the body, the
revelations inherent in its concreteness, and the power of its actions,
integrated with the wisdom of psyche can be the elixir for healing a
traumatized person of profound and pervasive suffering.

From Fact to "Fiction;" From My Story to "Mystory"

The above discussion of trauma and ritual theory helps to bridge
the gap between body and psyche that has been cultivated in Western
identity, providing a language of embodiment that is related to the

language of psychological experience. By attending to the wisdom of the body, my story moves beyond relaying the facts of what occurred chronologically and relatively objectively; a story of the "what" and "how," which may provoke affective or other responses, but neglects meaning and therefore contributes little to the healing of potentially traumatic experiences. Such a *logos* or ego-centered narrative serves as our beginning since it provides the events to be psychologized. However, such a narrative fails to "see through" what occurred for clues from the soul's meaning-filled perspective into "[psyche's] nature, structure, and purpose;" a perspective large enough to engage existential questions of life and death.[813] Meaning is nourished by reflection and imagination and enlivened by psychologizing questions: "Who is visiting?" "What is going on here?" "What might this symptom mean?" "What is the myth (or meaningful archetypal pattern) that is incarnating?" For the soul—understood as a reflective "perspective [...] which makes meaning possible"—the literal gives way to the imaginal, the metaphorical, and to the myth being unconsciously lived.[814] Revelation of the myth is a step towards a particular quality of freedom and healing based on imagination, which is the province of soul. The meaning and mystery concealed within the concrete body unfolds through reflective relating with manifest content.

As I have stated, for me, the particular myth—and the answer to "who is visiting"— revealed itself intuitively and symptomatically. Medusa's image emerged spontaneously and repeatedly in my psychic life so that in order to work with my story of endometriosis archetypally, I am compelled to view it through the context of Medusa (and Athene). Such an approach has the effect of "*deepening* events into [meaningful] experiences."[815] However, despite my sense of Medusa's presence in my disease, the overlay of purposeful choice and action I sometimes impose serves the telling but does not imply that any such level of awareness existed in me at the time I was choosing or acting; except when explicitly stated, the clarity and meaning which I superimpose onto the facts result from reflection through the lens of myth. As the philosopher Soren Kierkegaard observes, life is lived forwards, but understood backwards: the meaning I make here is hindsight and not causal. Again, I emphasize that linear causality between mythopoesis and the emergence or course of physical disease is a literalization that is incongruent with my purpose and beyond my scope of knowledge.

Girlhood in patriarchy: a mythic back story

Myth does not provide Medusa with a childhood; she first appears as a *parthenos*. Athene's childhood is obscured by her Olympian birth as the fully-grown *Parthenos* from Zeus's head. Luckily, we have glimpses of Athene's girlhood in other accounts. We know that she loses her mother, who, though wise and primordial is consumed by the power drives of ascending patriarchy. Athene suffers the effects of this unintended maternal abandonment in her suppression of her connection to her maternal, Earth origins, which she projects onto other females, perhaps engendering her need to integrate them into her. Recall, Athene's dear friend Pallas, the childhood foster-sister from Africa whom the goddess accidentally slays and whose identity Athene takes onto herself in the same way that the goddess later incorporates Medusa; both Pallas and the Gorgon serving as compensating *yin-yin* attitudes to Athene's powerful *yang* reality.

Stories also demonstrate that Athene is well acquainted with the threat of violation inherent in her *parthenos* state and the general threat of violence, particularly sexual violence, engendered in patriarchal views of masculine/male prerogative. She deals with these threats in various ways. Pre-Greek Athene, from a less phallocentric tradition, dispatches the perpetrating father figure with righteous agency and wears his flayed pelt as her protective *aegis*. Later, in Greek myth, she adapts the protective persona of Father's Daughter, handmaiden and shieldmaiden of Olympus. Despite her adaptation, Athene sometimes smolders with resentment against her father and, notably, preserves the chthonic feminine sacred—even its most demonic forms— covertly within the patriarchy, "hidden" in her temple center as the *Eumenides* and upon her breast as the Gorgoneion *aegis*. Much of who Athene may be is obscured by her Apollonian image so that she can easily literalize into a vision of the promise and prestige available to the woman who denies and rejects *yin* values; to its favorite daughters patriarchy bestows success, power, and inclusion. To fall into identification with this Athene is to risk petrifying perfectionism, but it can seem like such a small price to pay for the rewards.

If I reflect on my own childhood and young womanhood as revealed in Athene's mirror, I comprehend how I actively, if sometimes unconsciously, cultivated my position as a Father's Daughter, not only in my family of origin, but in my stance in the world. Unfortunately, my Athene was predominately the Father's Daughter, and, within the milieu of my culture and family, I took her denial of the feminine at face value. Athene's myth shows that the Father's Daughter role can serve as a survival mechanism; it did so for me. My affiliation with Athene runs deep. My childhood was also marked by early maternal attachment disruption, interpersonal trauma and violence, and the constant tension of feeling paternal estrangement and identification. I benefited from genuine parental affection (however imperfect), my father's powerful imagination, my mother's perseverance despite her own trauma, an abiding link to chthonic (instinctive, animal, Earth) nature, and an Athene-like temperament—strong, strategic, dexterous, protean, and self-reliant.

Within this childhood myth are the seeds of my pragmatic, objective, and unconsciously antagonistic relationship to my female body, its specifically female processes, and endometriosis. Psychologically, I was in thrall to a patriarchal version of Athene. Archetypally, Athene was visiting and her presence provided me pragmatic adaptability, strategic vigilance, and the power to succeed in "a man's world." Because of the unconscious nature of my communion, or perhaps more precisely, my ego-identification with a one-sided version of the goddess, I ascended to striving and perfectionism so that in attending her altar I both worshiped and defended against the dominant *yang* principle, taking on its "potentially overwhelming [...] power by assimilating it in [my] own being."[816] This assimilation replicated the patriarchal hierarchy within me so that my adopted, adaptive ego related to my female body by exploiting its "pleasuring giving" aspects while disciplining, controlling, and judging it, and suppressing its needs and symptoms as secondary inconveniences.

The Father's Daughter persona was belied by my female blood; Medusa in my veins and flowing from my body. Perhaps the only way I could look at the rage of my denigrated Gorgon heritage and my own wounding was reflected through my endometriosis— knowing Medusa through her awe-ful manifestations of blood, pain, and death. Rather than an empowering, "protective *aegis*," I wore my endometriotic Gorgoneion as a "defensive mask, made necessary by dread of annihilation" as the ever-threatened fate of the vulnerable *parthenos* for whom patriarchy has demonized feminine creativity and female agency and delimited her worth in sexual terms.[817] If I had looked fully upon the face of my own embodied misogyny I would have turned to stone—as encounters with chthonic rage will do. Perhaps my endometriotic Gorgoneion served as ironically apotropaic, deflecting the full force of ontic shame engendered in my gender. As a patriarchal female, the terrible Gorgoneion came to rest in the part of my body so frequently judged to be the face of terror, evil, shame, and sin; the embodied center of the dynamic tension of the feminine and her sex as "*sacra*, sacred and accursed:" the female reproductive organs and their blood processes.[818]

Myth tells us that seeing Medusa's face turns one to stone. But then, looking upon any goddess or god has a similarly overwhelming, annihilating effect according to mythologies throughout the world. Why is this dynamic demonized in the Gorgon Medusa's case? Medusa's dual nature as goddess and mortal seems relevant in pondering the question. We have seen how woman's prerogative to participate so overtly in life's creation and destruction through her biological capacity to bear children and menstruate (bleed without dying and seemingly, spontaneously heal) made her powerfully taboo so that the symbol of her reproductive organs, both internal and external, came to be seen as monstrous. Despite being misunderstood and marginalized by the ancient Greeks, females and their menstrual processes were still regarded as threateningly powerful, in many ways, more horror than mystery—the stony face of the terrible Gorgoneion. Misogynistic attitudes persist into the modern West (and elsewhere); finding their way into the psyches of women and men. Woman's most indigenous processes—menstruation, pregnancy, menopause—have become disease processes, medicalized and demonized as the bane of the female and proof of her original sin and defiled nature.

For me, it is as if, as I unconsciously align myself with dominant patriarchal values in order to function as a successful Father's Daughter, even my body takes on that perspective and when confronted with the reality of its divine, chthonic feminine nature through menses it is turned to stone, petrified like the patriarchal attitude that confronts Medusa in myths. In this way I perceive my endometriosis as metaphoric for embodied misogyny and Medusa as an image of the archetypal energy pattern expressing the deeply regenerative, chthonic sacred, literalized and scorned as femaleness.

At an early age, influenced by my temperament, experiences, and personality, I apprehended the victim-victimizer dynamic at play in the world and perceived the *yang* position as forcefully dominant and of superior power. In a dangerous, competitive world of scarcity and rigid standards, force and power can become of superior value to feeling and connection. I concretely—and metaphorically—aligned myself with the *yang* attitude such that I wore and internalized an *aegis* of feminine rage along with collective and personal stories of defilement. In compensation, my soul began its lifelong mythopoesis toward redeeming the wholeness of the feminine, and my dis-eased female body became the context. For Downing, it is Athene who represents "the repression of the feminine" and, conversely, "the undoing of the repression as a soul task [which] demands a courageous examination of our own participation in misogynous self-denial."[819] For me, endometriosis facilitates and Medusa mediates self-reflection while Athene offers an image of creative reconciliation and integration, a return to the wholeness of the feminine soul, in spirit and matter. Through the mythic mirror, endometriosis, still a physical disease with all that that implies and requires, deepens into a particular and meaningful visitation and I begin to apprehend it as a complicated life companion.

Womanhood: time to grow up

The reflections above emerge out of a reciprocal interaction between fact and fiction, personal event and myth. What unfolds is a re-storying of my early experience of endometriosis that allows a mythic sense of "the meaning" of my development of that particular condition. Now I explore other events, including the births and deaths of my children and my hysterectomy as meaningful experiences in a coherent mythopoetic narrative.

Birth and death and regeneration

The deaths of my infant sons were existentially disintegrating for me, while the unexpected grace of my own near-death experiences left a lingering sense of sacred integration. The twin experiences of devastation and grace juxtaposed in time and space created extreme psychic tension within me. Initially, pain dominated everything, and as I convalesced, the grief sometimes threatened to overwhelm me; I contemplated whether or not I had the strength to continue to live. However, the unrelenting love demonstrated by others and a stubborn idea that it was my responsibility to ameliorate rather than exacerbate the tragedy made more death untenable. In addition, there was the undeniable, incomprehensible *experience* of my encounter with my own death that persisted beneath the grief: an incongruent, awesome presence that had made reassurance irrelevant and yet, in its objectively relational potency, calmed and resourced me for the inevitable. This encounter with death revealed a new (for me) reality of source, or being—or Being, for there was an undeniable quality of the impersonal and trans-human present—which demanded that I hold loss and presence, agony and gratitude, and grief and joy simultaneously. The death aspect of the Great Goddess, for me a Medusan incarnation, was visiting. From her I ascertained that my long-standing panic around the idea of my death was, in part, enlivened by a much earlier experience of psychic annihilation, or terror of it, caused by an event which I experienced as traumatic abandonment as a baby. It is as if I had now twice encountered the Gorgon, archetype of the daemonic sacred. First, as a 15-month-old for whom it was terrible and yet quickened the seed of chthonic connection that has sustained me, like Athene, throughout my life, even when I was relatively unconscious of it and projected it outward onto other females and nature. And again, as I slipped into the arms of my approaching physical death and "She" revealed to me the irrelevance of my ego position and the deeper reality of my unsullied worthiness, my relational oneness with her as source and ending and source. That she was death, I had no doubt. That she was regeneration, I had yet to learn.

The traumatic intensity of these two encounters was perhaps as close as this human could come to looking upon Medusa's face unmediated. My other experiences of her have been relatively depotentiated, encounters or embodiments of the Gorgoneion. I have argued that endometriosis—as a disease that both protected from and embodied misogynistic threats to my femininity—can be imaged as such a mask. I believe I was also the beneficiary of Medusa's Gorgoneion apotropaic power in deflecting destructive sexual aggression as a vulnerable child as well. As Edelman's work shows, encounters with the Gorgon as the daemonic sacred may result in the crippling condition of being a "shamecarrier" for whom embodiment of and relationship with the divine lacks "*aidos* in Democritus' sense: reverence for self."[820] I recognize this "shamecarrier" aspect in myself as arising from my uninitiated encounters with the Gorgon, not only as the denigrated face of the sacred feminine but also "the dark side of the Holy, the *tremendum*, [...] which can manifest as the threat of psychological as well as physical catastrophe."[821] The illuminating paradox is that both the annihilating wounding to my self-reverence and its progressive restoration—the lived knowledge that I "have value *by virtue of [my] existence*"—emerge from my encounters with Medusa, her mythic blood both destructive and healing.[822]

The Gorgon compelled me into regeneration, but only after I surrendered to devastation, without compromise. For a long time, I entertained the thought that my sons had been a sacrificial offering ransoming familial generations of suppressed women. This narrative continues to resonate with mythopoesis; so large and objective a context that I am ever aware of its potential grandiosity. Beyond this story of metaphoric human sacrifice, I see a more personal, psychological offering, that of the attitude I thought I could not live without: control. I had believed that power was control and that by being in control and controlling life, I was safe (from it) and that perfectionism could exempt me from blame, the trigger for annihilating shame. Like Athene, I could move through the world with impunity disguised as the Father's Daughter. The Gorgon face of death ripped that illusion away. The encounter felt paradoxically relational; despite my ego's temporary shattering in surrender to the experience of approaching death and overwhelming pain, "I" was okay because my being was held by and in sacred presence; my soul was in Soul. What I felt, against all expectation, was calm; a peace not coming from me but into and through me. "I" was empty, yet present and completely permeated and contained in compassion. It was not ecstasy—because the portal was traumatic loss and suffering—but an abiding calm of surrender and trust. This encompassing acceptance was not agreement; somehow whether or not my ego agreed with what was happening did not matter at all. The sacred that was revealed to and through me was huge, so large that it filled my perceptual field and no other reality was as real as that presence, which included everything. I had been stripped to the bone and not found wanting, but rather held and loved. I was at the Great Mother's altar and she was *tremendum*, demonic only to my ego desires, and I was her creature, of her, and therefore blessed.

Later, she would welcome my beloved sons into her paradoxically fertile reality, where nothing grows but where life itself is born. And I remained in life, dazed, anguished to be left behind and yet, already the seeds of transformation were stirring within me. Stripped of the illusion of control I began to glimpse life's chthonic extremity in death and so the lovely maiden—like Ovid's Medusa, a creature of patriarchal appetite and scorn—transformed into her true snaky nature.

Reconciliation: body and self

The near-death experience described above evokes the pre-Greek Gorgon as the death and regeneration aspect of the Great Goddesses described by Gimbutas, Dexter, and others and discussed in Chapter 3. For this reason, I briefly diverge from the specific myths of Medusa and Athene into the more intact gynocentric mythology of Sumer, which predates ancient Greece. This foray into Sumer is not so great a departure from the mythic milieu of ancient Greece, as was revealed in the material about the origins and archetypal linkings of the Gorgon and Athene in traditions predating and outside of Greece. The Sumerian myth of Inanna's descent to the underworld (c. 3500-1600 BCE) provides a particularly feminine myth of descent and regeneration. For me, the Gorgon's beheading as restorative is only possible when preceded by a more embodied, symbolic (that is, shamanic) mythic enactment of the sacred experiences my mind has attempted to narrate. For, although I sense the problem—that I wear the Gorgoneion upon my female sex—I cannot force the resolution imaged by Athene with her Gorgoneion *aegis* upon her breast. Before I can embark on the adventure with Hermes and Perseus—heroic twins waiting to accompany me onto the Gorgon plane—I must go back to the more ancient story of Inanna and her chthonic sister, Ereshkigal.

In the text of *The Descent of Inanna,* Inanna, as Queen of Heaven and Earth, is a supreme deity incorporating many epitaphs and qualities, some of which she shares with Athene. For example, Inanna's central place is shared only slightly more peripherally by Athene on Olympus where the Greek goddess is often described as Zeus's favorite and prime agent. Athene also has in common Inanna's role as goddess of war[823] and, despite Inanna's association with sexual love and fertility, both goddesses signify *eros* (relatedness) as the "feminine beyond the merely maternal."[824] Inanna also masterfully applies persuasion in ways that are reminiscent of Athene's famed rhetorical skills.

Ereshkigal, Sumerian Goddess of Death, shares many qualities with Medusa, including "hair [that] swirls about her head like leeks," her rageful temper, and a sexual encounter with or rape by Enki "God of the Waters."[825] Dexter notes that, despite being deities of death, both Medusa and Ereshkigal give birth. Unlike the Greek myth, in the more ancient Sumerian story, "the Goddess of the Underworld did not have to die in the process of giving birth; she who presided over death presided over rebirth."[826] In fact, it was the deity of life, Inanna, who had to die in order to regenerate. Two millennia later, Medusa pays for the birth of her children with her own life. One way to understand this shift is that once she is demonized, along with death, the Gorgon's shamanic regenerative power is lost; her children must be freed from her body via a murderous cesarean section. Certainly the prevailing reading of the Greco-Roman Medusa myths favors Medusa as a monster who is necessarily vanquished, whose evil must be sublimated and controlled by Athene as the feminine in service to patriarchal values.

However, as demonstrated previously, a more soulful, healing interpretation is indicated by Athene's incorporation of the chthonic feminine. Ereshkigal's essential role in regeneration expands and concretizes an understanding of the nature of Medusa and provides a fruitful model for imaging a sort of psycho-embodied descent to encounter the Gorgon. A full recounting of the story with commentary is provided by Diane Wolkstein and Samuel Noah Kramer in *Inanna: Queen of Heaven and Earth*, and is well worth reading. A very brief summary must suffice for my purposes here.

The descent of Inanna

Inanna, Queen of Heaven and Earth, is compelled "Because ... of [her] elder sister" to go to the Underworld to witness the funeral of Ereshkigal's consort.[827] Ereshkigal, Queen of the Great Below, is outraged by Inanna's taboo visit to the Underworld, but allows Inanna to proceed, ritually stripping her sister of divine status until Inanna is "bowed low" before Ereshkigal's throne.[828] Judgment is pronounced, Inanna is rendered lifeless, and her flesh hung to rot on a hook. Inanna's death pangs are mirrored in Ereshkigal's birth pangs as the Queen of the Underworld is stricken, writhing on the floor in excruciating pain. Meanwhile, efforts to restore Inanna from the Underworld—efforts put in place by Inanna as precautionary—are unfolding above. Inanna's beloved and grieving companion, Ninshubur, travels from god to god pleading for their intervention on Inanna's behalf. Repeatedly she is rejected, chastised, and shamed. But, Ninshubur perseveres until Inanna's maternal grandfather, Enki, God of Wisdom (and the Waters) sends the *kurgarra* and *galatur*, genderless entities of pure empathy formed from the dirt under Enki's fingernails and disguised as common houseflies, to ameliorate Ereshkigal's pain. The *kurgarra* and *galatur* circle Ereshkigal, attuned and attending to her suffering with words that mirror her cries and exhortations. This compassionate intercession, generated by the cooperation of feminine and masculine divine forces, frees Ereshkigal from her suffering. The Goddess of Death is touched by her first experience of nonjudgmental empathy and deep rapport and in a gesture of gratitude releases Inanna at the request of the *kurgarra* and *galatur*. The Goddess of Heaven and Earth is restored to life. However, she is also transformed by her confrontation and reconciliation with her chthonic sister. Accompanied by the *galla*, spirits of the underworld, and carrying the deep wisdom of the Earth previously absent from her solar knowledge,[829] Inanna establishes eternal reciprocity between all realms by sacrificing her beloved consort Dumuzi through a cyclical fate of death and renewal that he shares with his sister Geshtinanna. Neglecting his relational values, Dumuzi has remained regally upon the throne in hubris despite Inanna's absence. His inability or refusal to recognize Inanna's transformation and his clinging to ego values of prestige and power compel Inanna to sacrifice him to his own transformative process of death and renewal. Despite her genuine love for him—she truly grieves his loss in the text—his psycho-spiritual maturation trumps personal attachments. However, Inanna tempers Dumuzi's fate by acquiescing to his sister Geshtinanna's compassionate pleas to take her instead. Personal love is not irrelevant and brings emotional reprieve and transforming comfort to human suffering (as Ninshubur's love did for Inanna and Ereshkigal) and so brother and sister share equally in the eternal cycle of descent and return.

Reflections on descent

The myth of Inanna's descent is a rendering of the shamanic activity of regeneration and healing as the reconciliation of opposing, but equally necessary, complementary realities. The story is also an eloquent model of the experience of descent into grief and bodily suffering; an encounter between ego and shadow. It speaks not only to psychic experience, but also to physical distress and concrete aspects of healing interventions. The narrative signifies the transformative effects of reconciling and integrating chthonic realities and the wisdom and cost of enhanced consciousness—upon her return, Inanna exercises the uncompromising clarity of objective relatedness even at the cost of her personal, subjective love for her consort, Dumuzi. Inanna emerging from the underworld with the *galla* all around her parallels Athene clothed in the Medusan Gorgoneion *aegis*. The deeper wisdom of death and regeneration is integrated and the change that the experience forges in one's identity is visible and most deeply affects the heart, that is, one's quality of relatedness. The integration of the chthonic divine feminine is the source of the sacred androgyny that expresses in Athene's wholeness; the *yin-yin* needed to balance the *yang-yin* she can too easily be identified with in patriarchal renderings.

For me, the story of Inanna's descent to Ereshkigal fills a mythic lacuna, such that, now, the image of Athene with Medusa's head transcends the split it previously signified and resonates with numinous beauty and restorative meaning. The Sumerian myth mediates reconciliation between self and body and, in my mind, provides the relational nuances and dynamics implied in the myths of Medusa and Athene, which are fundamental and prerequisite to integration.

Like Inanna and Ereshkigal, Athene and Medusa represent distinct, complementary realms that are paradoxically, inextricably connected. Overtly expressed as sisterhood in the Sumerian myth, Athene's kinship with Medusa drives the Gorgon's mythic life story and is explicitly expressed as Athene's Gorgoneion *aegis* and the epithet Athene Gorgopis. Inanna and Athene can be seen as representing ego reality—intellect and spirit—distinct and yet in functional relationship with Ereshkigal and Medusa as material reality—body (including affect and instinct) and matter. In terms of depth psychology, the relationship represents the ego-self axis, recovered when what was necessarily sundered in service to ego develop is related again.[830]

In these myths of the divided feminine reconciled, I see a blueprint for healing the split within the feminine self and female body. While the Greek myth of Athene's beheading of the Gorgon and incorporation of the Gorgoneion *aegis* provides an image of integration, the Sumerian myth lays out a fundamentally relational pathway that demonstrates reconciliation and integration of spirit and body through dis-ease and loss. The *yin-yin* archetypal energies including instinct, the body, and death represented by Ereshkigal and Medusa are portrayed and validated as difficult and painful, but not evil, and, above all, as essential and sacred. Medusa, like Ereshkigal contains a deep, primal sort of pain so potent that it drives away subjective *eros* and the transformative warmth of empathy. This, in part, illuminates what makes the Gorgon so threatening to the Western ethos in which the feminine is equated with subjective relatedness. There is a homeopathic relationship between the damage done by the shaming of instinctual, "unseemly" aspects of the so-called feminine: *eros* is what is damaged and *eros* is the repair. Like the *kurgarra* and the *galatur* coming to witness Ereshkigal in her agony, courageous, nonjudgmental empathy grounded in humility (the *kurgarra* and *galatur* are made from the humus under Enki's fingernails) and selflessness (Ninshubur's shameless devotion) is required to make contact with and soothe such a suffering feminine (or perhaps any) soul and female body. If like Inanna-Ereshkigal, one can go into the psychologically and physically wounded places; submit to being emptied of the attitude of ego supremacy, power, and control; deeply accept, feel, and express painful affect authentically without aggression against self or other; and be seen and validated empathically in a relationship which is both objectively and subjectively loving and devoid of ego needs to fix or judge, then the core wound of fundamental shamefulness as a soul wound may begin to heal. In the same way, if I enter into soulful relationship with my disease and body through myth with an attitude that is dehumanizing (seeing through the literal disease in my personal body to the archetypal and mythic), pathologizing (imagining the symptoms to be meaningful), and personifying (imaginally interacting with a chthonic goddess with guiding mythologies), the *psychoid* flesh wound of embodied misogyny may begin to heal.

Medusa, like Ereshkigal suffers alone in a dark cave of underworld alienation. As Marion Woodman suggests, "One aspect of the dark cave is the unconscious body, frozen as an iceberg, without personal feeling, made rigid [or petrified] by stress and driven-ness."[831] So, the body itself becomes a Medusan realm, and perhaps most vulnerable to becoming symptomatic are the rejected demonized organs of menstruation. Patriarchy ruptures connection with feeling "feminine" values because such values are *ir*-rational and condemned as inconvenient, unproductive, and potentially unpleasant. Similarly, physical processes and instincts are rendered shameful, disgusting, and conversely fascinating and titillating, the antipathy of decency and goodness. Sensitivity to natural cycles, emotions, and bodily needs conflict with linearity, driven-ness, productivity, efficiency, and other patriarchal values so that we live disembodied lives.

According to Woodman, "A disembodied woman is vulnerable to invasion by Medusa."[832] Rather than "invasion" I offer "visitation," for if encountered with consciousness and imagination, Medusa's presence, no matter how difficult, may be an opportunity for embodiment and wholeness. I do not deny that the process is painful, perhaps even treacherous. As Woodman observes, if a woman "commits herself to embodiment, she will experience the agony of the thaw as her molecules awaken to the pain of past and present."[833] However, refusal seems ultimately futile since the aspect of reality represented by goddesses like Medusa and Ereshkigal is essentially "things as they are;" concrete, amoral, paradoxically personal and impersonal, and inherently beyond our control[834] regardless of attempts by rational, patriarchal one-sidedness to demonize, sanitize, control, or deny these chthonic truths.

Woodman also associates women's sexuality with the Gorgon as a Medusan possession of a woman's sexuality within the suffering of life-denying anorexia. Medusa is seen as the antipathy to healing because she represents the rage manifest in perfectionism that destroys *eros*. The same observations seem apropos to endometriosis. But what if Medusa can be metaphorically reached, not identified with or denied but accepted in her real and necessary form as the mysterious *yin-yin* reality of death, which engenders regeneration; that is, the source of life? What if menstrual pain amplified by endometriosis is understood as Medusan calls to listen to a long forgotten feminine voice? A call to heal the splitting of *eros* itself into polarities of elevated subjective relatedness and demonized objective relatedness. Seeing through my lived experience by way of Inanna and Ereshkigal, with its pain and loss, fear and shame, the mind and body begin to come into functional relationship so that I can proceed with restorative dismemberment; Athene and the Gorgon can be made a relational unity.

Surgical "cure"

I now turn to the surgical intervention which seemingly (nine years out) eliminated my primary symptoms, including chronic pain, and released energy for the psycho-spiritual integration of which this book is the fruition. While the transformative work described above reveals substantial progress toward the reconciliation between feminine self and female body, the physical disease continued to rage within my body, once again threatening my life. The rules of nature typically proceed without compromise or exception even when mitigated by psycho-spiritual wisdom and efforts to expand one's consciousness. The organs of my pelvic girdle, like the petrified men and animals encountered by Perseus as he approached Medusa's cave, were irrevocably turned to stone. The only hope was to cut away the monstrous head of Medusa manifest in my tortured womb.

Despite hysterectomy's widespread acceptance and frequency— recall that an estimated 600,000 American woman undergo the procedure annually—it is not a benign or easy intervention in the short or long run. Any major surgery poses primary and secondary risks, including death from complications, infection, or adverse reactions to anesthesia. Radical hysterectomy, or castration, which includes the removal of the ovaries, adds lifelong health risk factors, some of which are serious. I discussed many medical, psychological, and social issues surrounding hysterectomy at length in Chapter 2 and will not repeat the material here. However, recall that female castration results in a precipitous loss of estrogen, instantly plunging a woman into medical menopause characterized by symptoms such as hot flashes, night sweats, insomnia, vaginal dryness, urinary tract infections, decreased sex drive, mood and cognitive disturbances, bladder control problems, fatigue, osteoporosis, heart disease, bowel obstruction due to surgical scarring, as well as grief and other psycho-spiritual complications.[835, 836, 837] Of course, hysterectomy may also provide the best and/or only intervention available to women who suffer from certain diseases and, when that is the case, the surgery is a necessary evil.

The medical story of hysterectomy, even when it offers the blessed "happy ending" of symptom relief does not engender healing for the feminine soul, which is wounded by this invasion. Hysterectomy may be an epic tale of heroic skill, concentration, and courage but it is simultaneously a bloody, penetrative assault on a chemically immobilized, but aware body and psyche. Perhaps the fundamental, guiding intention is restoration by controlled destruction. Here, I see the myth of Athene's beheading of the Gorgon Medusa.

My surgery was extensive and invasive. It resulted in both immense symptom relief and long-term health consequences, including bone mass loss. From a mythopoetic perspective, the surgery deftly excised the petrifying head of the Gorgon, which had the effect of liberating my creative spirit and facilitating renewal of my chthonic nature; delivering my Pegasos and Chrysaor. By cutting away the embodied misogyny, personified as a literalized Gorgoneion, I was freed from crushing, deadly symptoms and able to gestate psycho-spiritual children of my creative spirit. The myth of Inanna and Ereshkigal provided a template for approaching suffering so that I could "listen to" and empathize with my dis-eased womb, and accept, grieve, and ritualize the surgery. The myth of Medusa and Athene gives me a means of "repatterning" my disease experience.[838] Athene creates the Gorgon out of Medusa and then reclaims the Gorgoneion. Archetypally, my soul, as a *psychoid* phenomenon, incarnated my ravaged Medusan female-ness as Gorgon energy gone berserk—potentially regenerative tissue as uncontained and destructive. Through the surgery, the demonized-demonic Gorgon was depotentiated. Psyche's pathologizing has led me through metaphoric and concrete deconstruction and reconstruction of my body, the story of which is still unfolding. The Gorgon is freed from her monstrous manifestation as literalized evil and the deformity of non-male-ness. I can recognize her as the archetypal energy underlying the Gorgoneion masks of endometriosis and other denigrated or feared indigenous female body processes. Relating to her means "listening to" feelings, sensations, dreams, intuitions, and images as information (the way that pathologizing listens to symptoms as meaningful), engaging these phenomena through personification using imaginative tools like Jungian active imagination, journaling, art, movement, and shamanic journeying. Discerning and giving contained, creative, symbolic yet concrete form to embodied psycho-spiritual information requires relating to the material with non-judgmental acceptance and self-compassion. This *eros* approach, signified as Pallas Athene, raises the Medusan Gorgoneion from her literalized, diseased location in the cave of my body to her metaphorical place in my heart, where she can be honored and her impulses humanized.

In the most detailed telling of the story of Medusa's beheading, Perseus describes the task and takes the fullest measure of credit for the deed. I see this as the ego's version of the story and recognize its particular truth. My own integration of the Gorgon requires that my ego choose to both act and subordinate its desires in the process of relating to the needs of body and soul. But the story of Perseus can serve as a warning about the relationally destructive power of instinctive, chthonic energy when it is disconnected from any divine source. My emerging recognition of embodied misogyny can trigger rage against myself and outrage towards those I perceive of as defenders and beneficiaries of patriarchy. This rage ruptures relationship and engenders defense and attack rather than providing protection because it disrupts my ability to be present, discern what is true for me, and act accordingly. But, the terrible potency of the Gorgon, as the chthonic divine, is balanced when integrated as part of the wholeness of Athene as representative of the Great Goddess archetype. In fact, the chthonic divine completes Athene, giving the goddess her harmonious nature.

Perseus's version notwithstanding, from multiple accounts of Medusa's beheading, it is undeniably Athene who energizes and guides the affair, ultimately receiving the primary boon of Medusa's head. This archetypal truth resonates with my sense of being the recipient rather than the originator of this story of healing. I see Athene's discerning, highly effective action illuminating my assessment of my medical situation and execution of an option (to receive care in a different state) I would never have considered previously. The synchronicities guiding my choices of treatment, surgeon, and facility struck me even at the time. Like Athene, I was selective in my choice of hero and his methods.

Conclusion

While researching Athene for this book, I contemplated the possibility that she represented woman's adapted ego forming itself according to the patriarchal, rational, philosophical, religious, psychological, and social ideal of ego-hood. This was Athene as she might be lived out by patriarchal women, like me, through a one-sided ego stance; in Downing's words, Athene as the "exemplary female image" of the heroic-ego.[839] In this story, Medusa represented the female body as carrier of shadow and shame, the chthonic power concentrated in her head demonized, disembodied, and wielded in service to patriarchal desires for power—including the power to be inviolable. Athene was all rational reasonableness and Medusa irrational rage. I resented and admired Athene for her assimilation. I championed and loathed Medusa's rage.

The mythopoetic picture of Athene as feminine ego and Medusa as estranged female body expressed the split I had observed in myself and other women. However, the interpretation failed to foster healing, perhaps because it was the image of the split, emblematic of the tension, but not of what might emerge from the tension. Being focused on the split, I was caught in the dynamic of identifying with one pole or the other, that is, being possessed by the complexes constellated around my wounds. Neurobiologically, this behavior strengthens the neuropathways associated with the trauma and short circuits healing by reinforcing the neurochemistry of activation. From a depth psychological view, living the split defends against feeling the tension engendered by the schism, a tension that if felt can stimulate the healing transcendent function of the psyche. Then the psychological question that let me feel the tension rather than the split and facilitated resolution of the tension came to me: What is the meaning of the beheading? Is it the co-opting of female power/sexuality for use by the adapted feminine ego? Is it a reuniting of feminine wholeness?

In fact, Athene and the Gorgoneion Medusa are not split, they are a body, spirit, and soul—whole and complete. And this completeness is achieved by way of the beheading. Further, there is reciprocity within the relationship between Athene and Medusa. This reciprocity is the energy of functional wholeness. Athene Gorgopis is two-faced and whole, uniting, through chthonic and Olympic imagery, the divine androgyny manifest throughout creation and in the act of creating. Athene does not simply contain and wield the terrible Gorgoneion, channeling rage-filled affect for self-aggrandizement or destructive defensiveness. The Gorgon is part of Athene's identity, relating Athene to her own generative, gynocentric, chthonic beginnings and acting as apotropaic protection.

Edelman discerns a useful difference between the terms "protect" and "defend" with regards to *eros*. She sees protection as "an expression of the Eros function since, although it is protective, it still lies within the sphere of relationship;" that is, in relation to another and one's own sense of self-worth and self-knowledge, one discerns the appropriate level of vulnerability and openness within an exchange.[840] Conversely, defense "operates outside of the Eros function. It breaks and makes impossible any real relatedness—to others, since it isolates us behind a barricade, making our authentic self inaccessible; and to our own self, since psychic energy is being used to sustain the defensive position rather than to nourish the ego-self connection."[841] In other words, defensiveness is reactive; emerging out of a state of fear, it separates and ruptures interconnection. Protection is responsive; emerging out of self-love and respect (*aidos*), it discerns what is to be shared and what is to be contained in each particular exchange. Think of the protective nature of Athene's shield. Perseus uses the shield, which protects by reflecting the monstrous image of Medusa's denigrated form allowing him to excise it; an action requiring intimate proximity. Thanks to Athene, he does not employ his own defensive shield, a tool that would have separated him from Medusa and provided no true protection, rendering his task impossible. I think of the surgical video monitors reflecting images of endometriosis—difficult, if not impossible for the unaided human eye to see—allowing the surgeon's crafty excision of the diseased tissue.

Athene's action (with or without Perseus) does not render Medusa benign, for Athene's Gorgoneion is potently apotropaic and protective. The Gorgon expresses a chthonic, mysterious, non-rational reality; but not *necessarily* an evil. However, denigrated and scorned, the Gorgon manifests as "gratuitously destructive of whatever [comes] into view," including the organs of the human body.[842] Again, I do not claim that the psychological experience of misogyny literally causes endometriosis. What is efficacious for me is the mythopoetic interpretation of the disease as a meaningful visitation of the deity which engenders resolution of a sense of psychological victimhood. The resolution is not a physical cure, but a pattern of response available to me as demonstrated by Athene in her restoring of Medusa's honor and reverence at the level of the heart as the apotropaic Gorgoneion; not the Gorgoneion as the Evil Eye, but in her "dual role as protector and destroyer."[843] My own hysterectomy served as a Medusan decapitation, a cutting away of the "*form to which* [the feminine principle] *had been distorted*, in keeping with the truth that in every achievement of consciousness, something must die."[844] Edelman sees the beheading of Medusa as allowing Athene to raise the "Gorgon to consciousness and [restore] her to her proper place in the natural order."[845] Going a step further, Medusa's restoration is to the heart such that what is possible is a specific capacity of love—qualities of wisdom and compassion that facilitate reverential acceptance of the whole of creation including life and death, and are beyond ego preference, attraction, or aversion. This is a capacity of relationship that reunites subjective and objective *eros*.

Endometriosis has taught me this: as a sacred voice it revealed its meaning and guided or compelled my transformation until I could begin to wear my Medusan *aegis* properly, with the awe-ful regenerative Gorgoneion radiating from my heart. My dis-ease taught me compassion, courage, radical acceptance, surrender, love, and offered a path to reconciliation and integration into greater wholeness within my body, and the energy to take that reconciliation and integration to other wounded bodies—female, male, animal, and planet. The ecological aspects of the proven and hypothesized contributors to endometriosis imply to me a message of global desecration of the so-called feminine as a matter far beyond my personal suffering.

What I have come to understand is that this work has not been about proving that Medusa is the Goddess of Endometriosis through the law of association (although the associations are there) or through the analysis of compelling physical, psychological, social, and mythological parallels (although the parallels are compelling). Rather, to a great extent, my healing has been the realization that it was through my very human act of claiming Medusa as *my* Goddess of Endometriosis that she becomes so. By personifying my disease experience as Medusan, I put her at the center of my experience of the disease. That is, I made the experience sacred. Whether by choosing to see my endometriosis experience as meaningful I called in Medusa or simply recognized her presence, I do not know for sure. Regardless, my time at Medusa's altar has disillusioned me of the belief that I should, or could, redeem her from her fundamental nature by transforming her. In fact, it is she who is the redeemer; she who is the transformer. Her visitation has not been about transforming the Gorgon, but transforming myself through the acceptance of the forces she represents—including pain, disease, and mortality—and reverential love of chthonic reality as it is, within and outside of me. Clearly, apprehending and integrating Medusa's revelations is the work of a lifetime and it will always be a work in progress.

In closing, I return to a lovely episode in Ovid's narrative wherein the Gorgon's severed head becomes the source of coral. Recall that Perseus has heroically won Andromeda's freedom and love by defeating the sea monster threatening to devour her. Kneeling on the sand to wash after his labors and

> Fearing to bruise the Gorgon's snake-covered head on the hard sand, he softened the ground with leaves and covered it over with seaweed, to serve as a mat for the head of Medusa, the daughter of Phorcys. The fronds which were fresh and still abundant in spongy pith absorbed the force of the Gorgon and hardened under her touch, acquiring a strange new stiffness in all the stems and the foliage. The sea-nymphs tested this miracle out on additional fronds of seaweed. Excited to find this yielded the same result, they repeated the marvel by tossing the plant's seeds over the waves.[846]

Revealed in this story within a story are clues to the nature of the chthonic power of the Gorgon and the qualities of attitude required for an encounter with this force to be generative. First is the context of the marriage, the *hieros gamos*, which signifies the union of opposites. Like the image of Athene wearing her Gorgoneion *aegis*, the sacred marriage signifies the work of reconciling and integrating dynamic complements into a functional, creative whole. Next, within this restorative context, Perseus treats Medusa's head with uncharacteristic reverence and care. Rather than wielding the chthonic feminine lethality, he returns her to earth and verdancy (like Frothingham's vegetation Gorgoneion). Perseus's expressions of protection and reverence exemplify a masculine attitude devoid of scorn or appetite toward the archetypal feminine. In response to this treatment, Medusa's Great Goddess power to form and transform is creatively metamorphic. Finally, we have the female sea-nymphs; curious and excited by Medusa's generative, transforming effects they *play* with the magic, propagating the wonder and facilitating creation of an undersea ecosystem as fecund and diverse as any on the planet.

Two elements seem especially instructive. The essential nature of the Gorgon's magic does not change—she still petrifies. One way to consider this fact is that death is still death even when revered as a sacred part of the great round of life. Death engenders a fundamental metamorphosis which is deeply mysterious and perhaps inevitably frightening to the typical Western ego complex. The supple, living, green leaves become rigid, losing their fleshy moist aliveness as they transform into a form that, to the untrained eye, appears inanimate. But of course, this "death" is an illusion. Coral is a marine invertebrate that is very much alive, growing and reproducing. This is not to say that the lesson of this myth is physical immortality, rather, I see an alternative understanding of the potent—and often painful— realities of death and disease, one that recognizes the indigenous re-generativity of death and the reciprocity of the life-death continuum. Essential to this interpretation, according to the myth, is a particularly "feminine," equanimous playfulness represented by the blithe curiosity and creativity of the sea-nymphs in response to Medusa's power. I see this *play* as the antidote to the rigid, defensive perfectionism that emanates from a soul and body burdened by the paralyzing dread of ontic shame before the Evil Eye of misogynistic scorn of or objectifying appetite for the feminine. Medusa called to me through the wounding of my endometriotic flesh (as she did Athene through the wounded female legacy of that Father's Daughter) to accept and love the realities of my embodied femaleness, despite the risks or consequences. As I ponder these words, I gaze upon an image of Pallas Athene by the Austrian symbolist painter Gustav Klimt, the Gorgon glittering upon her heart, and I sense that akin to the trembling *aidos* experienced before the chthonic divine, is joy. Joy—as it arises spontaneously in response to apprehending the wonder and awe of *all* of life—is incarnated, embodied in lived experience through playful creativity and creative play, which the sea-nymphs reveal, are also gifts of the Gorgon.

ACKNOWLEDGMENTS

My deepest gratitude to the countless Ones, seen and unseen, who loved, taught, sustained, and challenged me in this work including my family, Debra Romero, Charlotte Carlson, Jerome Bernstein, Patrick Mahaffey, Dennis Patrick Slattery, Alexander J. Shaia, Dorothy Hudson, Robin van Loben Sels, and Dr. Javier F. Magrina. And my enduring appreciation to Jennifer Leigh Selig for guiding this book to fruition.

ABOUT THE AUTHOR

Jaffa Vernon Frank, Ph.D., is an archetypal mythologist, licensed mental health counselor, and a woman with over 40 years of experience living with endometriosis. She teaches courses in the psychology of altruism, archetypes, and the evolution of consciousness at Southwestern College in Santa Fe, New Mexico.

NOTES

[1] Hillman, James. *Re-Visioning Psychology.* New York: Harper & Row, 1975. Print. 55.

[2] Ibid, 80.

[3] Ibid, 34.

[4] Doty, William G. *Mythography: The Study of Myths and Rituals.* 2nd ed. Tuscaloosa: U of Alabama P, 2000. Print. xv.

[5] Campbell, Joseph. Interview by Bill Moyers. *The Power of Myth.* Ed. Betty Sue Flowers. New York: Doubleday, 1988. Print. 51.

[6] Cook, Andrew S. *Stop Endometriosis and Pelvic Pain: What Every Woman and Her Doctor Need to Know.* Los Gatos, CA: Femsana, 2012. Print. 13.

[7] McDermott, Rachel Fell. "Kālī's New Frontiers: A Hindu Goddess on the Internet." *Encountering Kālī: In the Margins, at the Center, in the West.* Eds. Rachel Fell McDermott and Jeffrey J. Kripal. Berkeley: U of California P, 2003. 273-295. Print. 285.

[8] Winkelman, Michael. "Shamanism: A Biogenetic Perspective." *Science, Religion, and Society: An Encyclopedia of History, Culture, and Controversy.* Vol. 2. Eds. Arri Eisen and Gary Laderman. Armonk, NY: M.E. Sharpe, 2007. 621-632. Print.

[9] Ibid, 632.

[10] Batt, Ronald E. *A History of Endometriosis.* London: Springer, 2011. Print. 183.

[11] Redwine, David B. *Googling Endometriosis: The Lost Centuries.* Bend, OR: David B. Redwine, MD, 2012. Print. 250.

[12] Bulun, Serdar E. "Endometriosis." *New England Journ. of Medicine,* vol. 360, 15 Jan. 2009, pp. 268-79. *NEJM Group,* doi: 10.1056/nejmRA0804690. Accessed 23 Nov. 2015.

[13] Ibid.

[14] Herington, Jennifer L. et al. "Immune Interactions in Endometriosis." *Expert Review of Clinical Immunology,* vol. 7, no. 5, Sept. 2011, pp. 611-26. *PMC/NIH-PA,* doi: 10.1586/eci.11.53. Accessed 6 Oct. 2015.

[15] Bulun, Serdar E. "Endometriosis." *New England Journ. of Medicine,* vol. 360, 15 Jan. 2009, pp. 268-79. *NEJM Group,* doi: 10.1056/nejmRA0804690. Accessed 23 Nov. 2015.

[16] Redwine, David B. *Googling Endometriosis: The Lost Centuries.* Bend, OR: David B. Redwine, MD, 2012. Print. v.

[17] "Home: Facts about Endometriosis." World Endometriosis Society, Sept. 2015. World Endometriosis Research Foundation, endometriosis.ca/Facts-about-endometriosis.pdf. Accessed 19 Jan. 2016.

[18] Sasson, Isaac E., and Hugh S. Taylor. "Stem Cells and the Pathogenesis of Endometriosis." *Annals of the New York Academy of Sciences*, vol. 1127, Apr. 2008, pp. 106–15. *PMC/NIH-PA*, doi: 10.1196/annals.1434.014. Accessed 6 Oct. 2015.

[19] Cook, Andrew S. *Stop Endometriosis and Pelvic Pain: What Every Woman and Her Doctor Need to Know.* Los Gatos, CA: Femsana, 2012. Print. 59.

[20] "Disease Information and Support: FAQs." *Endofound.org*, 2017. *Endometriosis Foundation of America*, www.endofound.org/faq. Accessed 9 Sept. 2015.

[21] Cook, Andrew S. *Stop Endometriosis and Pelvic Pain: What Every Woman and Her Doctor Need to Know.* Los Gatos, CA: Femsana, 2012. Print. 40.

[22] Ibid, 45.

[23] Redwine, David B. *Googling Endometriosis: The Lost Centuries.* Bend, OR: David B. Redwine, MD, 2012. Print. ii.

[24] Agarwal, Neha, and Arulselvi Subramanian. "Endometriosis— Morphology, Clinical Presentations and Molecular Pathology." *Journ. of Laboratory Physicians,* vol. 2, no.1, Jan.-June 2010, pp. 1-9, *PMC/Medknow Publications,* doi: 10.4103/0974-2727.66699. Accessed 29 Sept. 2015.

[25] Ballweg, Mary Lou. "Research Reveals Disease is Starting Younger, Diagnosis Delayed." *Endometriosis: The Complete Reference for Taking Charge of Your Health.* Ed. Ballweg. Chicago: Contemporary, 2003. 343-60. Print. 352.

[26] Hutchison, Robert. "'The Abdominal Woman:' An Address on the Chronic Abdomen." *The Endometriosis Sourcebook.* Ed. Mary Lou Ballweg. Chicago: Contemporary, 1995. 315-16. Print. 315.

[27] Redwine, David B. *Googling Endometriosis: The Lost Centuries.* Bend, OR: David B. Redwine, MD, 2012. Print. ii, 250.

[28] Ballweg, Mary Lou. "Endometriosis: A New Picture of the Disease Is Emerging." *The Endometriosis Sourcebook.* Ed. Ballweg. Chicago: Contemporary, 1995. 369-75. Print. 371.

[29] Ballweg, Mary Lou. "The Puzzle of Endometriosis." *The Endometriosis Sourcebook.* Ed. Ballweg. Chicago: Contemporary, 1995. 409-30. Print. 420.

[30] Delaney, Janice, Mary Jane Lupton, and Emily Toth. *The Curse: A Cultural History of Menstruation.* Urbana, IL: U of Illinois P, 1988. Print. 58.

[31] Ballweg, Mary Lou. "Endometriosis: A New Picture of the Disease Is Emerging." *The Endometriosis Sourcebook.* Ed. Ballweg. Chicago: Contemporary, 1995. 369-75. Print. 371.

[32] Hutchison, Robert. "'The Abdominal Woman:' An Address on the Chronic Abdomen." *The Endometriosis Sourcebook.* Ed. Mary Lou Ballweg. Chicago: Contemporary, 1995. 315-16. Print. 315.

[33] Ibid, 316.

[34] Ibid.

[35] Ibid.

[36] Ballweg, Mary Lou. "It's All in Your Head." *The Endometriosis Sourcebook.* Ed. Ballweg. Chicago: Contemporary, 1995. 295-321. Print. 305.

[37] Cook, Andrew S. *Stop Endometriosis and Pelvic Pain: What Every Woman and Her Doctor Need to Know.* Los Gatos, CA: Femsana, 2012. Print. 122.

[38] Ballweg, Mary Lou. "It's All in Your Head." *The Endometriosis Sourcebook.* Ed. Ballweg. Chicago: Contemporary, 1995. 295-321. Print. 298.

[39] "Somatoform Disorders." Diagnostic and Statistical Manual of Mental Disorders: DSM-IV-TR. 4th ed. Washington, DC: American Psychiatric Assn, 2000. 485-90. Print. 490.

[40] Ibid.

[41] Ibid, 488.

[42] Ballweg, Mary Lou. "Research Reveals Disease is Starting Younger, Diagnosis Delayed." *Endometriosis: The Complete Reference for Taking Charge of Your Health.* Ed. Ballweg. Chicago: Contemporary, 2003. 343-60. Print. 352.

[43] Ballweg, Mary Lou. "Endometriosis: A New Picture of the Disease Is Emerging." *The Endometriosis Sourcebook.* Ed. Ballweg. Chicago: Contemporary, 1995. 369-75. Print. 371.

[44] Ballard, Karen, Karen Lowton, and Jeremy Wright. "What's the Delay? A Qualitative Study of Women's Experiences of Reaching a Diagnosis of Endometriosis." *Fertility and Sterility: The American Society of Reproductive Medicine,* vol. 86, no. 5, Nov. 2006, pp. 1296-301. *Elsevier Inc,* doi: 10.1016/j.fertnstert.2006.04.054. Accessed 1 Oct. 2015.

[45] Ballweg, Mary Lou. "It's All in Your Head." *The Endometriosis Sourcebook.* Ed. Ballweg. Chicago: Contemporary, 1995. 295-321. Print. 301.

[46] Ballweg, Mary Lou. "The Puzzle of Endometriosis." *The Endometriosis Sourcebook.* Ed. Ballweg. Chicago: Contemporary, 1995. 409-30. Print. 425.

[47] Redwine, David B. *Googling Endometriosis: The Lost Centuries.* Bend, OR: David B. 425. Redwine, MD, 2012. Print. 110.

[48] Herington, Jennifer L. et al. "Immune Interactions in Endometriosis." *Expert Review of Clinical Immunology,* vol. 7, no. 5, Sept. 2011, pp. 611-26. *PMC/NIH-PA,* doi: 10.1586/eci.11.53. Accessed 6 Oct. 2015.

[49] Redwine, David B. *Googling Endometriosis: The Lost Centuries.* Bend, OR: David B. Redwine, MD, 2012. Print. 110.

[50] Campbell, P. Fay. "Endo: What a Pain It Is!" *Endometriosis: The Complete Reference for Taking Charge of Your Health.* Ed. Mary Lou Ballweg. Chicago: Contemporary, 2003. 9-28. Print. 11.

51 Agarwal, Neha, and Arulselvi Subramanian. "Endometriosis—
    Morphology, Clinical Presentations and Molecular Pathology." *Journ.
    of Laboratory Physicians,* vol. 2, no.1, Jan.-June 2010, pp. 1-9,
    PMC/Medknow Publications, doi: 10.4103/0974-2727.66699. Accessed
    29 Sept. 2015.

52 Ibid.

53 Herington, Jennifer L. et al. "Immune Interactions in Endometriosis."
    Expert Review of Clinical Immunology, vol. 7, no. 5, Sept. 2011, pp. 611-
    26. *PMC/NIH-PA,* doi: 10.1586/eci.11.53. Accessed 6 Oct. 2015.

54 Henderson, Lorraine, and Ros Wood. *Explaining Endometriosis.* St.
    Leonards, NSW: Allen & Unwin, 2000. Print. 17.

55 Mains, Barbara. "Endometriosis and Pain." *The Endometriosis Sourcebook.*
    Ed. Mary Lou Ballweg. Chicago: Contemporary, 1995. 35-40. Print.
    44.

56 Agarwal, Neha, and Arulselvi Subramanian. "Endometriosis—
    Morphology, Clinical Presentations and Molecular Pathology." *Journ.
    of Laboratory Physicians,* vol. 2, no.1, Jan.-June 2010, pp. 1-9,
    PMC/Medknow Publications, doi: 10.4103/0974-2727.66699. Accessed
    29 Sept. 2015.

57 Ballweg, Mary Lou. "What is Endometriosis?" Endometriosis: The
    Complete Reference for *Taking Charge of Your Health.* Ed. Ballweg.
    Chicago: Contemporary, 2003. 1-6. Print. 1.

58 Henderson, Lorraine, and Ros Wood. *Explaining Endometriosis.* St.
    Leonards, NSW: Allen & Unwin, 2000. Print. 17-18.

59 Agarwal, Neha, and Arulselvi Subramanian. "Endometriosis—
    Morphology, Clinical Presentations and Molecular Pathology." *Journ.
    of Laboratory Physicians,* vol. 2, no.1, Jan.-June 2010, pp. 1-9,
    PMC/Medknow Publications, doi: 10.4103/0974-2727.66699. Accessed
    29 Sept. 2015.

60 Redwine, David B. *Googling Endometriosis: The Lost Centuries.* Bend, OR:
    David B. Redwine, MD, 2012. Print. 224.

61 Ballweg, Mary Lou. "The Enigma Called Endometriosis." *The
    Endometriosis Sourcebook.* Ed. Ballweg. Chicago: Contemporary, 1995.
    10-15. Print. 10.

62 Henderson, Lorraine, and Ros Wood. *Explaining Endometriosis.* St.
    Leonards, NSW: Allen & Unwin, 2000. Print. 18.

63 Hummelshoj, Lone, ed. "About Endometriosis: Causes." *Endometriosis.org:
    The Global Forum for News and Information,* 5 Apr. 2011,
    endometriosis.org/endometriosis/causes/. Accessed 8 Sept. 2015.

64 Henderson, Lorraine, and Ros Wood. *Explaining Endometriosis.* St.
    Leonards, NSW: Allen & Unwin, 2000. Print. 18, 40.

65 Ibid, 18.

66 Mains, Barbara. "Endometriosis and Pain." *The Endometriosis Sourcebook.* Ed. Mary Lou Ballweg. Chicago: Contemporary, 1995. 35-40. Print. 42.

67 Agarwal, Neha, and Arulselvi Subramanian. "Endometriosis—Morphology, Clinical Presentations and Molecular Pathology." *Journ. of Laboratory Physicians,* vol. 2, no.1, Jan.-June 2010, pp. 1-9, *PMC/Medknow Publications,* doi: 10.4103/0974-2727.66699. Accessed 29 Sept. 2015.

68 Ibid.

69 Ballweg, Mary Lou. "The Puzzle of Endometriosis." *The Endometriosis Sourcebook.* Ed. Ballweg. Chicago: Contemporary, 1995. 409-30. Print. 412.

70 Campbell, P. Fay. "Endo: What a Pain It Is!" *Endometriosis: The Complete Reference for Taking Charge of Your Health.* Ed. Mary Lou Ballweg. Chicago: Contemporary, 2003. 9-28. Print. 13.

71 Ballweg, Mary Lou. "What is Endometriosis?" Endometriosis: The Complete Reference for *Taking Charge of Your Health.* Ed. Ballweg. Chicago: Contemporary, 2003. 1-6. Print. 2.

72 Henderson, Lorraine, and Ros Wood. *Explaining Endometriosis.* St. Leonards, NSW: Allen & Unwin, 2000. Print. 19.

73 Ballweg, Mary Lou. "Endometriosis and the Intestines." *The Endometriosis Sourcebook.* Ed. Ballweg. Chicago: Contemporary, 1995. 197-208. Print. 199-200.

74 Redwine, David B. *Googling Endometriosis: The Lost Centuries.* Bend, OR: David B. Redwine, MD, 2012. Print. 53.

75 Yap, Andrea Lea. "Endometriosis and the Urinary Tract." *The Endometriosis Sourcebook.* Ed. Mary Lou Ballweg. Chicago: Contemporary, 1995. 211-25. Print. 220.

76 Mains, Barbara. "Endometriosis and Pain." *The Endometriosis Sourcebook.* Ed. Mary Lou Ballweg. Chicago: Contemporary, 1995. 35-40. Print. 38.

77 Herington, Jennifer L. et al. "Immune Interactions in Endometriosis." *Expert Review of Clinical Immunology,* vol. 7, no. 5, Sept. 2011, pp. 611-26. *PMC/NIH-PA,* doi: 10.1586/eci.11.53. Accessed 6 Oct. 2015.

78 Cook, Andrew S. *Stop Endometriosis and Pelvic Pain: What Every Woman and Her Doctor Need to Know.* Los Gatos, CA: Femsana, 2012. Print. 124.

79 Migaki, Grace I. "The Immune System: Part and Parcel of Endo." *Endometriosis: The Complete Reference for Taking Charge of Your Health.* Ed. Mary Lou Ballweg. Chicago: Contemporary, 2003. 157-78. Print. 172.

80 Campbell, P. Fay. "Endo: What a Pain It Is!" *Endometriosis: The Complete Reference for Taking Charge of Your Health.* Ed. Mary Lou Ballweg. Chicago: Contemporary, 2003. 9-28. Print. 10.

81 Ibid, 11.
82 Mains, Barbara. "Endometriosis and Pain." *The Endometriosis Sourcebook*.
    Ed. Mary Lou Ballweg. Chicago: Contemporary, 1995. 35-40. Print.
    39.
83 Cook, Andrew S. *Stop Endometriosis and Pelvic Pain: What Every Woman and
    Her Doctor Need to Know*. Los Gatos, CA: Femsana, 2012. Print. 125.
84 Ibid, 124.
85 Campbell, P. Fay. "Endo: What a Pain It Is!" *Endometriosis: The Complete
    Reference for Taking Charge of Your Health*. Ed. Mary Lou Ballweg.
    Chicago: Contemporary, 2003. 9-28. Print. 11.
86 Cook, Andrew S. *Stop Endometriosis and Pelvic Pain: What Every Woman and
    Her Doctor Need to Know*. Los Gatos, CA: Femsana, 2012. Print. 125.
87 Olive, David qtd. in Mains, Barbara. "Endometriosis and Pain." *The
    Endometriosis Sourcebook*. Ed. Mary Lou Ballweg. Chicago:
    Contemporary, 1995. 35-40. Print. 38.
88 Mains, Barbara. "Endometriosis and Pain." *The Endometriosis Sourcebook*.
    Ed. Mary Lou Ballweg. Chicago: Contemporary, 1995. 35-40. Print.
    39.
89 Cook, Andrew S. *Stop Endometriosis and Pelvic Pain: What Every Woman and
    Her Doctor Need to Know*. Los Gatos, CA: Femsana, 2012. Print. 126-
    29.
90 Ibid, 127.
91 Ibid, 128.
92 Ibid. 34.
93 Ballard, Karen, Karen Lowton, and Jeremy Wright. "What's the Delay? A
    Qualitative Study of Women's Experiences of Reaching a Diagnosis
    of Endometriosis." *Fertility and Sterility: The American Society of
    Reproductive Medicine*, vol. 86, no. 5, Nov. 2006, pp. 1296-301. *Elsevier
    Inc*, doi: 10.1016/j.fertnstert.2006.04.054. Accessed 1 Oct. 2015.
94 Campbell, P. Fay. "Endo: What a Pain It Is!" *Endometriosis: The Complete
    Reference for Taking Charge of Your Health*. Ed. Mary Lou Ballweg.
    Chicago: Contemporary, 2003. 9-28. Print. 15.
95 Delaney, Janice, Mary Jane Lupton, and Emily Toth. *The Curse: A Cultural
    History of Menstruation*. Urbana, IL: U of Illinois P, 1988. Print. 7.
96 Houppert, Karen. *The Curse: Confronting the Last Unmentionable Taboo:
    Menstruation*. New York: Farrar, Straus and Giroux, 1999. Print. 6-7.
97 Ibid, 6.
98 Ibid, 7.
99 Ibid, 6-7.
100 Martin, Emily. *The Woman in the Body: A Cultural Analysis of Reproduction*.
    Boston: Beacon P, 1987. Print. 35.
101 Ibid, 45.

[102] Ibid, 46.

[103] Ibid, 47.

[104] Dougherty, Elizabeth. "Endometriosis and Infertility." *Endometriosis: The Complete Reference for Taking Charge of Your Health.* Ed. Mary Lou Ballweg. Chicago: Contemporary, 2003. 133-46. Print. 133.

[105] Corman, Cathy. "Infertility and Endometriosis." *The Endometriosis Sourcebook.* Ed. Mary Lou Ballweg. Chicago: Contemporary, 1995. 237-47. Print. 239.

[106] Ballweg, Mary Lou."Pregnancy, Labor, and Postpartum Experiences of Women with Endometriosis." *The Endometriosis Sourcebook.* Ed. Ballweg. Chicago: Contemporary, 1995. 248-57. Print. 249.

[107] Agarwal, Neha, and Arulselvi Subramanian. "Endometriosis—Morphology, Clinical Presentations and Molecular Pathology." *Journ. of Laboratory Physicians,* vol. 2, no.1, Jan.-June 2010, pp. 1-9, *PMC/Medknow Publications,* doi: 10.4103/0974-2727.66699. Accessed 29 Sept. 2015.

[108] Henderson, Lorraine, and Ros Wood. *Explaining Endometriosis.* St. Leonards, NSW: Allen & Unwin, 2000. Print. 115-116.

[109] Dougherty, Elizabeth. "Endometriosis and Infertility." *Endometriosis: The Complete Reference for Taking Charge of Your Health.* Ed. Mary Lou Ballweg. Chicago: Contemporary, 2003. 133-46. Print. 134.

[110] Bulun, Serdar E. "Endometriosis." *New England Journ. of Medicine,* vol. 360, 15 Jan. 2009, pp. 268-79. *NEJM Group,* doi: 10.1056/nejmRA0804690. Accessed 23 Nov. 2015.

[111] Ibid.

[112] Dougherty, Elizabeth. "Endometriosis and Infertility." *Endometriosis: The Complete Reference for Taking Charge of Your Health.* Ed. Mary Lou Ballweg. Chicago: Contemporary, 2003. 133-46. Print. 134-35.

[113] Ballweg, Mary Lou. "Pregnancy, Labor, and Postpartum Experiences of Women with Endometriosis." *The Endometriosis Sourcebook.* Ed. Ballweg. Chicago: Contemporary, 1995. 248-57. Print. 255.

[114] Bulun, Serdar E. "Endometriosis." *New England Journ. of Medicine,* vol. 360, 15 Jan. 2009, pp. 268-79. *NEJM Group,* doi: 10.1056/nejmRA0804690. Accessed 23 Nov. 2015.

[115] Herington, Jennifer L. et al. "Immune Interactions in Endometriosis." *Expert Review of Clinical Immunology,* vol. 7, no. 5, Sept. 2011, pp. 611-26. *PMC/NIH-PA,* doi: 10.1586/eci.11.53. Accessed 6 Oct. 2015.

[116] Cook, Andrew S. *Stop Endometriosis and Pelvic Pain: What Every Woman and Her Doctor Need to Know.* Los Gatos, CA: Femsana, 2012. Print. 34.

[117] Redwine, David B. *Googling Endometriosis: The Lost Centuries.* Bend, OR: David B. Redwine, MD, 2012. Print. 18.

[118] Astruc, Jean qtd. in Redwine, David B. *Googling Endometriosis: The Lost Centuries*. Bend, OR: David B. Redwine, MD, 2012. Print. 68.

[119] Redwine, David B. *Googling Endometriosis: The Lost Centuries*. Bend, OR: David B. Redwine, MD, 2012. Print. 208.

[120] Ibid, 18.

[121] Ibid, 11.

[122] Trota of Salerno qtd. in Redwine, David B. *Googling Endometriosis: The Lost Centuries*. Bend, OR: David B. Redwine, MD, 2012. Print. 52.

[123] Redwine, David B. *Googling Endometriosis: The Lost Centuries*. Bend, OR: David B. Redwine, MD, 2012. Print. 73.

[124] Mains, Barbara. "Pain Management." *The Endometriosis Sourcebook*. Ed. Mary Lou Ballweg. Chicago: Contemporary, 1995. 46-48. Print. 48.

[125] Redwine, David B. *Googling Endometriosis: The Lost Centuries*. Bend, OR: David B. Redwine, MD, 2012. Print. 137.

[126] Gunning, Bedford qtd. in Redwine, David B. *Googling Endometriosis: The Lost Centuries*. Bend, OR: David B. Redwine, MD, 2012. Print. 134-35.

[127] Astruc, Jean qtd. in Redwine, David B. *Googling Endometriosis: The Lost Centuries*. Bend, OR: David B. Redwine, MD, 2012. Print. 69.

[128] Aristotle qtd. in Delaney, Janice, Mary Jane Lupton, and Emily Toth. *The Curse: A Cultural History of Menstruation*. Urbana, IL: U of Illinois P, 1988. Print. 46.

[129] Delaney, Janice, Mary Jane Lupton, and Emily Toth. *The Curse: A Cultural History of Menstruation*. Urbana, IL: U of Illinois P, 1988. Print. 47.

[130] Ibid.

[131] Ibid, 48.

[132] Schwebach, Lynn S. "Learning to Cope with Endometriosis." *The Endometriosis Sourcebook*. Ed. Mary Lou Ballweg. Chicago: Contemporary, 1995. 277-93. Print. 286.

[133] Ballweg, Mary Lou. "It's All in Your Head." *The Endometriosis Sourcebook*. Ed. Ballweg. Chicago: Contemporary, 1995. 295-321. Print. 304.

[134] Ibid, 309.

[135] Cook, Andrew S. *Stop Endometriosis and Pelvic Pain: What Every Woman and Her Doctor Need to Know*. Los Gatos, CA: Femsana, 2012. Print. 34.

[136] Ballweg, Mary Lou. "It's All in Your Head." *The Endometriosis Sourcebook*. Ed. Ballweg. Chicago: Contemporary, 1995. 295-321. Print. 306.

[137] Batt, Ronald E. *A History of Endometriosis*. London: Springer, 2011. Print. xiii.

[138] Ibid, xxiv.

[139] Ibid, xxiv n10.

[140] Herington, Jennifer L. et al. "Immune Interactions in Endometriosis." *Expert Review of Clinical Immunology*, vol. 7, no. 5, Sept. 2011, pp. 611-26. *PMC/NIH-PA*, doi: 10.1586/eci.11.53. Accessed 6 Oct. 2015.

[141] Cook, Andrew S. *Stop Endometriosis and Pelvic Pain: What Every Woman and Her Doctor Need to Know*. Los Gatos, CA: Femsana, 2012. Print. 86.

[142] Sasson, Isaac E., and Hugh S. Taylor. "Stem Cells and the Pathogenesis of Endometriosis." *Annals of the New York Academy of Sciences*, vol. 1127, Apr. 2008, pp. 106–15. *PMC/NIH-PA*, doi: 10.1196/annals.1434.014. Accessed 6 Oct. 2015.

[143] Batt, Ronald E. *A History of Endometriosis*. London: Springer, 2011. Print. 179.

[144] Sasson, Isaac E., and Hugh S. Taylor. "Stem Cells and the Pathogenesis of Endometriosis." *Annals of the New York Academy of Sciences*, vol. 1127, Apr. 2008, pp. 106–15. *PMC/NIH-PA*, doi: 10.1196/annals.1434.014. Accessed 6 Oct. 2015.

[145] Bulun, Serdar E. "Endometriosis." *New England Journ. of Medicine*, vol. 360, 15 Jan. 2009, pp. 268-79. *NEJM Group*, doi: 10.1056/nejmRA0804690. Accessed 23 Nov. 2015.

[146] Ibid.

[147] Agarwal, Neha, and Arulselvi Subramanian. "Endometriosis—Morphology, Clinical Presentations and Molecular Pathology." *Journ. of Laboratory Physicians*, vol. 2, no.1, Jan.-June 2010, pp. 1-9, *PMC/Medknow Publications*, doi: 10.4103/0974-2727.66699. Accessed 29 Sept. 2015.

[148] Sasson, Isaac E., and Hugh S. Taylor. "Stem Cells and the Pathogenesis of Endometriosis." *Annals of the New York Academy of Sciences*, vol. 1127, Apr. 2008, pp. 106–15. *PMC/NIH-PA*, doi: 10.1196/annals.1434.014. Accessed 6 Oct. 2015.

[149] Batt, Ronald E. *A History of Endometriosis*. London: Springer, 2011. Print. 182.

[150] Ibid, 190-91.

[151] Bulun, Serdar E. "Endometriosis." *New England Journ. of Medicine*, vol. 360, 15 Jan. 2009, pp. 268-79. *NEJM Group*, doi: 10.1056/nejmRA0804690. Accessed 23 Nov. 2015.

[152] Redwine, David B. *Googling Endometriosis: The Lost Centuries*. Bend, OR: David B. Redwine, MD, 2012. Print. 19.

[153] Ibid, 249.

[154] Ibid.

[155] Batt, Ronald E. *A History of Endometriosis*. London: Springer, 2011. Print. 179.

[156] Ibid, 180.

[157] Ibid, 203.

158 Agarwal, Neha, and Arulselvi Subramanian. "Endometriosis—
    Morphology, Clinical Presentations and Molecular Pathology." *Journ.
    of Laboratory Physicians,* vol. 2, no.1, Jan.-June 2010, pp. 1-9,
    PMC/Medknow Publications, doi: 10.4103/0974-2727.66699. Accessed
    29 Sept. 2015.
159 Henderson, Lorraine, and Ros Wood. *Explaining Endometriosis.* St.
    Leonards, NSW: Allen & Unwin, 2000. Print. 111.
160 Sasson, Isaac E., and Hugh S. Taylor. "Stem Cells and the Pathogenesis
    of Endometriosis." *Annals of the New York Academy of Sciences,* vol.
    1127, Apr. 2008, pp. 106–15. *PMC/NIH-PA,* doi:
    10.1196/annals.1434.014. Accessed 6 Oct. 2015.
161 Agarwal, Neha, and Arulselvi Subramanian. "Endometriosis—
    Morphology, Clinical Presentations and Molecular Pathology." *Journ.
    of Laboratory Physicians,* vol. 2, no.1, Jan.-June 2010, pp. 1-9,
    PMC/Medknow Publications, doi: 10.4103/0974-2727.66699. Accessed
    29 Sept. 2015.
162 Ballweg, Mary Lou. "The Enigma Called Endometriosis." *The
    Endometriosis Sourcebook.* Ed. Ballweg. Chicago: Contemporary, 1995.
    10-15. Print. 11.
163 Agarwal, Neha, and Arulselvi Subramanian. "Endometriosis—
    Morphology, Clinical Presentations and Molecular Pathology." *Journ.
    of Laboratory Physicians,* vol. 2, no.1, Jan.-June 2010, pp. 1-9,
    PMC/Medknow Publications, doi: 10.4103/0974-2727.66699. Accessed
    29 Sept. 2015.
164 Sasson, Isaac E., and Hugh S. Taylor. "Stem Cells and the Pathogenesis
    of Endometriosis." *Annals of the New York Academy of Sciences,* vol.
    1127, Apr. 2008, pp. 106–15. *PMC/NIH-PA,* doi:
    10.1196/annals.1434.014. Accessed 6 Oct. 2015.
165 Ibid.
166 Ibid.
167 Ibid.
168 Ibid.
169 Ibid.
170 Ibid.
171 "Epigenomics." *National Human Genome Research Institute,* 1 Apr. 2016.
    National Institutes of Health, www.genome.gov/27532724/. Accessed
    19 Oct. 2015.
172 "Epigenetics." *Learn.Genetics,* 15 July 2013. *Genetic Science Learning
    Center/U of Utah Health Sciences,*
    learn.genetics.utah.edu/content/epigenetics/. *Accessed 19 Oct. 2015.*
173 Cook, Andrew S. *Stop Endometriosis and Pelvic Pain: What Every Woman and
    Her Doctor Need to Know.* Los Gatos, CA: Femsana, 2012. Print. 18.

174 Hummelshoj, Lone, ed. "About Endometriosis: Causes."
Endometriosis.org: The Global Forum for News and Information, 5 Apr. 2011,
endometriosis.org/endometriosis/causes/. Accessed 8 Sept. 2015.

175 Frisch, Rose qtd. in "Preventing Endometriosis: It May Be Possible!"
Endometriosis: The Complete Reference for Taking Charge of Your Health. Ed.
Mary Lou Ballweg. Chicago: Contemporary, 2003. 305-40. Print. 308.

176 Sasson, Isaac E., and Hugh S. Taylor. "Stem Cells and the Pathogenesis
of Endometriosis." *Annals of the New York Academy of Sciences*, vol.
1127, Apr. 2008, pp. 106–15. *PMC/NIH-PA*, doi:
10.1196/annals.1434.014. Accessed 6 Oct. 2015.

177 Migaki, Grace I. "The Immune System: Part and Parcel of Endo."
Endometriosis: The Complete Reference for Taking Charge of Your Health. Ed.
Mary Lou Ballweg. Chicago: Contemporary, 2003. 157-78. Print. 168.

178 Ibid, 169-73.

179 Ibid, 175.

180 Herington, Jennifer L. et al. "Immune Interactions in Endometriosis."
Expert Review of Clinical Immunology, vol. 7, no. 5, Sept. 2011, pp. 611-
26. *PMC/NIH-PA,* doi: 10.1586/eci.11.53. Accessed 6 Oct. 2015.

181 Ibid.

182 Ibid.

183 Migaki, Grace I. "The Immune System: Part and Parcel of Endo."
Endometriosis: The Complete Reference for Taking Charge of Your Health. Ed.
Mary Lou Ballweg. Chicago: Contemporary, 2003. 157-78. Print. 174.

184 Herington, Jennifer L. et al. "Immune Interactions in Endometriosis."
Expert Review of Clinical Immunology, vol. 7, no. 5, Sept. 2011, pp. 611-
26. *PMC/NIH-PA,* doi: 10.1586/eci.11.53. Accessed 6 Oct. 2015.

185 Cook, Andrew S. *Stop Endometriosis and Pelvic Pain: What Every Woman and
Her Doctor Need to Know*. Los Gatos, CA: Femsana, 2012. Print. 138-
39, 142.

186 Campbell, P. Fay. "Endo: What a Pain It Is!" *Endometriosis: The Complete
Reference for Taking Charge of Your Health*. Ed. Mary Lou Ballweg.
Chicago: Contemporary, 2003. 9-28. Print. 12.

187 Migaki, Grace I. "The Immune System: Part and Parcel of Endo."
Endometriosis: The Complete Reference for Taking Charge of Your Health. Ed.
Mary Lou Ballweg. Chicago: Contemporary, 2003. 157-78. Print. 163.

188 Herington, Jennifer L. et al. "Immune Interactions in Endometriosis."
Expert Review of Clinical Immunology, vol. 7, no. 5, Sept. 2011, pp. 611-
26. *PMC/NIH-PA,* doi: 10.1586/eci.11.53. Accessed 6 Oct. 2015.

189 Ballweg, Mary Lou. "Research Reveals Disease is Starting Younger,
Diagnosis Delayed." *Endometriosis: The Complete Reference for Taking
Charge of Your Health*. Ed. Ballweg. Chicago: Contemporary, 2003.
343-60. Print. 352.

190 Ballweg, Mary Lou. "Endometriosis and Environmental Toxins." *The Endometriosis Sourcebook.* Ed. Ballweg. Chicago: Contemporary, 1995. 377-82. Print. 377.

191 Ibid.

192 Bulun, Serdar E. "Endometriosis." *New England Journ. of Medicine,* vol. 360, 15 Jan. 2009, pp. 268-79. *NEJM Group,* doi: 10.1056/nejmRA0804690. Accessed 23 Nov. 2015.

193 "Diethylstilbestrol (DES) and Cancer." *National Cancer Institute* 5 Oct. 2011, *National Institutes of Health,* www.cancer.gov/about-cancer/causes-prevention/risk/hormones/des-fact-sheet. Accessed 23 Nov. 2015.

194 Ibid.

195 Herington, Jennifer L. et al. "Immune Interactions in Endometriosis." *Expert Review of Clinical Immunology,* vol. 7, no. 5, Sept. 2011, pp. 611-26. *PMC/NIH-PA,* doi: 10.1586/eci.11.53. Accessed 6 Oct. 2015.

196 Cook, Andrew S. *Stop Endometriosis and Pelvic Pain: What Every Woman and Her Doctor Need to Know.* Los Gatos, CA: Femsana, 2012. Print. 21-22.

197 Ballweg, Mary Lou. "Endometriosis and Environmental Toxins." *The Endometriosis Sourcebook.* Ed. Ballweg. Chicago: Contemporary, 1995. 377-82. Print. 377.

198 Cook, Andrew S. *Stop Endometriosis and Pelvic Pain: What Every Woman and Her Doctor Need to Know.* Los Gatos, CA: Femsana, 2012. Print. 21.

199 Ballweg, Mary Lou. "Endometriosis and Environmental Toxins." *The Endometriosis Sourcebook.* Ed. Ballweg. Chicago: Contemporary, 1995. 377-98. Print. 389.

200 Ibid, 379.

201 Herington, Jennifer L. et al. "Immune Interactions in Endometriosis." *Expert Review of Clinical Immunology,* vol. 7, no. 5, Sept. 2011, pp. 611-26. *PMC/NIH-PA,* doi: 10.1586/eci.11.53. Accessed 6 Oct. 2015.

202 Ibid.

203 "IARC Monographs on the Evaluation of Carcinogenic Risks to Humans." *International Agency for Research on Cancer,* vol. 69, 4-11 Feb. 1997, pp. 339-40, World Health Organization, monographs.iarc.fr/ENG/Monographs/vol69/mono69-5E.pdf. Accessed13 Nov. 2015.

204 Cook, Andrew S. *Stop Endometriosis and Pelvic Pain: What Every Woman and Her Doctor Need to Know.* Los Gatos, CA: Femsana, 2012. Print. 22.

205 Ballweg, Mary Lou. "Dioxins, PCBs, and Endometriosis—What Do We Need to Know to Protect Ourselves?" *The Endometriosis Sourcebook.* Ed. Ballweg. Chicago: Contemporary, 1995. 385-94. Print. 388.

206 Herington, Jennifer L. et al. "Immune Interactions in Endometriosis." *Expert Review of Clinical Immunology*, vol. 7, no. 5, Sept. 2011, pp. 611-26. *PMC/NIH-PA*, doi: 10.1586/eci.11.53. Accessed 6 Oct. 2015.

207 "IARC Monographs on the Evaluation of Carcinogenic Risks to Humans." *International Agency for Research on Cancer*, vol. 69, 4-11 Feb. 1997, pp. 339-40, World Health Organization, monographs.iarc.fr/ENG/Monographs/vol69/mono69-5E.pdf. Accessed13 Nov. 2015.

208 Ballweg, Mary Lou. "Dioxins, PCBs, and Endometriosis—What Do We Need to Know to Protect Ourselves?" *The Endometriosis Sourcebook*. Ed. Ballweg. Chicago: Contemporary, 1995. 385-94. Print. 386.

209 "IARC Monographs on the Evaluation of Carcinogenic Risks to Humans." *International Agency for Research on Cancer*, vol. 69, 4-11 Feb. 1997, pp. 339-40, World Health Organization, monographs.iarc.fr/ENG/Monographs/vol69/mono69-5E.pdf. Accessed13 Nov. 2015.

210 "Dioxin: A Fact Sheet." *Center for Health, Environment & Justice,*17 Feb. 2012. *People's Action Institute*, chej.org/wp-content/uploads/Documents/DioxinFactSheet.pdf. Accessed 13 Nov. 2015.

211 "IARC Monographs on the Evaluation of Carcinogenic Risks to Humans." *International Agency for Research on Cancer*, vol. 69, 4-11 Feb. 1997, pp. 339-40, World Health Organization, monographs.iarc.fr/ENG/Monographs/vol69/mono69-5E.pdf. Accessed13 Nov. 2015. 339-40.

212 Ballweg, Mary Lou. "Dioxins, PCBs, and Endometriosis—What Do We Need to Know to Protect Ourselves?" *The Endometriosis Sourcebook*. Ed. Ballweg. Chicago: Contemporary, 1995. 385-94. Print. 386.

213 Ibid.

214 Agarwal, Neha, and Arulselvi Subramanian. "Endometriosis—Morphology, Clinical Presentations and Molecular Pathology." *Journ. of Laboratory Physicians,* vol. 2, no.1, Jan.-June 2010, pp. 1-9, *PMC/Medknow Publications,* doi: 10.4103/0974-2727.66699. Accessed 29 Sept. 2015.

215 Henderson, Lorraine, and Ros Wood. *Explaining Endometriosis*. St. Leonards, NSW: Allen & Unwin, 2000. Print. 38.

216 Agarwal, Neha, and Arulselvi Subramanian. "Endometriosis—Morphology, Clinical Presentations and Molecular Pathology." *Journ. of Laboratory Physicians,* vol. 2, no.1, Jan.-June 2010, pp. 1-9, *PMC/Medknow Publications,* doi: 10.4103/0974-2727.66699. Accessed 29 Sept. 2015.

217 Ballard, Karen, Karen Lowton, and Jeremy Wright. "What's the Delay?
A Qualitative Study of Women's Experiences of Reaching a
Diagnosis of Endometriosis." *Fertility and Sterility: The American Society
of Reproductive Medicine,* vol. 86, no. 5, Nov. 2006, pp. 1296-301. *Elsevier
Inc,* doi: 10.1016/j.fertnstert.2006.04.054. Accessed 1 Oct. 2015.

218 Cook, Andrew S. *Stop Endometriosis and Pelvic Pain: What Every Woman and
Her Doctor Need to Know.* Los Gatos, CA: Femsana, 2012. Print. 63.

219 Henderson, Lorraine, and Ros Wood. *Explaining Endometriosis.* St.
Leonards, NSW: Allen & Unwin, 2000. Print. 37.

220 Ballweg, Mary Lou. "What is Endometriosis?" Endometriosis: The
Complete Reference for *Taking Charge of Your Health.* Ed. Mary Lou
Ballweg. Chicago: Contemporary, 2003. 1-6. Print. 3.

221 Redwine, David B. *Googling Endometriosis: The Lost Centuries.* Bend, OR:
David B. Redwine, MD, 2012. Print. 111.

222 Mains, Barbara. "Endometriosis and Pain." *The Endometriosis Sourcebook.*
Ed. Mary Lou Ballweg. Chicago: Contemporary, 1995. 35-40. Print.
38.

223 Cook, Andrew S. *Stop Endometriosis and Pelvic Pain: What Every Woman and
Her Doctor Need to Know.* Los Gatos, CA: Femsana, 2012. Print. 126.

224 Agarwal, Neha, and Arulselvi Subramanian. "Endometriosis—
Morphology, Clinical Presentations and Molecular Pathology." *Journ.
of Laboratory Physicians,* vol. 2, no.1, Jan.-June 2010, pp. 1-9,
PMC/Medknow Publications, doi: 10.4103/0974-2727.66699. Accessed
29 Sept. 2015.

225 Olive, David qtd. in Mains, Barbara. "Endometriosis and Pain." *The
Endometriosis Sourcebook.* Ed. Mary Lou Ballweg. Chicago:
Contemporary, 1995. 35-40. Print. 38.

226 Agarwal, Neha, and Arulselvi Subramanian. "Endometriosis—
Morphology, Clinical Presentations and Molecular Pathology." *Journ.
of Laboratory Physicians,* vol. 2, no.1, Jan.-June 2010, pp. 1-9,
PMC/Medknow Publications, doi: 10.4103/0974-2727.66699. Accessed
29 Sept. 2015.

227 Ballard, Karen, Karen Lowton, and Jeremy Wright. "What's the Delay?
A Qualitative Study of Women's Experiences of Reaching a
Diagnosis of Endometriosis." *Fertility and Sterility: The American Society
of Reproductive Medicine,* vol. 86, no. 5, Nov. 2006, pp. 1296-301. *Elsevier
Inc,* doi: 10.1016/j.fertnstert.2006.04.054. Accessed 1 Oct. 2015.

228 Ibid.

229 Ibid.

230 Ibid.

231 Ibid.

232 Campbell, P. Fay. "Endo: What a Pain It Is!" *Endometriosis: The Complete Reference for Taking Charge of Your Health.* Ed. Mary Lou Ballweg. Chicago: Contemporary, 2003. 9-28. Print. 13.

233 Ibid, 16.

234 Ballweg, Mary Lou. "The Puzzle of Endometriosis." *The Endometriosis Sourcebook.* Ed. Mary Lou Ballweg. Chicago: Contemporary, 1995. 409-30. Print. 424-25.

235 Campbell, P. Fay. "Endo: What a Pain It Is!" *Endometriosis: The Complete Reference for Taking Charge of Your Health.* Ed. Mary Lou Ballweg. Chicago: Contemporary, 2003. 9-28. Print. 13.

236 Ballweg, Mary Lou. "It's All in Your Head." *The Endometriosis Sourcebook.* Ed. Ballweg. Chicago: Contemporary, 1995. 295-321. Print. 312.

237 Ibid, 313.

238 Ibid, 314.

239 Ibid.

240 Ballard, Karen, Karen Lowton, and Jeremy Wright. "What's the Delay? A Qualitative Study of Women's Experiences of Reaching a Diagnosis of Endometriosis." *Fertility and Sterility: The American Society of Reproductive Medicine,* vol. 86, no. 5, Nov. 2006, pp. 1296-301. *Elsevier Inc,* doi: 10.1016/j.fertnstert.2006.04.054. Accessed 1 Oct. 2015.

241 Ballweg, Mary Lou. "Research Reveals Disease is Starting Younger, Diagnosis Delayed." *Endometriosis: The Complete Reference for Taking Charge of Your Health.* Ed. Ballweg. Chicago: Contemporary, 2003. 343-60. Print. 357, 358.

242 Lamb, Karen, Lyle J. Breitkopf, and Karen Hamilton. "Does Hysterectomy and Removal of the Ovaries Offer a Cure for Endometriosis? An Exploratory Study." *The Endometriosis Sourcebook.* Ed. Mary Lou Ballweg. Chicago: Contemporary, 1995. 130-43. Print. 141.

243 Campbell, P. Fay. "Endo: What a Pain It Is!" *Endometriosis: The Complete Reference for Taking Charge of Your Health.* Ed. Mary Lou Ballweg. Chicago: Contemporary, 2003. 9-28. Print. 15.

244 Birnbaum, Michael D. "Menstrual Cramps Are Not Normal." *The Endometriosis Sourcebook.* Ed. Mary Lou Ballweg. Chicago: Contemporary, 1995. Print. 322.

245 Ballweg, Mary Lou. "It's All in Your Head." *The Endometriosis Sourcebook.* Ed. Ballweg. Chicago: Contemporary, 1995. 295-321. Print. 301.

246 Ibid, 299.

247 Ballweg, Mary Lou. "The Puzzle of Endometriosis." *The Endometriosis Sourcebook.* Ed. Ballweg. Chicago: Contemporary, 1995. 409-30. Print. 423.

248 Cook, Andrew S. *Stop Endometriosis and Pelvic Pain: What Every Woman and Her Doctor Need to Know*. Los Gatos, CA: Femsana, 2012. Print. 2-3.

249 Redwine, David B. *Googling Endometriosis: The Lost Centuries*. Bend, OR: David B. Redwine, MD, 2012. Print. 137.

250 Campbell, P. Fay. "Endo: What a Pain It Is!" *Endometriosis: The Complete Reference for Taking Charge of Your Health*. Ed. Mary Lou Ballweg. Chicago: Contemporary, 2003. 9-28. Print. 12.

251 Mains, Barbara. "Endometriosis and Pain." *The Endometriosis Sourcebook*. Ed. Mary Lou Ballweg. Chicago: Contemporary, 1995. 35-40. Print. 36.

252 Campbell, P. Fay. "Endo: What a Pain It Is!" *Endometriosis: The Complete Reference for Taking Charge of Your Health*. Ed. Mary Lou Ballweg. Chicago: Contemporary, 2003. 9-28. Print. 13.

253 Cook, Andrew S. *Stop Endometriosis and Pelvic Pain: What Every Woman and Her Doctor Need to Know*. Los Gatos, CA: Femsana, 2012. Print. 26.

254 Ballard, Karen, Karen Lowton, and Jeremy Wright. "What's the Delay? A Qualitative Study of Women's Experiences of Reaching a Diagnosis of Endometriosis." *Fertility and Sterility: The American Society of Reproductive Medicine,* vol. 86, no. 5, Nov. 2006, pp. 1296-301. *Elsevier Inc,* doi: 10.1016/j.fertnstert.2006.04.054. Accessed 1 Oct. 2015.

255 Ibid.

256 Ibid.

257 Jaffe, Russell. Foreword. *Endometriosis: The Complete Reference for Taking Charge of Your Health*. Ed. Mary Lou Ballweg. Chicago: Contemporary, 2003. xv-xvii. Print. xv.

258 Cook, Andrew S. *Stop Endometriosis and Pelvic Pain: What Every Woman and Her Doctor Need to Know*. Los Gatos, CA: Femsana, 2012. Print. 88.

259 Ibid, 14.

260 Henderson, Lorraine, and Ros Wood. *Explaining Endometriosis*. St. Leonards, NSW: Allen & Unwin, 2000. Print. 48, 50.

261 Agarwal, Neha, and Arulselvi Subramanian. "Endometriosis—Morphology, Clinical Presentations and Molecular Pathology." *Journ. of Laboratory Physicians,* vol. 2, no.1, Jan.-June 2010, pp. 1-9, *PMC/Medknow Publications,* doi: 10.4103/0974-2727.66699. Accessed 29 Sept. 2015.

262 Ibid.

263 Henderson, Lorraine, and Ros Wood. *Explaining Endometriosis*. St. Leonards, NSW: Allen & Unwin, 2000. Print. 50.

264 Mains, Barbara. "GnRH Update." *The Endometriosis Sourcebook*. Ed. Mary Lou Ballweg. Chicago: Contemporary, 1995. 162-80. Print. 167.

265 Bulun, Serdar E. "Endometriosis." *New England Journ. of Medicine,* vol. 360, 15 Jan. 2009, pp. 268-79. *NEJM Group,* doi: 10.1056/nejmRA0804690. Accessed 23 Nov. 2015.

266 Henderson, Lorraine, and Ros Wood. *Explaining Endometriosis.* St. Leonards, NSW: Allen & Unwin, 2000. Print. 119.

267 Redwine, David qtd. in Agger, Ellen. "Menopause and Endometriosis." *Endometriosis: The Complete Reference for Taking Charge of Your Health.* Ed. Mary Lou Ballweg. Chicago: Contemporary, 2003:275-304. Print. 280.

268 Henderson, Lorraine, and Ros Wood. *Explaining Endometriosis.* St. Leonards, NSW: Allen & Unwin, 2000. Print. 119.

269 Agger, Ellen. "Menopause and Endometriosis." *Endometriosis: The Complete Reference for Taking Charge of Your Health.* Ed. Mary Lou Ballweg. Chicago: Contemporary, 2003:275-304. Print. 281.

270 Cook, Andrew S. *Stop Endometriosis and Pelvic Pain: What Every Woman and Her Doctor Need to Know.* Los Gatos, CA: Femsana, 2012. Print. 41, 42.

271 Ballweg, Mary Lou. "Pregnancy, Labor, and Postpartum Experiences of Women with Endometriosis." *The Endometriosis Sourcebook.* Ed. Ballweg. Chicago: Contemporary, 1995. 248-57. Print. 252.

272 Henderson, Lorraine, and Ros Wood. *Explaining Endometriosis.* St. Leonards, NSW: Allen & Unwin, 2000. Print. 119.

273 Redwine, David B. *Googling Endometriosis: The Lost Centuries.* Bend, OR: David B. Redwine, MD, 2012. Print. 79.

274 Ballweg, Mary Lou. "Pregnancy, Labor, and Postpartum Experiences of Women with Endometriosis." *The Endometriosis Sourcebook.* Ed. Ballweg. Chicago: Contemporary, 1995. 248-57. Print. 249.

275 Ballweg, Mary Lou. "The Enigma Called Endometriosis." *The Endometriosis Sourcebook.* Ed. Ballweg. Chicago: Contemporary, 1995. 10-15. Print. 12.

276 Ballweg, Mary Lou. "Pregnancy, Labor, and Postpartum Experiences of Women with Endometriosis." *The Endometriosis Sourcebook.* Ed. Ballweg. Chicago: Contemporary, 1995. 248-57. Print. 252-57.

277 Ballweg, Mary Lou. "Immunotherapy: The Newest Treatment for Endometriosis." *Endometriosis: The Complete Reference for Taking Charge of Your Health.* Ed. Ballweg. Chicago: Contemporary, 2003. 81-106. Print. 82.

278 Henderson, Lorraine, and Ros Wood. *Explaining Endometriosis.* St. Leonards, NSW: Allen & Unwin, 2000. Print. 93-102.

279 Cook, Andrew S. *Stop Endometriosis and Pelvic Pain: What Every Woman and Her Doctor Need to Know.* Los Gatos, CA: Femsana, 2012. Print. 139.

280 Redwine, David B. *Googling Endometriosis: The Lost Centuries.* Bend, OR: David B. Redwine, MD, 2012. Print. 202.

281 Ibid, 203.

282 Ibid, 225.

283 Ibid, 226.

284 Ibid, 202.

285 Ibid, iv, 7.

286 Thorburn, John qtd. in Redwine, David B. *Googling Endometriosis: The Lost Centuries*. Bend, OR: David B. Redwine, MD, 2012. Print. 203.

287 Oppenheimer, L.S. qtd. In Redwine, David B. *Googling Endometriosis: The Lost Centuries*. Bend, OR: David B. Redwine, MD, 2012. Print. 176.

288 Main, Barbara. "Pain Management." *The Endometriosis Sourcebook*. Ed. Mary Lou Ballweg. Chicago: Contemporary, 1995. 46-48. Print. 48.

289 Ballweg, Mary Lou. "It's All in Your Head." *The Endometriosis Sourcebook*. Ed. Ballweg. Chicago: Contemporary, 1995. 295-321. Print. 308.

290 Henderson, Lorraine, and Ros Wood. *Explaining Endometriosis*. St. Leonards, NSW: Allen & Unwin, 2000. Print. 105.

291 Ibid, 105-08.

292 Cook, Andrew S. *Stop Endometriosis and Pelvic Pain: What Every Woman and Her Doctor Need to Know*. Los Gatos, CA: Femsana, 2012. Print. 134-35.

293 Ibid, 133-34.

294 Park, Ki, and Anthony A Bavry. "Risk of Stroke Associated with Nonsteroidal Anti-Inflammatory Drugs." *Vascular Health and Risk Management*, vol. 10, 2014, pp. 25–32. *PMC*, doi: 10.2147/VHRM.S54159. Accessed 2 Dec. 2015.

295 Bulun, Serdar E. "Endometriosis." *New England Journ. of Medicine*, vol. 360, 15 Jan. 2009, pp. 268-79. *NEJM Group*, doi: 10.1056/nejmRA0804690. Accessed 23 Nov. 2015.

296 Olive, David L. "What You Need to Know About Treating Endometriosis Medically." *Endometriosis: The Complete Reference for Taking Charge of Your Health*. Ed. Mary Lou Ballweg. Chicago: Contemporary, 2003. 29-46. Print. 37.

297 Cook, Andrew S. *Stop Endometriosis and Pelvic Pain: What Every Woman and Her Doctor Need to Know*. Los Gatos, CA: Femsana, 2012. Print. 84.

298 Ibid.

299 Ibid.

300 Olive, David L. "What You Need to Know About Treating Endometriosis Medically." *Endometriosis: The Complete Reference for Taking Charge of Your Health*. Ed. Mary Lou Ballweg. Chicago: Contemporary, 2003. 29-46. Print. 37.

301 Henderson, Lorraine, and Ros Wood. *Explaining Endometriosis*. St. Leonards, NSW: Allen & Unwin, 2000. Print. 52-54.

302 Olive, David L. "What You Need to Know About Treating Endometriosis Medically." *Endometriosis: The Complete Reference for*

Taking Charge of Your Health. Ed. Mary Lou Ballweg. Chicago: Contemporary, 2003. 29-46. Print. 34.

[303] Ibid, 36.

[304] Ibid, 35.

[305] Cook, Andrew S. *Stop Endometriosis and Pelvic Pain: What Every Woman and Her Doctor Need to Know*. Los Gatos, CA: Femsana, 2012. Print. 89.

[306] Henderson, Lorraine, and Ros Wood. *Explaining Endometriosis*. St. Leonards, NSW: Allen & Unwin, 2000. Print. 58.

[307] Olive, David L. "What You Need to Know About Treating Endometriosis Medically." *Endometriosis: The Complete Reference for Taking Charge of Your Health*. Ed. Mary Lou Ballweg. Chicago: Contemporary, 2003. 29-46. Print. 32.

[308] Norcum, Mona Trempe. "Danazol Revisited: Does an 'Old' Drug Have 'New' Tricks?" *The Endometriosis Sourcebook*. Ed. Mary Lou Ballweg. Chicago: Contemporary, 1995. 185-96. Print. 193.

[309] Ibid, 188.

[310] Ibid, 187-88.

[311] Olive, David L. "What You Need to Know About Treating Endometriosis Medically." *Endometriosis: The Complete Reference for Taking Charge of Your Health*. Ed. Mary Lou Ballweg. Chicago: Contemporary, 2003. 29-46. Print. 32-33.

[312] Henderson, Lorraine, and Ros Wood. *Explaining Endometriosis*. St. Leonards, NSW: Allen & Unwin, 2000. Print. 59-60.

[313] Cook, Andrew S. *Stop Endometriosis and Pelvic Pain: What Every Woman and Her Doctor Need to Know*. Los Gatos, CA: Femsana, 2012. Print. 89.

[314] Olive, David L. "What You Need to Know About Treating Endometriosis Medically." *Endometriosis: The Complete Reference for Taking Charge of Your Health*. Ed. Mary Lou Ballweg. Chicago: Contemporary, 2003. 29-46. Print. 33.

[315] Norcum, Mona Trempe. "Danazol Revisited: Does an 'Old' Drug Have 'New' Tricks?" *The Endometriosis Sourcebook*. Ed. Mary Lou Ballweg. Chicago: Contemporary, 1995. 185-96. Print. 192.

[316] Olive, David L. "What You Need to Know About Treating Endometriosis Medically." *Endometriosis: The Complete Reference for Taking Charge of Your Health*. Ed. Mary Lou Ballweg. Chicago: Contemporary, 2003. 29-46. Print. 38.

[317] Herington, Jennifer L. et al. "Immune Interactions in Endometriosis." *Expert Review of Clinical Immunology*, vol. 7, no. 5, Sept. 2011, pp. 611-26. *PMC/NIH-PA*, doi: 10.1586/eci.11.53. Accessed 6 Oct. 2015.

[318] Mains, Barbara. "GnRH Update." *The Endometriosis Sourcebook*. Ed. Mary Lou Ballweg. Chicago: Contemporary, 1995. 162-80. Print. 167.

[319] Ibid, 166.

320 Ibid, 170.

321 Ibid, 173.

322 Ibid, 175.

323 Olive, David L. "What You Need to Know About Treating Endometriosis Medically." *Endometriosis: The Complete Reference for Taking Charge of Your Health.* Ed. Mary Lou Ballweg. Chicago: Contemporary, 2003. 29-46. Print. 38.

324 Mains, Barbara. "GnRH Update." *The Endometriosis Sourcebook.* Ed. Mary Lou Ballweg. Chicago: Contemporary, 1995. 162-80. Print. 174.

325 Ibid, 167.

326 Cook, Andrew S. *Stop Endometriosis and Pelvic Pain: What Every Woman and Her Doctor Need to Know.* Los Gatos, CA: Femsana, 2012. Print. 40-41.

327 Ibid, 90.

328 Olive, David L. "What You Need to Know About Treating Endometriosis Medically." *Endometriosis: The Complete Reference for Taking Charge of Your Health.* Ed. Mary Lou Ballweg. Chicago: Contemporary, 2003. 29-46. Print. 43.

329 Ibid, 40-44.

330 Cook, Andrew S. *Stop Endometriosis and Pelvic Pain: What Every Woman and Her Doctor Need to Know.* Los Gatos, CA: Femsana, 2012. Print. 90.

331 Ballweg, Mary Lou. "Emerging Principles of Surgery for Endometriosis." *The Endometriosis Sourcebook.* Ed. Ballweg. Chicago: Contemporary, 1995. Print. 81.

332 Ibid.

333 Miller, Charles E., and Mary Lou Ballweg. "Surgical Treatments. Surgery Through the Laparoscope: The Future Has Arrived." *The Endometriosis Sourcebook.* Ed. Ballweg. Chicago: Contemporary, 1995. 61-78. Print. 64.

334 Ballweg, Mary Lou. "Choosing a Laparoscopic Surgeon." *The Endometriosis Sourcebook.* Ed. Ballweg. Chicago: Contemporary, 1995. 86-90. Print. 86-87.

335 Miller, Charles E., and Mary Lou Ballweg. "Surgical Treatments. Surgery Through the Laparoscope: The Future Has Arrived." *The Endometriosis Sourcebook.* Ed. Ballweg. Chicago: Contemporary, 1995. 61-78. Print. 78.

336 Cook, Andrew S. *Stop Endometriosis and Pelvic Pain: What Every Woman and Her Doctor Need to Know.* Los Gatos, CA: Femsana, 2012. Print. 93.

337 Ibid, 91.

338 Bulun, Serdar E. "Endometriosis." *New England Journ. of Medicine,* vol. 360, 15 Jan. 2009, pp. 268-79. *NEJM Group,* doi: 10.1056/nejmRA0804690. Accessed 23 Nov. 2015.

339 "Disease Information and Support: About Endometriosis." *Endofound.org*, 2015. *Endometriosis Foundation of America*, www.endofound.org/endometriosis. Accessed 9 Sept. 2015.

340 Henderson, Lorraine, and Ros Wood. *Explaining Endometriosis*. St. Leonards, NSW: Allen & Unwin, 2000. Print. 85.

341 Lamb, Karen, Lyle J. Breitkopf, and Karen Hamilton. "Does Hysterectomy and Removal of the Ovaries Offer a Cure for Endometriosis? An Exploratory Study." *The Endometriosis Sourcebook*. Ed. Mary Lou Ballweg. Chicago: Contemporary, 1995. 130-43. Print. 141.

342 Redwine, David qtd. in Agger, Ellen. "Menopause and Endometriosis." *Endometriosis: The Complete Reference for Taking Charge of Your Health*. Ed. Mary Lou Ballweg. Chicago: Contemporary, 2003:275-304. Print. 280.

343 Redwine, David B. *Googling Endometriosis: The Lost Centuries*. Bend, OR: David B. Redwine, MD, 2012. Print. 85.

344 Agger, Ellen. "Surgery and Endometriosis: Expanding Horizons." *Endometriosis: The Complete Reference for Taking Charge of Your Health*. Ed. Mary Lou Ballweg. Chicago: Contemporary, 2003. 51-79. Print. 75.

345 Ballweg, Mary Lou. "Hysterectomy and Endometriosis: Overview." *The Endometriosis Sourcebook*. Ed. Ballweg. Chicago: Contemporary, 1995. 101-08. Print. 106.

346 Agger, Ellen. "Menopause and Endometriosis." *Endometriosis: The Complete Reference for Taking Charge of Your Health*. Ed. Mary Lou Ballweg. Chicago: Contemporary, 2003:275-304. Print. 279.

347 Zimlicki, Paula M. "Hysterectomy: The Loneliest Decision of All." *The Endometriosis Sourcebook*. Ed. Mary Lou Ballweg. Chicago: Contemporary, 1995. 109-21. Print. 111, 116.

348 Ibid, 112.

349 Agger, Ellen. "Menopause and Endometriosis." *Endometriosis: The Complete Reference for Taking Charge of Your Health*. Ed. Mary Lou Ballweg. Chicago: Contemporary, 2003:275-304. Print. 280.

350 Ibid, 279.

351 Lamb, Karen, Lyle J. Breitkopf, and Karen Hamilton. "Does Hysterectomy and Removal of the Ovaries Offer a Cure for Endometriosis? An Exploratory Study." *The Endometriosis Sourcebook*. Ed. Mary Lou Ballweg. Chicago: Contemporary, 1995. 130-43. Print. 141-42.

352 Ballweg, Mary Lou. "Hysterectomy and Endometriosis: Overview." *The Endometriosis Sourcebook*. Ed. Ballweg. Chicago: Contemporary, 1995. 101-08. Print. 108.

353 Redwine, David B. *Googling Endometriosis: The Lost Centuries*. Bend, OR: David B. Redwine, MD, 2012. Print. 216.

354 Leonard, C. H. qtd. in Redwine, David B. *Googling Endometriosis: The Lost Centuries*. Bend, OR: David B. Redwine, MD, 2012. Print. 216.

355 Ballweg, Mary Lou. "Hysterectomy and Endometriosis: Overview." *The Endometriosis Sourcebook*. Ed. Ballweg. Chicago: Contemporary, 1995. 101-08. Print. 107.

356 "Reproductive Health: Data and Statistics: Hysterectomy." *Centers for Disease Control and Prevention,* 9 May 2016, U.S. Division of Reproductive Health, www.cdc.gov/reproductivehealth/data_stats/index.htm. Accessed 13 Nov. 2015.

357 Ballweg, Mary Lou. "Hysterectomy and Endometriosis: Overview." *The Endometriosis Sourcebook*. Ed. Ballweg. Chicago: Contemporary, 1995. 101-08. Print. 107.

358 Redwine, David B. *Googling Endometriosis: The Lost Centuries*. Bend, OR: David B. Redwine, MD, 2012. Print. 217.

359 Zimlicki, Paula M. "Hysterectomy: The Loneliest Decision of All." *The Endometriosis Sourcebook*. Ed. Mary Lou Ballweg. Chicago: Contemporary, 1995. 109-21. Print. 117.

360 Miller, Charles E., and Mary Lou Ballweg. "Surgical Treatments. Surgery Through the Laparoscope: The Future Has Arrived." *The Endometriosis Sourcebook*. Ed. Ballweg. Chicago: Contemporary, 1995. 61-78. Print. 74.

361 Ibid, 80.

362 Bulun, Serdar E. "Endometriosis." *New England Journ. of Medicine,* vol. 360, 15 Jan. 2009, pp. 268-79. *NEJM Group*, doi: 10.1056/nejmRA0804690. Accessed 23 Nov. 2015.

363 Henderson, Lorraine, and Ros Wood. *Explaining Endometriosis*. St. Leonards, NSW: Allen & Unwin, 2000. Print. 117.

364 Ibid.

365 Corman, Cathy. "Infertility and Endometriosis." *The Endometriosis Sourcebook*. Ed. Mary Lou Ballweg. Chicago: Contemporary, 1995. 237-47. Print. 241.

366 Ibid, 243.

367 Agarwal, Neha, and Arulselvi Subramanian. "Endometriosis— Morphology, Clinical Presentations and Molecular Pathology." *Journ. of Laboratory Physicians,* vol. 2, no.1, Jan.-June 2010, pp. 1-9, *PMC/Medknow Publications,* doi: 10.4103/0974-2727.66699. Accessed 29 Sept. 2015.

368 Lyttleton, Jane. *Treatment of Infertility with Chinese Medicine*. Edinburgh: Churchill Livingstone, 2004. Print. 175.

369 Ibid, 4-5.

370 Ibid, 3.

371 Ni, Daoshing qtd. in JoHanson, Kathleen. "Traditional Chinese Medicine and Endometriosis: An Interview with Daoshing Ni, LAc, PhD, DOM, Dipl. CH." *The Endometriosis Sourcebook*. Ed. Mary Lou Ballweg. Chicago: Contemporary, 1995. 267-71. Print. 267.

372 Shattuck, Arthur D. "Traditional Chinese Medicine and the Treatment of Endometriosis." *The Endometriosis Sourcebook*. Ed. Mary Lou Ballweg. Chicago: Contemporary, 1995. 259-66. Print. 262.

373 Ibid, 262, 264-65.

374 Lyttleton, Jane. *Treatment of Infertility with Chinese Medicine*. Edinburgh: Churchill Livingstone, 2004. Print. 9-10.

375 Ibid, xv, 21.

376 Shattuck, Arthur D. "Traditional Chinese Medicine and the Treatment of Endometriosis." *The Endometriosis Sourcebook*. Ed. Mary Lou Ballweg. Chicago: Contemporary, 1995. 259-66. Print. 263.

377 Lyttleton, Jane. *Treatment of Infertility with Chinese Medicine*. Edinburgh: Churchill Livingstone, 2004. Print. vx, 9-10.

378 Shattuck, Arthur D. "Traditional Chinese Medicine and the Treatment of Endometriosis." *The Endometriosis Sourcebook*. Ed. Mary Lou Ballweg. Chicago: Contemporary, 1995. 259-66. Print. 262.

379 Lyttleton, Jane. *Treatment of Infertility with Chinese Medicine*. Edinburgh: Churchill Livingstone, 2004. Print. 10.

380 Ibid, 175.

381 Shattuck, Arthur D. "Traditional Chinese Medicine and the Treatment of Endometriosis." *The Endometriosis Sourcebook*. Ed. Mary Lou Ballweg. Chicago: Contemporary, 1995. 259-66. Print. 266.

382 Ni, Daoshing qtd. in JoHanson, Kathleen. "Traditional Chinese Medicine and Endometriosis: An Interview with Daoshing Ni, LAc, PhD, DOM, Dipl. CH." *The Endometriosis Sourcebook*. Ed. Mary Lou Ballweg. Chicago: Contemporary, 1995. 267-71. Print. 269.

383 Lyttleton, Jane. *Treatment of Infertility with Chinese Medicine*. Edinburgh: Churchill Livingstone, 2004. Print. 170.

384 Ibid, 175.

385 Ibid, xv.

386 Ni, Daoshing qtd. in JoHanson, Kathleen. "Traditional Chinese Medicine and Endometriosis: An Interview with Daoshing Ni, LAc, PhD, DOM, Dipl. CH." *The Endometriosis Sourcebook*. Ed. Mary Lou Ballweg. Chicago: Contemporary, 1995. 267-71. Print. 267.

387 Redwine, David B. *Googling Endometriosis: The Lost Centuries*. Bend, OR: David B. Redwine, MD, 2012. Print. 75.

388 Ballweg, Mary Lou. "The Puzzle of Endometriosis." *The Endometriosis Sourcebook*. Ed. Ballweg. Chicago: Contemporary, 1995. 409-30. Print. 423.

389 Delaney, Janice, Mary Jane Lupton, and Emily Toth. *The Curse: A Cultural History of Menstruation*. Urbana, IL: U of Illinois P, 1988. Print. 7-8.

390 Ibid, 8.

391 Redwine, David B. *Googling Endometriosis: The Lost Centuries*. Bend, OR: David B. Redwine, MD, 2012. Print. 7.

392 Ibid, 6, 42.

393 Hillman, James. *Re-Visioning Psychology*. New York: Harper & Row, 1975. Print. 137.

394 Redwine, David B. *Googling Endometriosis: The Lost Centuries*. Bend, OR: David B. Redwine, MD, 2012. Print. 7.

395 Downing, Christine. *Gods in Our Midst: Mythological Images of the Masculine: A Woman's View*. New York: Crossroad, 1993. Print. 30.

396 Ibid, 21.

397 Root, Ileen Brennan. *Redeeming the Gorgon: Reclaiming the* Medusa Function *of Psyche*. Diss. Pacifica Graduate Institute, 2007. Carpinteria, CA: ProQuest, 2007. Print. 32.

398 Ibid.

399 Neumann, Erich. *The Great Mother; an Analysis of the Archetype*. Trans. Ralph Manheim. New York: Pantheon Books, 1955. Print. 275.

400 Garber, Marjorie B., and Nancy J. Vickers, eds. *The Medusa Reader*. New York: Routledge, 2003. Print. 3.

401 Dexter, Miriam Robbins. "The Ferocious and the Erotic 'Beautiful' Medusa and the Neolithic Bird and Snake." *Journ. of Feminist Studies in Religion*, vol. 26, no. 1, Spring 2010, pp. 25-41. *Indiana U P/UCLA Library*, doi:10.2979/fsr.2010.26.1.25. Accessed 5 Aug. 2016. 25.

402 Shuttle, Penelope, and Peter Redgrove. *The Wise Wound: Menstruation and Everywoman*. London: Marion Boyars, 2005. Print. 248.

403 Garber, Marjorie B., and Nancy J. Vickers, eds. *The Medusa Reader*. New York: Routledge, 2003. Print. 21.

404 Ibid, 26.

405 Diodorus Siculus qtd. in Garber, Marjorie B., and Nancy J. Vickers, eds. *The Medusa Reader*. New York: Routledge, 2003. Print. 26.

406 Ibid, 29.

407 Pausanias qtd. in Garber, Marjorie B., and Nancy J. Vickers, eds. *The Medusa Reader*. New York: Routledge, 2003. Print. 44.

408 Gibmutas, Marija. *The Language of the Goddess*. New York: Thames & Hudson, 1989. Print. 318.

409 Kerényi, C. *The Gods of the Greeks*. London: Thames and Hudson, 1982. Print. 49.

410 Chevalier, Jean, and Alain Gheerbrant. *A Dictionary of Symbols*. London: Penguin, 1996. Print. 1081.

411 Ibid, 1088.

412 Hesiod. *Theogony*. Trans. Richmond Lattimore. *Works and Days; Theogony; The Shield of Herakles*. Ann Arbor, MI: U of Michigan P, 1991. 119-86. Print. Line 282.

413 Chevalier, Jean, and Alain Gheerbrant. *A Dictionary of Symbols*. London: Penguin, 1996. Print. 1086.

414 Atsma, Aaron J. "Keto." *Theoi Greek Mythology*, compiler Atsma, Theoi Project, 2000-2017, www.theoi.com/Pontios/Keto.html. Accessed 17 Oct. 2016.

415 Chevalier, Jean, and Alain Gheerbrant. A Dictionary of Symbols. London: Penguin, 1996. Print. 516.

416 Dexter, Miriam Robbins. "The Ferocious and the Erotic 'Beautiful' Medusa and the Neolithic Bird and Snake." *Journ. of Feminist Studies in Religion*, vol. 26, no. 1, Spring 2010, pp. 25-41. *Indiana U P/UCLA Library*, doi:10.2979/fsr.2010.26.1.25. Accessed 5 Aug. 2016. 33.

417 Ibid, 36.

418 Chevalier, Jean, and Alain Gheerbrant. A Dictionary of Symbols. London: Penguin, 1996. Print. 516-26.

419 Dexter, Miriam Robbins. *Whence the Goddesses: A Source Book*. New York: Pergamon P, 1990. Print. 5, 18, 119, 177-80.

420 Kerényi, C. *The Gods of the Greeks*. London: Thames and Hudson, 1982. Print. 54-55.

421 Graves, Robert. *The Greek Myths: The Complete and Definitive Edition*. New York: Penguin, 2011. Print. 129.

422 Gimbutas, Marija. *The Goddesses and Gods of Old Europe: Myths and Cult Images*. Berkeley: U of California P, 1982. Print. 152.

423 Downing, Christine. *Gods in Our Midst: Mythological Images of the Masculine: A Woman's View*. New York: Crossroad, 1993. Print. 124.

424 Smith, Barbara. "Greece." *The Feminist Companion to Mythology*. Ed. Carolyne Larrington. London: Pandora, 1992. 65-101. Print. 92.

425 Campbell, Joseph. Interview by Bill Moyers. *The Power of Myth*. Ed. Betty Sue Flowers. New York: Doubleday, 1988. Print. 222.

426 Atsma, Aaron J. "Gorgones and Medousa." *Theoi Greek Mythology*, compiler Atsma, Theoi Project, 2000-2017, www.theoi.com/Pontios/Gorgones.html. Accessed 17 Oct. 2016.

427 Dexter, Miriam Robbins. "The Ferocious and the Erotic 'Beautiful' Medusa and the Neolithic Bird and Snake." *Journ. of Feminist Studies in Religion*, vol. 26, no. 1, Spring 2010, pp. 25-41. *Indiana U P/UCLA Library*, doi:10.2979/fsr.2010.26.1.25. Accessed 5 Aug. 2016. 25.

428 Shuttle, Penelope, and Peter Redgrove. *The Wise Wound: Menstruation and Everywoman*. London: Marion Boyars, 2005. Print. 248.

429 Harrison, Jane Ellen. *Prolegomena to the Study of Greek Religion*. Princeton, NJ: Princeton U P, 1991. Print. 191.

430 Kerényi, C. *The Gods of the Greeks*. London: Thames and Hudson, 1982. Print. 49.

431 Ibid, 185.

432 Harrison, Jane Ellen. *Prolegomena to the Study of Greek Religion*. Princeton, NJ: Princeton U P, 1991. Print. 225.

433 Ibid, 212.

434 Ibid.

435 Ibid.

436 Ibid.

437 Ibid.

438 Lubell, Winifred Milius. *The Metamorphosis of Baubo: Myths of Woman's Sexual Energy*. Nashville: Vanderbilt U P, 1994. Print. 110.

439 Harrison, Jane Ellen. *Prolegomena to the Study of Greek Religion*. Princeton, NJ: Princeton U P, 1991. Print. 188.

440 Atsma, Aaron J. "Themis." *Theoi Greek Mythology*, compiler Atsma, Theoi Project, 2000-2017, www.theoi.com/Titan/TitanisThemis.html. Accessed 17 Oct. 2016.

441 von Franz, Marie-Louise. *The Feminine in Fairy Tales*. Rev. ed. Boston: Shambhala, 1993. Print. 39.

442 Gimbutas, Marija. *The Language of the Goddess*. New York: Thames & Hudson, 1989. Print. 207.

443 Neumann, Erich. *The Great Mother: An Analysis of the Archetype*. Trans. Ralph Manheim. New York: Pantheon Books, 1955. Print. 275.

444 Harrison, Jane Ellen. *Prolegomena to the Study of Greek Religion*. Princeton, NJ: Princeton U P, 1991. Print. 194.

445 Gimbutas, Marija. *The Language of the Goddess*. New York: Thames & Hudson, 1989. Print. xxii, 207-08.

446 Smith, Barbara. "Greece." *The Feminist Companion to Mythology*. Ed. Carolyne Larrington. London: Pandora, 1992. 65-101. Print. 93.

447 Edelman, Sandra. *Turning the Gorgon: A Meditation on Shame*. Woodstock, CT: Spring Publications, Inc. 1998. Print. 161

448 Dexter, Miriam Robbins. *Whence the Goddesses: A Source Book*. New York: Pergamon P, 1990. Print. 119.

449 Edelman, Sandra. *Turning the Gorgon: A Meditation on Shame*. Woodstock, CT: Spring Publications, Inc. 1998. Print. 61.

450 Downing, Christine. *The Goddess: Mythological Images of the Feminine*. New York: Author's Choice P, 1981. Print. 124.

451 Siebers, Tobin. *The Mirror of Medusa*. Christchurch, NZ: Cybereditions, 2000. Print. 44-45.

452 Kerényi, C. *The Gods of the Greeks*. London: Thames and Hudson, 1982. Print. 45.

453 Graves, Robert. *The Greek Myths: The Complete and Definitive Edition*. New York: Penguin, 2011. Print. 129.

454 Atsma, Aaron J. "Gorgones and Medousa." *Theoi Greek Mythology*, compiler Atsma, Theoi Project, 2000-2017, www.theoi.com/Pontios/Gorgones.html. Accessed 17 Oct. 2016.

455 Kerényi, C. *The Gods of the Greeks*. London: Thames and Hudson, 1982. Print. 49.

456 Graves, Robert. *The Greek Myths: The Complete and Definitive Edition*. New York: Penguin, 2011. Print. 129.

457 Ibid.

458 Gimbutas, Marija. *The Goddesses and Gods of Old Europe: Myths and Cult Images*. Berkeley: U of California P, 1982. Print. 211.

459 Ibid, 214-15.

460 Lubell, Winifred Milius. *The Metamorphosis of Baubo: Myths of Woman's Sexual Energy*. Nashville: Vanderbilt U P, 1994. Print. 5-7.

461 Root, Ileen Brennan. *Redeeming the Gorgon: Reclaiming the Medusa Function of Psyche*. Diss. Pacifica Graduate Institute, 2007. Carpinteria, CA: ProQuest, 2007. Print. 10.

462 Dexter, Miriam Robbins. "The Ferocious and the Erotic 'Beautiful' Medusa and the Neolithic Bird and Snake." *Journ. of Feminist Studies in Religion*, vol. 26, no. 1, Spring 2010, pp. 25-41. *Indiana U P/UCLA Library*, doi:10.2979/fsr.2010.26.1.25. Accessed 5 Aug. 2016. 32.

463 Ibid, 32.

464 Gibmutas, Marija. *The Language of the Goddess*. New York: Thames & Hudson, 1989. Print. 208.

465 Campbell, Joseph qtd. in Root, Ileen Brennan. *Redeeming the Gorgon: Reclaiming the Medusa Function of Psyche*. Diss. Pacifica Graduate Institute, 2007. Carpinteria, CA: ProQuest, 2007. Print. 57.

466 Harrison, Jane Ellen. *Prolegomena to the Study of Greek Religion*. Princeton, NJ: Princeton U P, 1991. Print. 194.

467 Gibmutas, Marija. *The Language of the Goddess*. New York: Thames & Hudson, 1989. Print. xix.

468 Gimbutas, Marija. *The Goddesses and Gods of Old Europe: Myths and Cult Images*. Berkeley: U of California P, 1982. Print. 66.

469 Gibmutas, Marija. *The Language of the Goddess*. New York: Thames & Hudson, 1989. Print. xxiii, 208.

470 Ibid, 132.

471 Gimbutas, Marija. *The Goddesses and Gods of Old Europe: Myths and Cult Images*. Berkeley: U of California P, 1982. Print. 12.

472 Graves, Robert. *The Greek Myths: The Complete and Definitive Edition*. New
      York: Penguin, 2011. Print. 45.
473 Edelman, Sandra. *Turning the Gorgon: A Meditation on Shame*. Woodstock,
      CT: Spring Publications, Inc. 1998. Print. 140
474 Ibid, 59.
475 Graves, Robert. *The Greek Myths: The Complete and Definitive Edition*. New
      York: Penguin, 2011. Print. 45.
476 Lubell, Winifred Milius. *The Metamorphosis of Baubo: Myths of Woman's
      Sexual Energy*. Nashville: Vanderbilt U P, 1994. Print. 5.
477 Dexter, Miriam Robbins. "The Ferocious and the Erotic 'Beautiful'
      Medusa and the Neolithic Bird and Snake." *Journ. of Feminist Studies in
      Religion*, vol. 26, no. 1, Spring 2010, pp. 25-41. *Indiana U P/UCLA
      Library*, doi:10.2979/fsr.2010.26.1.25. Accessed 5 Aug. 2016. 33.
478 Gibmutas, Marija. *The Language of the Goddess*. New York: Thames &
      Hudson, 1989. Print. 185.
479 Ibid, 121.
480 Ibid.
481 Ibid, 207.
482 Edelman, Sandra. *Turning the Gorgon: A Meditation on Shame*. Woodstock,
      CT: Spring Publications, Inc. 1998. Print. 61
483 Ibid.
484 Gibmutas, Marija. *The Language of the Goddess*. New York: Thames &
      Hudson, 1989. Print. 132.
485 Ibid, 185.
486 Dexter, Miriam Robbins. "The Ferocious and the Erotic 'Beautiful'
      Medusa and the Neolithic Bird and Snake." *Journ. of Feminist Studies in
      Religion*, vol. 26, no. 1, Spring 2010, pp. 25-41. *Indiana U P/UCLA
      Library*, doi:10.2979/fsr.2010.26.1.25. Accessed 5 Aug. 2016. 32.
487 Ibid, 33.
488 Ibid, 29.
489 Lubell, Winifred Milius. *The Metamorphosis of Baubo: Myths of Woman's
      Sexual Energy*. Nashville: Vanderbilt U P, 1994. Print. 5.
490 Root, Ileen Brennan. *Redeeming the Gorgon: Reclaiming the* Medusa Function
      of Psyche. Diss. Pacifica Graduate Institute, 2007. Carpinteria, CA:
      ProQuest, 2007. Print. 211.
491 Dexter, Miriam Robbins. "The Ferocious and the Erotic 'Beautiful'
      Medusa and the Neolithic Bird and Snake." *Journ. of Feminist Studies in
      Religion*, vol. 26, no. 1, Spring 2010, pp. 25-41. *Indiana U P/UCLA
      Library*, doi:10.2979/fsr.2010.26.1.25. Accessed 5 Aug. 2016. 35.
492 Ibid, 31.

[493] Coomaraswamy, A. "Sir Gawain and the Green Knight," *Speculum*, vol. 19, no. 1, Jan. 1944, pp. 104-25. *JSTOR/Medieval Academy of America*, www.jstor.org/stable/2856858. Accessed 22 Jan. 2015. 113.

[494] Dexter, Miriam Robbins. "The Ferocious and the Erotic 'Beautiful' Medusa and the Neolithic Bird and Snake." *Journ. of Feminist Studies in Religion*, vol. 26, no. 1, Spring 2010, pp. 25-41. *Indiana U P/UCLA Library*, doi:10.2979/fsr.2010.26.1.25. Accessed 5 Aug. 2016. 33.

[495] Root, Ileen Brennan. *Redeeming the Gorgon: Reclaiming the* Medusa Function *of Psyche*. Diss. Pacifica Graduate Institute, 2007. Carpinteria, CA: ProQuest, 2007. Print. 32.

[496] Siebers, Tobin. The Mirror of Medusa. Christchurch, NZ: Cybereditions, 2000. Print. 54.

[497] Edelman, Sandra. *Turning the Gorgon: A Meditation on Shame*. Woodstock, CT: Spring Publications, Inc. 1998. Print. 60.

[498] Siebers, Tobin. The Mirror of Medusa. Christchurch, NZ: Cybereditions, 2000. Print. 9.

[499] Harrison, Jane Ellen. *Prolegomena to the Study of Greek Religion*. Princeton, NJ: Princeton U P, 1991. Print. 196.

[500] Ibid, 195.

[501] Siebers, Tobin. The Mirror of Medusa. Christchurch, NZ: Cybereditions, 2000. Print. 38.

[502] Harrison, Jane Ellen. *Prolegomena to the Study of Greek Religion*. Princeton, NJ: Princeton U P, 1991. Print. 187-88, 190.

[503] Graves, Robert. *The Greek Myths: The Complete and Definitive Edition*. New York: Penguin, 2011. Print. 129.

[504] Harrison, Jane Ellen. *Prolegomena to the Study of Greek Religion*. Princeton, NJ: Princeton U P, 1991. Print. 188.

[505] Siebers, Tobin. *The Mirror of Medusa*. Christchurch, NZ: Cybereditions, 2000. Print. 38.

[506] Ibid, 23.

[507] Ibid, 178, 26.

[508] Ibid, 69, 20.

[509] Moss, Leonard and Cappannari, Stephen qtd. in Siebers, Tobin. *The Mirror of Medusa*. Christchurch, NZ: Cybereditions, 2000. Print. 24.

[510] Delaney, Janice, Mary Jane Lupton, and Emily Toth. *The Curse: A Cultural History of Menstruation*. Urbana, IL: U of Illinois P, 1988. Print. 7.

[511] Shuttle, Penelope, and Peter Redgrove. *The Wise Wound: Menstruation and Everywoman*. London: Marion Boyars, 2005. Print. 60.

[512] Delaney, Janice, Mary Jane Lupton, and Emily Toth. *The Curse: A Cultural History of Menstruation*. Urbana, IL: U of Illinois P, 1988. Print. 7.

513 Lubell, Winifred Milius. *The Metamorphosis of Baubo: Myths of Woman's Sexual Energy*. Nashville: Vanderbilt U P, 1994. Print. 110.

514 Pliny qtd. in Delaney, Janice, Mary Jane Lupton, and Emily Toth. *The Curse: A Cultural History of Menstruation*. Urbana, IL: U of Illinois P, 1988. Print. 9.

515 Ibid.

516 Ibid.

517 Thomson, George qtd. in Delaney, Janice, Mary Jane Lupton, and Emily Toth. *The Curse: A Cultural History of Menstruation*. Urbana, IL: U of Illinois P, 1988. Print. 8.

518 Smith, Barbara. "Greece." *The Feminist Companion to Mythology*. Ed. Carolyne Larrington. London: Pandora, 1992. 65-101. Print. 476.

519 Edelman, Sandra. *Turning the Gorgon: A Meditation on Shame*. Woodstock, CT: Spring Publications 38., Inc. 1998. Print. 73.

520 Ibid, 76.

521 Snell, Bruno. *The Discovery of the Mind*. Trans. T.G. Rosenmeyer. Cambridge, MA: Harvard U P, 1953. 167.

522 Edelman, Sandra. *Turning the Gorgon: A Meditation on Shame*. Woodstock, CT: Spring Publications, Inc. 1998. Print. 91.

523 Ibid, 71.

524 Ibid, 91.

525 Ibid.

526 Herman, Nini qtd. in Edelman, Sandra. *Turning the Gorgon: A Meditation on Shame*. Woodstock, CT: Spring Publications, Inc. 1998. Print. 92.

527 Edelman, Sandra. *Turning the Gorgon: A Meditation on Shame*. Woodstock, CT: Spring Publications, Inc. 1998. Print. 92.

528 Ibid, 88.

529 Ibid, 90.

530 Ricouer, Paul qtd. in Edelman, Sandra. *Turning the Gorgon: A Meditation on Shame*. Woodstock, CT: Spring Publications, Inc. 1998. Print. 93.

531 Houppert, Karen. *The Curse: Confronting the Last Unmentionable Taboo: Menstruation*. New York: Farrar, Straus and Giroux, 1999. Print. 7.

532 Ibid, 6.

533 Shuttle, Penelope, and Peter Redgrove. *The Wise Wound: Menstruation and Everywoman*. London: Marion Boyars, 2005. Print. 41.

534 Ibid, 2.

535 Gibmutas, Marija. *The Language of the Goddess*. New York: Thames & Hudson, 1989. Print. 51, 63.

536 Aeschylus. *The Eumenides*. Aeschylus I. Eds. David Grene and Richmond Lattimore. Trans. Lattimore. Chicago: U of Chicago P, 1953. 133-71. Print. Line 54.

537 Shuttle, Penelope, and Peter Redgrove. *The Wise Wound: Menstruation and Everywoman*. London: Marion Boyars, 2005. Print. 75.

538 Lubell, Winifred Milius. *The Metamorphosis of Baubo: Myths of Woman's Sexual Energy*. Nashville: Vanderbilt U P, 1994. Print. 110.

539 Gibmutas, Marija. *The Language of the Goddess*. New York: Thames & Hudson, 1989. Print. 207-08.

540 Harrison, Jane Ellen. *Prolegomena to the Study of Greek Religion*. Princeton, NJ: Princeton U P, 1991. Print. 187.

541 Ovid. *Metamorphoses*. Trans. David Raeburn. London: Penguin, 2004. Print. 4.780-81.

542 Freud, Sigmund. "Medusa's Head." PEP Archive, translator James Strachey, 1922. EBSCO,pgi.idm.oclc.org/login?url=http://search.edscohost.com/login.aspx?direct=true&db=pph&AN=SE.018.0273A&site=ehost-live&scope=site. Accessed 26 Apr. 2016.

543 Edelman, Sandra. *Turning the Gorgon: A Meditation on Shame*. Woodstock, CT: Spring Publications, Inc. 1998. Print. 62.

544 Smith, Barbara. "Greece." *The Feminist Companion to Mythology*. Ed. Carolyne Larrington. London: Pandora, 1992. 65-101. Print. 65-101.

545 Aeschylus. *The Eumenides*. Aeschylus I. Eds. David Grene and Richmond Lattimore. Trans. Lattimore. Chicago: U of Chicago P, 1953. 133-71. Print. Lines 658-61.

546 Edelman, Sandra. *Turning the Gorgon: A Meditation on Shame*. Woodstock, CT: Spring Publications, Inc. 1998. Print. 63.

547 Frothingham, A. L. *"Medusa II. The Vegetation Gorgoneion." American Journ. of Archaeology, vol. 19, no. 1, Jan.-Mar. 1915, pp. 13-23*. JSTOR, www.jstor.org/stable/497260. Accessed 28 Sept. 2016. 22.

548 Ibid.

549 Ibid, 13.

550 Ibid.

551 Ibid, 15.

552 Ibid, 17.

553 Ibid, 15, 16, 18, 21.

554 Ibid, 13.

555 Ibid, 18.

556 Ibid, 22.

557 Burkert, Walter qtd. in Lubell, Winifred Milius. *The Metamorphosis of Baubo: Myths of Woman's Sexual Energy*. Nashville: Vanderbilt U P, 1994. Print. 37.

558 Shuttle, Penelope, and Peter Redgrove. *The Wise Wound: Menstruation and Everywoman*. London: Marion Boyars, 2005. Print. 22, 248.

559 Harrison, Jane Ellen. *Prolegomena to the Study of Greek Religion*. Princeton, NJ: Princeton U P, 1991. Print. 234.

560 Gibmutas, Marija. *The Language of the Goddess*. New York: Thames & Hudson, 1989. Print. 207-08.

561 Homer. *The Iliad*. Trans. Robert Fagles. New York: Penguin, 1990. Print. 5.849-50.

562 Ibid, 11.39-40.

563 Ibid, 8.398.

564 Homer. *The Odyssey*. Trans. Albert Cook. 2nd ed. New York: W.W. Norton, 1993. Print. 11.634-35.

565 Dexter, Miriam Robbins. "The Ferocious and the Erotic 'Beautiful' Medusa and the Neolithic Bird and Snake." *Journ. of Feminist Studies in Religion*, vol. 26, no. 1, Spring 2010, pp. 25-41. *Indiana U P/UCLA Library*, doi:10.2979/fsr.2010.26.1.25. Accessed 5 Aug. 2016. 27.

566 Edelman, Sandra. *Turning the Gorgon: A Meditation on Shame*. Woodstock, CT: Spring Publications, Inc. 1998. Print. 140-141.

567 Ibid, 141.

568 Ibid.

569 Ibid, 60.

570 Hesiod. *Theogony*. Trans. Richmond Lattimore. *Works and Days; Theogony; The Shield of Herakles*. Ann Arbor, MI: U of Michigan P, 1991. 119-86. Print. Line 275.

571 Edelman, Sandra. *Turning the Gorgon: A Meditation on Shame*. Woodstock, CT: Spring Publications, Inc. 1998. Print. 59

572 Hesiod. *Theogony*. Trans. Richmond Lattimore. *Works and Days; Theogony; The Shield of Herakles*. Ann Arbor, MI: U of Michigan P, 1991. 119-86. Print. Line 279.

573 Ibid, Line 282.

574 Hesiod. *The Shield of Herakles*. Trans. Richmond Lattimore. *Works and Days; Theogony; The Shield of Herakles*. Ann Arbor, MI: U of Michigan P, 1991. 187-220. Print. Line 230.

575 Ibid, Lines 223-24.

576 Atsma, Aaron J. "Phorkys." *Theoi Greek Mythology*, compiler Atsma, Theoi Project, 2000-2017, www.theoi.com/Pontios/Phorkys.html. Accessed 5 Oct. 2016.

577 Atsma, Aaron J. "Keto." *Theoi Greek Mythology*, compiler Atsma, Theoi Project, 2000-2017, www.theoi.com/Pontios/Keto.html. Accessed 17 Oct. 2016.

578 Apollodorus. *The Library of Greek Mythology*. Trans. Robin Hard. Oxford: Oxford U P, 1997. Print. II.5.12.

579 Ibid, II.4.2.

580 Ibid.

[581] Ibid, II.4.

[582] Ibid, II.7.3.

[583] Ibid.

[584] Ibid, III.10.3.

[585] Dexter, Miriam Robbins. *Whence the Goddesses: A Source Book*. New York: Pergamon P, 1990. Print. 179.

[586] Root, Ileen Brennan. *Redeeming the Gorgon: Reclaiming the* Medusa Function *of Psyche*. Diss. Pacifica Graduate Institute, 2007. Carpinteria, CA: ProQuest, 2007. Print. 7.

[587] Edelman, Sandra. *Turning the Gorgon: A Meditation on Shame*. Woodstock, CT: Spring Publications, Inc. 1998. Print. 62-63.

[588] Dexter, Miriam Robbins. "The Ferocious and the Erotic 'Beautiful' Medusa and the Neolithic Bird and Snake." *Journ. of Feminist Studies in Religion*, vol. 26, no. 1, Spring 2010, pp. 25-41. *Indiana U P/UCLA Library*, doi:10.2979/fsr.2010.26.1.25. Accessed 5 Aug. 2016. 31.

[589] Edelman, Sandra. *Turning the Gorgon: A Meditation on Shame*. Woodstock, CT: Spring Publications, Inc. 1998. Print. 42.

[590] Ovid. *Metamorphoses*. Trans. David Raeburn. London: Penguin, 2004. Print. 4.616.

[591] Ibid, 4.674.

[592] Ibid, 4.781.

[593] Ibid, 4.799-800.

[594] Ibid, 5.258-59.

[595] Dexter, Miriam Robbins. *Whence the Goddesses: A Source Book*. New York: Pergamon P, 1990. Print. x-xi.

[596] Lucan qtd. in Garber, Marjorie B., and Nancy J. Vickers, eds. *The Medusa Reader*. New York: Routledge, 2003. Print. 40.

[597] Ibid, 41-42.

[598] Ibid, 42.

[599] Ibid, 41.

[600] Ibid, 40-42.

[601] Ibid, 40-41.

[602] Ibid, 40.

[603] Edelman, Sandra. *Turning the Gorgon: A Meditation on Shame*. Woodstock, CT: Spring Publications, Inc. 1998. Print. 92

[604] Lucian qtd. in Garber, Marjorie B., and Nancy J. Vickers, eds. *The Medusa Reader*. New York: Routledge, 2003. Print. 42.

[605] Ibid, 43.

[606] Pindar qtd. in Garber, Marjorie B., and Nancy J. Vickers, eds. *The Medusa Reader*. New York: Routledge, 2003. Print. 15.

607 Aeschylus. *The Eumenides*. Aeschylus I. Eds. David Grene and Richmond
     Lattimore. Trans. Lattimore. Chicago: U of Chicago P, 1953. 133-71.
     Print. Lines 48-51.

608 Harrison, Jane Ellen. *Prolegomena to the Study of Greek Religion*. Princeton,
     NJ: Princeton U P, 1991. Print. 223-24.

609 Euripides. *Ion*. *Internet Sacred Text Archive*, translator Robert Potter,
     compiler John Bruno Hare, no line numbers, 2011. *Evinity Publishing*,
     www.sacred-texts.com/cla/eurip/ion.htm. Accessed 13 Mar. 2016.

610 Harrison, Jane Ellen. *Prolegomena to the Study of Greek Religion*. Princeton,
     NJ: Princeton U P, 1991. Print. 225.

611 Kerényi, C. *The Gods of the Greeks*. London: Thames and Hudson, 1982.
     Print. 185.

612 Harrison, Jane Ellen. *Prolegomena to the Study of Greek Religion*. Princeton,
     NJ: Princeton U P, 1991. Print. 224.

613 Ibid.

614 Hesiod. *Theogony*. Trans. Richmond Lattimore. *Works and Days*; *Theogony*;
     The Shield of Herakles. Ann Arbor, MI: U of Michigan P, 1991. 119-86.
     Print. Lines 585, 589.

615 Ibid, Line 610.

616 Keuls, Eva qtd. in Lubell, Winifred Milius. *The Metamorphosis of Baubo:
     Myths of Woman's Sexual Energy*. Nashville: Vanderbilt U P, 1994. Print.
     104.

617 Lubell, Winifred Milius. *The Metamorphosis of Baubo: Myths of Woman's
     Sexual Energy*. Nashville: Vanderbilt U P, 1994. Print. 111.

618 Blundell, Sue. *Women in Classical Athens*. London: Bristol Classical P.,
     2001. Print. 19.

619 Ibid, 16.

620 Ibid, 30.

621 Ibid, 41.

622 Ibid, 29.

623 Shuttle, Penelope, and Peter Redgrove. *The Wise Wound: Menstruation and
     Everywoman*. London: Marion Boyars, 2005. Print. 129, 248.

624 Smith, Barbara. "Greece." *The Feminist Companion to Mythology*. Ed.
     Carolyne Larrington. London: Pandora, 1992. 65-101. Print. 87.

625 Redwine, David B. *Googling Endometriosis: The Lost Centuries*. Bend, OR:
     David B. Redwine, MD, 2012. Print. 20.

626 Aristotle qtd. in Blundell, Sue. *Women in Classical Athens*. London: Bristol
     Classical P., 2001. Print. 45.

627 Smith, Barbara. "Greece." *The Feminist Companion to Mythology*. Ed.
     Carolyne Larrington. London: Pandora, 1992. 65-101. Print. 87.

628 Blundell, Sue. *Women in Classical Athens*. London: Bristol Classical P.,
     2001. Print. 49.

629 Smith, Barbara. "Greece." *The Feminist Companion to Mythology.* Ed.
    Carolyne Larrington. London: Pandora, 1992. 65-101. Print. 87.

630 Ibid, 87, 92.

631 Ibid, 87-88.

632 Ibid, 88.

633 Blundell, Sue. *Women in Classical Athens.* London: Bristol Classical P.,
    2001. Print. 24.

634 Redwine, David B. *Googling Endometriosis: The Lost Centuries.* Bend, OR:
    David B. Redwine, MD, 2012. Print. 24, 26-27, 28.

635 Witt, Charlotte, and Shapiro, Lisa, "Feminist History of Philosophy." *The
    Stanford Encyclopedia of Philosophy, editor* Edward N. Zalta, Spring 2017,
    plato.stanford.edu/archives/spr2017/entries/feminism-femhist/>.
    Accessed 5 Mar. 2016.

636 Aristotle qtd. in Witt, Charlotte, and Shapiro, Lisa, "Feminist History of
    Philosophy." *The Stanford Encyclopedia of Philosophy, editor* Edward N.
    Zalta, Spring 2017,
    plato.stanford.edu/archives/spr2017/entries/feminism-femhist/>.
    Accessed 5 Mar. 2016.

637 Redwine, David B. *Googling Endometriosis: The Lost Centuries.* Bend, OR:
    David B. Redwine, MD, 2012. Print. 29.

638 Witt, Charlotte, and Shapiro, Lisa, "Feminist History of Philosophy." *The
    Stanford Encyclopedia of Philosophy, editor* Edward N. Zalta, Spring 2017,
    plato.stanford.edu/archives/spr2017/entries/feminism-femhist/>.
    Accessed 5 Mar. 2016.

639 Jaegar, Werner qtd. in Edelman, Sandra. *Turning the Gorgon: A Meditation
    on Shame.* Woodstock, CT: Spring Publications, Inc. 1998. Print. 43.

640 Garber, Marjorie B., and Nancy J. Vickers, eds. *The Medusa Reader.* New
    York: Routledge, 2003. Print. 7.

641 Ibid, 1.

642 Hesiod qtd. in Downing, Christine. *The Goddess: Mythological Images of the
    Feminine.* New York: Author's Choice P, 1981. Print. 100.

643 Kerényi, C. *The Gods of the Greeks.* London: Thames and Hudson, 1982.
    Print. 128.

644 Gimbutas, Marija. *The Goddesses and Gods of Old Europe: Myths and Cult
    Images.* Berkeley: U of California P, 1982. Print. 149.

645 Edelman, Sandra. *Turning the Gorgon: A Meditation on Shame.* Woodstock,
    CT: Spring Publications, Inc. 1998. Print. 146.

646 Downing, Christine. *The Goddess: Mythological Images of the Feminine.* New
    York: Author's Choice P, 1981. Print. 115.

647 Graves, Robert. *The Greek Myths: The Complete and Definitive Edition.* New
    York: Penguin, 2011. Print. 46.

648 Harrison, Jane Ellen. *Prolegomena to the Study of Greek Religion*. Princeton, NJ: Princeton U P, 1991. Print. 302.

649 Aeschylus. *The Eumenides*. Aeschylus I. Eds. David Grene and Richmond Lattimore. Trans. Lattimore. Chicago: U of Chicago P, 1953. 133-71. Print. Lines 736-38.

650 Homer. "Homeric Hymn 28." *Theoi Texts Library*, translator H. G. Evelyn-White, compiler A. J. Atsma, Theoi Project, 2000-2017, www.theoi.com/Text/HomericHymns1.html. Accessed 21 Nov. 2016.

651 Hesiod. *Theogony*. Trans. Richmond Lattimore. *Works and Days; Theogony; The Shield of Herakles*. Ann Arbor, MI: U of Michigan P, 1991. 119-86. Print. Lines 925-930.

652 Kerényi, C. *The Gods of the Greeks*. London: Thames and Hudson, 1982. Print. 128.

653 Hesiod. *Theogony*. Trans. Richmond Lattimore. *Works and Days; Theogony; The Shield of Herakles*. Ann Arbor, MI: U of Michigan P, 1991. 119-86. Print. Line 887.

654 Graves, Robert. *The Greek Myths: The Complete and Definitive Edition*. New York: Penguin, 2011. Print. 30.

655 Hesiod. *Theogony*. Trans. Richmond Lattimore. *Works and Days; Theogony; The Shield of Herakles*. Ann Arbor, MI: U of Michigan P, 1991. 119-86. Print. Line 887.

656 Kerényi, C. *The Gods of the Greeks*. London: Thames and Hudson, 1982. Print. 118.

657 Hesiod. *Theogony*. Trans. Richmond Lattimore. *Works and Days; Theogony; The Shield of Herakles*. Ann Arbor, MI: U of Michigan P, 1991. 119-86. Print. Lines 889-90.

658 Kerényi, C. *The Gods of the Greeks*. London: Thames and Hudson, 1982. Print. 119.

659 Graves, Robert. *The Greek Myths: The Complete and Definitive Edition*. New York: Penguin, 2011. Print. 46.

660 Harrison, Jane Ellen. *Prolegomena to the Study of Greek Religion*. Princeton, NJ: Princeton U P, 1991. Print. 301.

661 Kerényi, C. *The Gods of the Greeks*. London: Thames and Hudson, 1982. Print. 128.

662 Gimbutas, Marija. *The Goddesses and Gods of Old Europe: Myths and Cult Images*. Berkeley: U of California P, 1982. Print. 149, 9.

663 Ibid, 147-48.

664 Harrison, Jane Ellen. *Prolegomena to the Study of Greek Religion*. Princeton, NJ: Princeton U P, 1991. Print. 304.

665 Kerényi, C. *The Gods of the Greeks*. London: Thames and Hudson, 1982. Print. 128.

666 Harrison, Jane Ellen. *Prolegomena to the Study of Greek Religion*. Princeton, NJ: Princeton U P, 1991. Print. 304.

667 Gimbutas, Marija. *The Goddesses and Gods of Old Europe: Myths and Cult Images*. Berkeley: U of California P, 1982. Print. 149.

668 Harrison, Jane Ellen. *Prolegomena to the Study of Greek Religion*. Princeton, NJ: Princeton U P, 1991. Print. 305.

669 Dexter, Miriam Robbins. *Whence the Goddesses: A Source Book*. New York: Pergamon P, 1990. Print. 119.

670 Harrison, Jane Ellen. *Prolegomena to the Study of Greek Religion*. Princeton, NJ: Princeton U P, 1991. Print. 306.

671 Dexter, Miriam Robbins. *Whence the Goddesses: A Source Book*. New York: Pergamon P, 1990. Print. 119.

672 Smith, Barbara. "Greece." *The Feminist Companion to Mythology*. Ed. Carolyne Larrington. London: Pandora, 1992. 65-101. Print. 73.

673 Ibid.

674 Dexter, Miriam Robbins. *Whence the Goddesses: A Source Book*. New York: Pergamon P, 1990. Print. 119.

675 Graves, Robert. *The Greek Myths: The Complete and Definitive Edition*. New York: Penguin, 2011. Print. 44.

676 Herodotus. *The History of Herodotus."* *Internet Sacred Text Archive*, translator G. C. Macaulay, compiler John Bruno Hare, 2011, 4.180-89. *Evinity Publishing*, www.sacred-texts.com/cla/hh/hh4180.htm. Accessed 21 June 2016. 4.180.

677 Gimbutas, Marija. *The Goddesses and Gods of Old Europe: Myths and Cult Images*. Berkeley: U of California P, 1982. Print. 149.

678 Edelman, Sandra. *Turning the Gorgon: A Meditation on Shame*. Woodstock, CT: Spring Publications, Inc. 1998. Print. 135.

679 Ibid, 139.

680 Gimbutas, Marija. *The Goddesses and Gods of Old Europe: Myths and Cult Images*. Berkeley: U of California P, 1982. Print. 18.

681 Edelman, Sandra. *Turning the Gorgon: A Meditation on Shame*. Woodstock, CT: Spring Publications, Inc. 1998. Print. 136.

682 Ibid.

683 Ibid.

684 Ibid, 61.

685 Hesiod. *Theogony*. Trans. Richmond Lattimore. *Works and Days; Theogony; The Shield of Herakles*. Ann Arbor, MI: U of Michigan P, 1991. 119-86. Print. Lines 896-97.

686 Smith, Barbara. "Greece." *The Feminist Companion to Mythology*. Ed. Carolyne Larrington. London: Pandora, 1992. 65-101. Print. 87.

687 Harrison, Jane Ellen. *Prolegomena to the Study of Greek Religion*. Princeton, NJ: Princeton U P, 1991. Print. 300.

688 Shuttle, Penelope, and Peter Redgrove. *The Wise Wound: Menstruation and Everywoman*. London: Marion Boyars, 2005. Print. 248.

689 Kerényi, C. *The Gods of the Greeks*. London: Thames and Hudson, 1982. Print. 121.

690 Ibid, 121, 123

691 Herodotus. *The History of Herodotus."* *Internet Sacred Text Archive*, translator G. C. Macaulay, compiler John Bruno Hare, 2011, 4.180-89. *Evinity Publishing*, www.sacred-texts.com/cla/hh/hh4180.htm. Accessed 21 June 2016. 4.180.

692 Ibid.

693 Downing, Christine. *The Goddess: Mythological Images of the Feminine*. New York: Author's Choice P, 1981. Print. 113.

694 Seelig, Beth J. "The Rape of Medusa in the Temple Of Athena: Aspects Of Triangulation in the Girl." *The International Journ. of Psychoanalysis*, vol. 83, no. 4, Jan. 2002, pp. 895–911. *E-Journals*, doi: 10.1516/00207570260172975. Accessed 13 June 2016. 898.

695Herodotus. *The History of Herodotus."* *Internet Sacred Text Archive*, translator G. C. Macaulay, compiler John Bruno Hare, 2011, 4.180-89. *Evinity Publishing*, www.sacred-texts.com/cla/hh/hh4180.htm. Accessed 21 June 2016. 4.189.

696 Graves, Robert. *The Greek Myths: The Complete and Definitive Edition*. New York: Penguin, 2011. Print. 47.

697 Ibid, 44.

698 Harrison, Jane Ellen. *Prolegomena to the Study of Greek Religion*. Princeton, NJ: Princeton U P, 1991. Print. 192.

699 Harding, M. Esther. *Woman's Mysteries: Ancient & Modern*. Boston, MA: Shambhala, 1971. Print. 104.

700 Ibid, 103.

701 Harrison, Jane Ellen. *Prolegomena to the Study of Greek Religion*. Princeton, NJ: Princeton U P, 1991. Print. 192.

702 Kerényi, C. *The Gods of the Greeks*. London: Thames and Hudson, 1982. Print. 123.

703 Edelman, Sandra. *Turning the Gorgon: A Meditation on Shame*. Woodstock, CT: Spring Publications, Inc. 1998. Print. 51.

704 Ibid, 138.

705 Graves, Robert. *The Greek Myths: The Complete and Definitive Edition*. New York: Penguin, 2011. Print. 34.

706 Downing, Christine. *The Goddess: Mythological Images of the Feminine*. New York: Author's Choice P, 1981. Print. 118.

707 Harrison, Jane Ellen. *Prolegomena to the Study of Greek Religion*. Princeton, NJ: Princeton U P, 1991. Print. 300.

708 Ibid, 228.

[709] Edelman, Sandra. *Turning the Gorgon: A Meditation on Shame.* Woodstock, CT: Spring Publications, Inc. 1998. Print. 55, 56.

[710] Ibid, 142.

[711] Downing, Christine. *The Goddess: Mythological Images of the Feminine.* New York: Author's Choice P, 1981. Print. 118.

[712] Edelman, Sandra. *Turning the Gorgon: A Meditation on Shame.* Woodstock, CT: Spring Publications, Inc. 1998. Print. 57.

[713] Homer. *The Odyssey.* Trans. Albert Cook. 2nd ed. New York: W.W. Norton, 1993. Print. XXIII.156-58.

[714] Homer. *The Iliad.* Trans. Robert Fagles. New York: Penguin, 1990. Print. 4.26-27.

[715] Ibid, 8.426-27.

[716] Ibid, 8.463-64.

[717] Ibid, 8.526.

[718] Ibid, 8.412-13.

[719] Edelman, Sandra. *Turning the Gorgon: A Meditation on Shame.* Woodstock, CT: Spring Publications, Inc. 1998. Print. 12.

[720] Monaghan, Patricia. *Encyclopedia of Goddesses and Heroines.* Novato, CA: New World Library, 2014. Print. 223.

[721] Edelman, Sandra. *Turning the Gorgon: A Meditation on Shame.* Woodstock, CT: Spring Publications, Inc. 1998. Print. 38.

[722] Ibid.

[723] Ibid, 47.

[724] Schneider, Carl qtd. in Edelman, Sandra. *Turning the Gorgon: A Meditation on Shame.* Woodstock, CT: Spring Publications, Inc. 1998. Print. 62.

[725] Edelman, Sandra. *Turning the Gorgon: A Meditation on Shame.* Woodstock, CT: Spring Publications, Inc. 1998. Print. 47.

[726] Ibid.

[727] Ibid, 45-46.

[728] Ibid, 46.

[729] Ibid, 48.

[730] Snell, Bruno. *The Discovery of the Mind.* Trans. T.G. Rosenmeyer. Cambridge, MA: Harvard U P, 1953. 168.

[731] Ibid, 167.

[732] Edelman, Sandra. *Turning the Gorgon: A Meditation on Shame.* Woodstock, CT: Spring Publications, Inc. 1998. Print. 48.

[733] Snell, Bruno. *The Discovery of the Mind.* Trans. T.G. Rosenmeyer. Cambridge, MA: Harvard U P, 1953. 167.

[734] Edelman, Sandra. *Turning the Gorgon: A Meditation on Shame.* Woodstock, CT: Spring Publications, Inc. 1998. Print. 58.

[735] Ibid, 47.

[736] Ibid, 39.

737 Shuttle, Penelope, and Peter Redgrove. *The Wise Wound: Menstruation and Everywoman*. London: Marion Boyars, 2005. Print. 22.

738 Lubell, Winifred Milius. *The Metamorphosis of Baubo: Myths of Woman's Sexual Energy*. Nashville: Vanderbilt U P, 1994. Print. 17, 84.

739 Ibid, 35-36.

740 Ibid, 26.

741 Ibid, 3-4.

742 Ibid, 179-80.

743 Plutarch qtd. in Lubell, Winifred Milius. *The Metamorphosis of Baubo: Myths of Woman's Sexual Energy*. Nashville: Vanderbilt U P, 1994. Print. 184.

744 Lubell, Winifred Milius. *The Metamorphosis of Baubo: Myths of Woman's Sexual Energy*. Nashville: Vanderbilt U P, 1994. Print. 184.

745 Ibid, 184-85

746 Schneider, Carl qtd. in Edelman, Sandra. *Turning the Gorgon: A Meditation on Shame*. Woodstock, CT: Spring Publications, Inc. 1998. Print. 62.

747 Aristotle qtd. in Witt, Charlotte, and Shapiro, Lisa, "Feminist History of Philosophy." *The Stanford Encyclopedia of Philosophy, editor* Edward N. Zalta, Spring 2017, plato.stanford.edu/archives/spr2017/entries/feminism-femhist/>. Accessed 5 Mar. 2016.

748 Freud, Sigmund. "Medusa's Head." PEP Archive, translator James Strachey, 1922. EBSCO,pgi.idm.oclc.org/login?url=http://search.edscohost.com/login.aspx?direct=true&db=pph&AN=SE.018.0273A&site=ehost-live&scope=site. Accessed 26 Apr. 2016.

749 Ibid.

750 Cixous, Hélène. "The Laugh of the Medusa." *Signs: Journ. of Women in Culture and Society*, translators Keith Cohen and Paula Cohen, vol. 1, no. 4, Summer 1976, pp. 875–93. *JSTOR/U of Chicago P*, doi: 10.1086/493306. Accessed 1 June 2016. 885.

751 Freud, Sigmund. "Medusa's Head." PEP Archive, translator James Strachey, 1922. EBSCO,pgi.idm.oclc.org/login?url=http://search.edscohost.com/login.aspx?direct=true&db=pph&AN=SE.018.0273A&site=ehost-live&scope=site. Accessed 26 Apr. 2016.

752 Harrison, Jane Ellen. *Prolegomena to the Study of Greek Religion*. Princeton, NJ: Princeton U P, 1991. Print. 303.

753 Edelman, Sandra. *Turning the Gorgon: A Meditation on Shame*. Woodstock, CT: Spring Publications, Inc. 1998. Print. 50-51.

754 Henderson, Joseph qtd. in Edelman, Sandra. *Turning the Gorgon: A Meditation on Shame*. Woodstock, CT: Spring Publications, Inc. 1998. Print. 54.

[755] Eliade, Mircea qtd. in Edelman, Sandra. *Turning the Gorgon: A Meditation on Shame*. Woodstock, CT: Spring Publications, Inc. 1998. Print. 54.

[756] Harrison, Jane Ellen. *Prolegomena to the Study of Greek Religion*. Princeton, NJ: Princeton U P, 1991. Print. 302.

[757] Edelman, Sandra. *Turning the Gorgon: A Meditation on Shame*. Woodstock, CT: Spring Publications, Inc. 1998. Print. 53.

[758] Ibid, 54.

[759] Ibid, 50, 52.

[760] Harding, M. Esther. *Woman's Mysteries: Ancient & Modern*. Boston, MA: Shambhala, 1971. Print. 33.

[761] Jung, C. G. *The Essential Jung: Selected Writings*. Ed. Anthony Storr. Princeton, NJ: Princeton UP, 1983. Print. 111.

[762] Luke, Helen. *The Way of Woman: Awakening the Perennial Feminine*. NY: Image Doubleday, 1995. Print. 45.

[763] Edelman, Sandra. *Turning the Gorgon: A Meditation on Shame*. Woodstock, CT: Spring Publications, Inc. 1998. Print. 50.

[764] Apollodorus. *The Library of Greek Mythology*. Trans. Robin Hard. Oxford: Oxford U P, 1997. Print. E5.22 - E6.6.

[765] Harding, M. Esther. *Woman's Mysteries: Ancient & Modern*. Boston, MA: Shambhala, 1971. Print. 103.

[766] Downing, Christine. *The Goddess: Mythological Images of the Feminine*. New York: Author's Choice P, 1981. Print. 109.

[767] Edelman, Sandra. *Turning the Gorgon: A Meditation on Shame*. Woodstock, CT: Spring Publications, Inc. 1998. Print. 50.

[768] Aeschylus. *The Eumenides*. Aeschylus I. Eds. David Grene and Richmond Lattimore. Trans. Lattimore. Chicago: U of Chicago P, 1953. 133-71. Print. Lines 681-84.

[769] Edelman, Sandra. *Turning the Gorgon: A Meditation on Shame*. Woodstock, CT: Spring Publications, Inc. 1998. Print. 53.

[770] Ibid, 52-53.

[771] Ibid, 53.

[772] Siegel, Daniel J. *The Neurobiology of 'We:' How Relationships, the Mind, and the Brain Interact to Shape Who We Are*. Unabridged. Boulder, CO: Sounds True, 2011. Audiobook CD. 7 discs. *Track 6*.

[773] Olson, Tillie Olson qtd. in Downing, Christine. *The Goddess: Mythological Images of the Feminine*. New York: Author's Choice P, 1981. Print. 115.

[774] Odajnyk, V. Walter. "The Archetypal Interpretation of Fairy Tales: Bluebeard." Part two. *Psychological Perspectives* 47.2 (2004): 247-74. Print. 252.

[775] Wilhelm, Richard, and Cary Baynes, trans. *The I Ching or the Book of Changes*. 3rd ed., Princeton U P, 1967. 10.

[776] Ibid, 3.

777 Odajnyk, V. Walter. "The Archetypal Interpretation of Fairy Tales: Bluebeard." Part two. *Psychological Perspectives* 47.2 (2004): 247-74. Print. 252.

778 Ibid.

779 Schatten, G. and Schatten, H. qtd. in Beldecos, Athena et al. "The Importance of Feminist Critique for Contemporary Cell Biology." *Hypatia*, copyright Scott Gilbert, vol. 3, no. 1, Spring 1988, pp. 61-76. *JSTOR*, classes.mathewjbrown.net/teaching-files/svd-phd/2-gender/BGSG.pdf. Accessed 9 Dec. 2016. 66.

780 Beldecos, Athena et al. "The Importance of Feminist Critique for Contemporary Cell Biology." *Hypatia*, copyright Scott Gilbert, vol. 3, no. 1, Spring 1988, pp. 61-76. *JSTOR*, classes.mathewjbrown.net/teaching-files/svd-phd/2-gender/BGSG.pdf. Accessed 9 Dec. 2016. 66.

781 Martin, Emily. "The Egg and the Sperm: How Science Has Constructed a Romance Based on Stereotypical Male-Female Roles." *Signs*, vol. 16, no. 3, Spring 1991, pp. 485-501. *JSTOR/U of Chicago P*, www.jstor.org/stable/3174586. Accessed 9 Dec. 2016. 492-93.

782 Ibid, 494.

783 Ibid, 496.

784 Ibid.

785 Wassarman, Paul qtd. in Martin, Emily. "The Egg and the Sperm: How Science Has Constructed a Romance Based on Stereotypical Male-Female Roles." *Signs*, vol. 16, no. 3, Spring 1991, pp. 485-501. *JSTOR/U of Chicago P*, www.jstor.org/stable/3174586. Accessed 9 Dec. 2016. 496.

786 Beldecos, Athena et al. "The Importance of Feminist Critique for Contemporary Cell Biology." *Hypatia*, copyright Scott Gilbert, vol. 3, no. 1, Spring 1988, pp. 61-76. *JSTOR*, classes.mathewjbrown.net/teaching-files/svd-phd/2-gender/BGSG.pdf. Accessed 9 Dec. 2016. 61.

787 Martin, Emily. "The Egg and the Sperm: How Science Has Constructed a Romance Based on Stereotypical Male-Female Roles." *Signs*, vol. 16, no. 3, Spring 1991, pp. 485-501. *JSTOR/U of Chicago P*, www.jstor.org/stable/3174586. Accessed 9 Dec. 2016. 498.

788 Ibid.

789 Downing, Christine. *The Goddess: Mythological Images of the Feminine*. New York: Author's Choice P, 1981. Print. 104.

790 Ibid, 113.

791 Corbett, Lionel qtd. in Root, Ileen Brennan. *Redeeming the Gorgon: Reclaiming the* Medusa Function *of Psyche*. Diss. Pacifica Graduate Institute, 2007. Carpinteria, CA: ProQuest, 2007. Print. 4.

[792] Dexter, Miriam Robbins. "The Ferocious and the Erotic 'Beautiful' Medusa and the Neolithic Bird and Snake." *Journ. of Feminist Studies in Religion*, vol. 26, no. 1, Spring 2010, pp. 25-41. *Indiana U P/UCLA Library*, doi:10.2979/fsr.2010.26.1.25. Accessed 5 Aug. 2016. 29.

[793] Paris, Ginette. *Pagan Grace*. Dallas, TX: Spring Publications, 1990. Print. 84.

[794] Slattery, Dennis Patrick. *The Wounded Body: Remembering the Markings of Flesh*. Albany, NY: State U of New York P, 2000. 207-235. Print. 134.

[795] Levine, Peter A., and Ann Frederick. *Waking the Tiger: Healing Trauma*. Berkeley: North Atlantic Books, 1997. Print. 119.

[796] Hillman, James. *Re-Visioning Psychology*. New York: Harper & Row, 1975. Print. x.

[797] Slattery, Dennis Patrick. *The Wounded Body: Remembering the Markings of Flesh*. Albany, NY: State U of New York P, 2000. 207-235. Print. 7.

[798] Agarwal, Neha, and Arulselvi Subramanian. "Endometriosis— Morphology, Clinical Presentations and Molecular Pathology." *Journ. of Laboratory Physicians,* vol. 2, no.1, Jan.-June 2010, pp. 1-9, *PMC/Medknow Publications,* doi: 10.4103/0974-2727.66699. Accessed 29 Sept. 2015.

[799] Hillman, James. *Re-Visioning Psychology*. New York: Harper & Row, 1975. Print. 174.

[800] Ibid, 137.

[801] Ibid.

[802] Ibid, 174.

[803] Norris, Rebecca Sachs. "Examining the Structure and Role of Emotion: Contributions of Neurobiology to the Study of Embodied Religious Experience." *Zygon*, vol. 40, no. 1, Mar. 2005, pp. 181-200. *EBSCOhost,* pgi.idm.oclc.org/login?url=http://search.ebscohost.com/login.aspx?direct=true&db=eoah&AN=6937927&site=pfi-live. Accessed 28 Mar. 2012. 196.

[804] Winkelman, Michael. "Shamanism: A Biogenetic Perspective." *Science, Religion, and Society: An Encyclopedia of History, Culture, and Controversy.* Vol. 2. Eds. Arri Eisen and Gary Laderman. Armonk, NY: M.E. Sharpe, 2007. 621-632. Print. 632.

[805] Hillman, James. *Re-Visioning Psychology*. New York: Harper & Row, 1975. Print. 80.

[806] Levine, Peter A., and Ann Frederick. *Waking the Tiger: Healing Trauma*. Berkeley: North Atlantic Books, 1997. Print. 16.

[807] Ibid, 20.

[808] Ibid.

809 Winkelman, Michael. "Shamanism: A Biogenetic Perspective." *Science, Religion, and Society: An Encyclopedia of History, Culture, and Controversy.* Vol. 2. Eds. Arri Eisen and Gary Laderman. Armonk, NY: M.E. Sharpe, 2007. 621-632. Print. 626.

810 Lévi-Strauss, Claude. "The Effectiveness of Symbols." *Readings in Ritual Studies.* Ed. Ronald L. Grimes. New Jersey: Prentice Hall, 1996. 368-378. Print. 374-77.

811 Calhoun, Lawrence G., and Richard G. Tedeschi. "Posttraumatic Growth: The Positive Lessons of Loss." *Meaning Reconstruction & the Experience of Loss.* Ed. Robert A. Neimeyer. Washington DC: American Psychological Assn, 2001. 157-72. Print. 160.

812 Kalsched, Donald. *The Inner World of Trauma: Archetypal Defenses of the Personal Spirit.* London: Routledge, 1996. Print. 6.

813 Hillman, James. *Re-Visioning Psychology.* New York: Harper & Row, 1975. Print. 117.

814 Ibid, x.

815 Ibid.

816 Downing, Christine. *The Goddess: Mythological Images of the Feminine.* New York: Author's Choice P, 1981. Print. 113.

817 Edelman, Sandra. *Turning the Gorgon: A Meditation on Shame.* Woodstock, CT: Spring Publications, Inc. 1998. Print. 111.

818 Thomson, George qtd. in Delaney, Janice, Mary Jane Lupton, and Emily Toth. *The Curse: A Cultural History of Menstruation.* Urbana, IL: U of Illinois P, 1988. Print. 8.

819 Downing, Christine. *The Goddess: Mythological Images of the Feminine.* New York: Author's Choice P, 1981. Print. 110.

820 Edelman, Sandra. *Turning the Gorgon: A Meditation on Shame.* Woodstock, CT: Spring Publications, Inc. 1998. Print. 122.

821 Ibid, 123.

822 Ibid, 122.

823 Wolkstein, Diana, and Samuel Noah Kramer. *Inanna, Queen of Heaven and Earth: Her Stories and Hymns from Sumer.* New York: Harper & Row, 1983. Print. 82.

824 Perera, Sylvia Brinton. *Descent to the Goddess: A Way of Initiation for Women.* Toronto, Can.: Inner City Books, 1981. Print. 16.

825 Wolkstein, Diana, and Samuel Noah Kramer. *Inanna, Queen of Heaven and Earth: Her Stories and Hymns from Sumer.* New York: Harper & Row, 1983. Print. 64, 140.

826 Dexter, Miriam Robbins. "The Ferocious and the Erotic 'Beautiful' Medusa and the Neolithic Bird and Snake." *Journ. of Feminist Studies in Religion*, vol. 26, no. 1, Spring 2010, pp. 25-41. *Indiana U P/UCLA Library*, doi:10.2979/fsr.2010.26.1.25. Accessed 5 Aug. 2016. 33.

827 Wolkstein, Diana, and Samuel Noah Kramer. *Inanna, Queen of Heaven and Earth: Her Stories and Hymns from Sumer.* New York: Harper & Row, 1983. Print. 55.

828 Ibid, 57.

829 Ibid, 156.

830 Edinger, Edward F. *The Eternal Drama: The Inner Meaning of Greek Mythology.* Boston: Shambhala, 1994. Print. 5, 56.

831 Woodman, Marion. *The Ravaged Bridegroom: Masculinity in Women.* Toronto, Can.: Inner City Books, 1990. Print. 176.

832 Ibid, 177.

833 Ibid.

834 Perera, Sylvia Brinton. *Descent to the Goddess: A Way of Initiation for Women.* Toronto, Can.: Inner City Books, 1981. Print. 25.

835 Agger, Ellen. "Menopause and Endometriosis." *Endometriosis: The Complete Reference for Taking Charge of Your Health.* Ed. Mary Lou Ballweg. Chicago: Contemporary, 2003:275-304. Print. 279.

836 Zimlicki, Paula M. "Hysterectomy: The Loneliest Decision of All." *The Endometriosis Sourcebook.* Ed. Mary Lou Ballweg. Chicago: Contemporary, 1995. 109-21. Print. 111, 116, 117.

837 Redwine, David B. *Googling Endometriosis: The Lost Centuries.* Bend, OR: David B. Redwine, MD, 2012. Print. 217.

838 Slattery, Dennis Patrick. *The Wounded Body: Remembering the Markings of Flesh.* Albany, NY: State U of New York P, 2000. 207-235. Print. 134.

839 Downing, Christine. *The Goddess: Mythological Images of the Feminine.* New York: Author's Choice P, 1981. Print. 103.

840 Edelman, Sandra. *Turning the Gorgon: A Meditation on Shame.* Woodstock, CT: Spring Publications, Inc. 1998. Print. 111.

841 Ibid.

842 Ibid, 106.

843 Ibid.

844 Ibid.

845 Ibid, 107.

846 Ovid. *Metamorphoses.* Trans. David Raeburn. London: Penguin, 2004. Print. 4.740-49.

www.ingramcontent.com/pod-product-compliance
Lightning Source LLC
Chambersburg PA
CBHW060046100426
42742CB00014B/2719